CHRISTIANS IN THE FACE
OF INJUSTICE

Ricardo Antoncich

CHRISTIANS IN THE FACE OF INJUSTICE

A LATIN AMERICAN READING OF CATHOLIC SOCIAL TEACHING

Translated from the Spanish by
Matthew J. O'Connell

ORBIS BOOKS

Maryknoll, New York 10545

The Catholic Foreign Mission Society of America (Maryknoll) recruits and trains people for overseas missionary service. Through Orbis Books Maryknoll aims to foster the international dialogue that is essential to mission. The books published, however, reflect the opinions of their authors and are not meant to represent the official position of the society.

Originally published as *Los cristianos ante la injusticia: Hacia una lectura latinoamericana de la doctrina social de la Iglesia*, © 1980 by Ediciones Grupo Social, Bogotá, Colombia

English translation © 1987 by Orbis Books, Maryknoll, NY 10545

Library of Congress Cataloging-in-Publication Data

Antoncich, Ricardo.
  Christians in the face of injustice.

  Translation of: Los cristianos ante la injusticia.
  Bibliography: p.
  Includes index.
  1. Sociology, Christian (Catholic)   2. Christianity
and justice—Latin America.   3. Church and social
problems—Latin America.   4. Catholic Church—Latin
America.   5. Latin America—Church history.   I. Title.
BX1753.A5813   1987   261.8   86-23529
ISBN 0-88344-413-5 (pbk.)

To
Alberto Ignacio Koenigsknecht, M.M.
Prelate of Juli, Peru
1917–1986

The people he led as a pastor has remembered him in the following words.

Thank you for . . . having been so devoted to God, to our Holy Mother Mary, to prayer; for having been a loyal, "all-around missionary," and a missionary totally committed to his ministry; for having been the friend of the *campesino*; for having been the voice of the oppressed—and having given them back their own voice as well; for having been a simple, lovable, human being; for having been such a solid rock in your convictions and your options. Thank you for having lived your convictions to the hilt, regardless of the consequences of your commitment to the poor; for having loved the poor as persons; for having shown in word and work how great a privilege of God it is to serve the poor; for having promoted the role of woman in the church; for having always had time for everyone. Thank you for your tireless quest for justice for your neighbor. Thank you for having sown good seed in the church of Juli. We promise to see to the harvest.

Yes, Alberto, you are gone now. You have answered the call of your Lord and Master to come aside and rest a while. But your works remain. Your cause is not over, nor will it be over. It must go on. Please fill us with your love for others, your gifts of yourself, your concern for the cause of the poor, that we may follow the same Jesus Christ in whose way you walked, giving witness to him with our lives to the death, just as you have done—and so meet again one day, in the joy of resurrection.

CONTENTS

PREFACE

The text presented in these pages is the result of several years' reflection on the social teaching of the church and the reality of the Latin American situation. The main concern of the book is: How are we to read and interpret the social teaching of the church in the Latin American context so that the challenge of gospel values may reach us with undiminished force?

I have expounded my reflections to quite diverse audiences in various countries and have seen with gratitude that my ideas have never caused a paralysis of action but on the contrary have led to a discovery of Christian identity and to a deeper love of the church.

As will be clear to the reader, the social teaching of the church has not been presented to my audiences as a veiled way of giving legitimacy to the social injustices that Latin America is suffering or as an invitation to revolutionary violence, but rather as a call to make faith and life a consistent whole. I am speaking of the consistency that Pope John Paul II asked of Christians in his homily in the Cathedral of Mexico City in January 1979:

> Consistency . . . means being conscious of your Catholic identity and manifesting it in a completely respectful way, yet without wavering or fear.
> The Church of today needs Christians who are ready to bear clear witness to their allegiance and who will play their part in the Church's mission in the world by being a leaven for religion, justice, and the advancement of human dignity in every social context and by endeavoring to supply the world with a "supplement of soul" so that it may be a more human and fraternal place from which man may look toward God [HCMC, p. 204].

The purpose of the first chapter is to summarize the experience of the years immediately preceding and following the Puebla conference and to reread that experience in the light of the messages of Pope John Paul II in Mexico and his encyclical *Redemptor hominis* (RH) as well as of other documents that convey his teaching. Its purpose is also to introduce the thought of the Latin American bishops, especially as expressed in their third general conference held in Puebla. The desire to provide Latin American Christians with a tool for reading and applying the social teaching of the church motivates this effort to rescue the prophetic power of many of their texts, a power that is perhaps concealed from Latin Americans by the style of the documents and the period in which they were written.

Chapters 2 and 3 present an overall view that shows the main coordinates of my thinking. My aim is not simply to present the documents of the church's social teaching but to convey an understanding of the hermeneutical problem that always arises when a text is read in a concrete situation. Having explained the general hermeneutical problem in chapter 2 and the meaning of "social teaching" in chapter 3, I then proceed to what constitutes the heart of this book: the search for hermeneutical criteria that will guide a reading of the documents containing the social teachings (chaps. 4–7), documents that are historical in nature (chap. 4), ethical in character (chap. 5), and socioeconomic and political in subject matter (chap. 6). If these teachings are to direct the action of Christians for liberation, as Pope John Paul II desires, they must also be read in the context of the process of liberation (chap. 7).

The final four chapters (8–11) are essays in the application of these hermeneutical criteria. Private property and the class struggle are sources of conflict because when the church defends property and expresses reservations about the class struggle, it seems to incline toward capitalism, and because, on the other hand, when it points out the limitations and social functions of property and acknowledges in an objective way the existence of social conflicts and of oppressive and repressive situations, it is accused of yielding to the attractions of Marxist ideology.

Ideology and politics are the last subjects discussed (chaps. 10–11) as I try to sum up the teaching of Puebla on these two points. These two chapters were lectures given at a theological meeting in Panama City in January 1980 and are printed here with minor changes.

May the maternal presence of Mary, the model of those who do not passively accept present circumstances, point ahead to the new Magnificat that our people will sing when the project of the poor and the lowly in behalf of justice has become a historical reality, while the projects of the unjust oppressors who worship the god of wealth or of power have proved empty and meaningless.

PREFACE TO THE ENGLISH EDITION

A reader adventurous enough to take up a book on the unfamiliar subject of the social doctrine of the church—and a book that addresses that subject from something of an unusual viewpoint, the Latin American—surely deserves some consideration on the part of the author by way of an explanation of why the book is being translated into English.

We know that the United States and the countries of Latin America are linked by intimate historical, social, economic, and political bonds. In this book we shall examine mainly their religious bonds. So many North American missionaries who have come to Latin America to share the faith have found themselves enriched in the process, as they shared the history, the culture, and the suffering of the Latin American peoples.

As I write these lines I have before me a picture of Alberto Ignacio Koenigsknecht, Maryknoll missionary, Vicar Apostolic of Juli in Peru. Bishop Alberto headed his church from March 1975 until February 9, 1986, and has left it a beautiful testimonial of joy, faith, hope, and the yearning for justice.

The bond of faith that unites so many Christians of North and South, in life and in death, enables us to encounter one another on the common ground of our obedience to the gospel and the teachings of the magisterium of the church. It is our common hope that the economic, political, and social ties that link the United States and Latin America may be marked by the Christian spirit. Then let us have a book that will speak to us on the teachings of the magisterium of the church in these areas.

We need the spirit of the gospel to help us see many of the relationships between our peoples in a different way than we are accustomed to seeing them. The uneasiness with which so many Latin Americans perceive socioeconomic and political relations with the United States springs from some concrete facts: the foreign debt, military intervention, and the United States' defense of its interests without any apparent concern for the interests of Latin America. In other words, the danger of mutual misunderstanding is ever present, and even threatens to disturb relations between good neighbors, not to mention relations of genuine human and Christian fellowship.

It will be helpful, then, to be able to read the social doctrine of the church in dialogue with a Latin American viewpoint. Our Latin American countries are *dependent*, either on capitalism or on socialism. Thus they are not the best examples of what their respective ideologies can offer. Reality on the periphery is very different from reality at the center, regardless of the operative ideology.

The reader will occasionally encounter the expression "peripheral capitalism" in this book. There is an enormous difference between our Latin American experience of capitalism and that of the average citizen in the United States. For example, North American society is characterized by an extensive middle class. There is no parallel here with the miniscule middle class of Latin American peripheral capitalism, in which the condition of very wealthy minorities stands in stark and shocking contrast to that of very poor majorities. We hear a great deal about the influence of Marxism in Latin American thinking. In my opinion, an objective appraisal of this phenomenon will have to take account of objective conditions of social inequality resulting from a capitalism that offers the most advantages to those who wield the greatest power of decision. Hence the crying injustice of the international foreign debt. Unless the voice of poor peoples is heard, a catastrophic movement of social conflict is in store, and a conflict that will poison relations between countries that have been good neighbors. Nor will this movement be the fruit of some manner of "subversion." It will be the fruit of free and voluntary decisions on the part of world capital.

The author's purpose in this book has been to offer the Latin American public some "hermeneutical criteria"—principles of interpretation—for an understanding of the teachings of the magisterium *in our reality*. The proposal by Orbis Books that this book be made available to the people of the United States as well, in English translation, will now make it possible to foster *dialogue* between North and South—and East and West—if the magisterium of the church, which is universal by calling and hence must transcend social and political systems, has anything to say to the world of today.

Since the publication of this book in Spanish, two important things have happened in the church. The first was the appearance of *Laborem exercens*, Pope John Paul II's encylical on labor. Some of the main points in this book are considerably supported by the Holy Father's thinking. Indeed the entire book could have been reworked in light of the encyclical. It seems to me that *Laborem exercens* takes a new approach to the social doctrine of the church. I would summarize the change as a shift of interest (1) from property to labor, and (2) from a preoccupation with doctrine to an analysis of historical facts.

Systematic presentations of social doctrine have invariably assigned priority to the Catholic teaching on property as an expression of the dignity of the human person. Labor has come in for very little emphasis. *Laborem exercens* reverses the order of precedence, and proposes an understanding of property as a right flowing from work, subordinate to work, and hence never legitimately utilized as a tool for the exploitation of work.

Laborem exercens evinces a new awareness on the part of the magisterium of the importance of historical conflicts as the starting point for an exposition of the social doctrine of the church. The encyclical accepts the interpretation that these conflicts are basically those of capital and labor. To be sure, it does not restrict the meaning of the class struggle to that of the social, economic, and political apsects of these class conflicts. It goes beyond the conflicts in their profane meaning to the very meaning of the human being as such, in all of the ethical radicality of that meaning, as the basis of a value difference between solidarity in work (regardless of the nature of the work or the social class of the worker) and a selfish holding of capital (when property is not in the service of labor but a form of exploitation of the same).

The second event to which we refer is the debate on the theology of liberation. The Roman Curia has made an official pronouncement on the subject in its "Instruction." A careful analysis of this document reveals a distinction between a *liberative pastoral ministry*, which emerges from the very nature of the church as an evangelizing organism, and the *theology of liberation*, whose function is to supply that ministry with its theoretical underpinnings. The animadversions of the Congregation for the Doctrine of the Faith are directed against neither of these two elements. Both are reaffirmed. The Congregation's misgivings in the "Instruction" bear on the use of Marxism in theology. By way of synthesis, we may say that the observations in the document concentrate on the philosophical aspects of Marxism, especially in the latter's view of conflict as essential to human nature: this would entail unacceptable consequences for christology, ecclesiology, and so on.

This warning is legitimate and necessary. It would have been less open to ideological abuse, however, if it had also set forth, in parallel fashion—as other magisterial documents do—the inacceptability of a view of human nature as intrinsically comporting individual interest (the philosophy of laissez-faire liberalism). There is another limitation as well. We must insist that the problem of Marxism cannot be limited to the problem of the *use* of its analytical tools in theology, or to the connections these tools have with Marxist philosophical theories. There is something more. Christianity must take cognizance of Marxism's grave, profound challenge to the whole Christian faith. The reader will note in this book an approach to the Marxist challenge calculated to arrive at an apprehension of reality that will be more faithful not only to the gospel but to the social pronouncements of the magisterium itself. Marxism confronts us with deep questions when it asserts that the church takes sides with capitalistic interests by teaching that private property is a "natural right." Marxism calls us to account with its claim that the church has no concern for the lot of the poor because it condemns the class struggle. Marxism challenges us when it describes the Christian faith as a "religious alienation" that withdraws men and women from a commitment to history. Unless it is willing to confront these questions, these challenges, the social magisterium will risk the status of an organ of oppression, when it should be a path of liberation.

If we are to take the admonitions of the church on the meaning of Marxism in contemporary culture seriously, then we must transcend the framework of the "use" of Marxist analytical tools and pass to a more complex, global horizon: we must "give an account of our faith" (cf. 1 Pet. 3:15) in the face of the questions posed by Marxism—as a social, cultural, political, and economic phenomenon—to the modern world.

But an answer to these questions will also involve an altogether honest examination of conscience on the presence of the church in the various forms of capitalism, both that of the center (in the developed capitalistic countries) and that of the periphery (in the underdeveloped countries). The voice of the church must manifest the *unity* of the spirit of the gospel despite a diversity of situations. For our faith is one, as the Lord is one and his people are one. We hope that this book will make a contribution to this examination of conscience.

The author owes much to the fellowship and common faith he shares with his many Hispanic brothers and sisters living in the United States. He has found them filled with two mighty yearnings. They hope that they will be adaptable—that they will be successfully assimilated into their new world with its new values. They want to be able to "feel at home" among their new people. But they hope, too, that they will be able to maintain their Hispanic cultural roots, which are not only so precious to them, but which could constitue a valuable contribution to the complex society of that great melting pot to the North where so many different cultural traditions have already met and married.

It has likewise been a great joy and pleasure to see the Catholic Church of the United States—especially in the pastoral letters of its bishops concerning Hispanic problems—so concerned for the defense of the cultural wealth of the Hispanic tradition, while at the same time urging the incorporation of this wealth into the cultural legacy of the North American people. We offer this book in grateful homage to this ecclesial sense of catholicity. We have a beautiful concrete expression of this sensitivity in the person of Bishop Alberto Ignacio Koenigsknecht.

1

THE LATIN AMERICAN RELEVANCE OF THE CHURCH'S SOCIAL TEACHING

As a result of the message and actions of Pope John Paul II and the bishops at Puebla the social teaching of the church is once again proving to be extraordinarily relevant to present-day Latin America. For, as the pope said, this teaching can provide norms for an authentically liberating activity.

Let me begin by recalling the teaching of Paul VI in his *Octogesima adveniens* (OA). Then we shall go on to see how the call of John Paul II has given this teaching new relevance and demanded its urgent application to the Latin American situation.

THE SOCIAL TEACHING OF *OCTOGESIMA ADVENIENS*

In this letter, written to commemorate the eightieth anniversary of the encyclical *Rerum novarum* (RN), Paul VI made some important points about the way in which the church's social teaching is to be understood at the present time.

The pope emphasizes the fact that the application of this teaching must be regarded as the task of the entire ecclesial community, in accordance with the changing and very diversified situations that arise. He points out how different these situations in fact are:

In some places they [Christians] are reduced to silence, regarded with suspicion and as it were kept on the fringe of society, enclosed without freedom in a totalitarian system. In other places they are a weak minority whose voice makes itself heard with difficulty. In some other nations, where the Church sees her place recognized, sometimes officially so, she too finds herself subjected to the repercussions of the crisis which is unsettling society; some of her members are tempted by radical and violent solutions from which they believe they can expect a happier outcome. While some people, unaware of present injustices, strive to prolong the existing situation, others allow themselves to be beguiled by revolutionary ideologies which promise them, not without delusion, a definitively better world.

In the face of such widely varying situations it is difficult for us to utter a unified message and to put forward a solution which has universal validity. Such is not our ambition, nor is it our mission. It is up to the Christian communities to analyze with objectivity the situation which is proper to their own country, to shed on it the light of the Gospel's unalterable words and to draw principles of reflection, norms of judgment, and directives for action from the social teaching of the Church. This teaching has been worked out in the course of history and notably, in this industrial era, since the historic date of the message of Pope Leo XIII on "the condition of the workers," and it is an honor and joy for us to celebrate today the anniversary of that message [OA 3–4].

The church's social teaching, then, does not provide an ideology that is to guide us as a social model of universal application. Consequently, the choices to be made and the commitments to be undertaken by Christians must be decided in the light of concrete circumstances:

> It is up to these Christian communities, with the help of the Holy Spirit, in communion with the bishops who hold responsibility and in dialogue with other Christian brethren and all men of good will, to discern the options and commitments which are called for in order to bring about the social, political, and economic changes seen in many cases to be urgently needed [OA 4].

> It is with all its dynamism that the social teaching of the Church accompanies men in their search. If it does not intervene to authenticate a given structure or to propose a ready-made model, it does not thereby limit itself to recalling general principles. It develops through reflection applied to the changing situations of this world, under the driving force of the Gospel as the source of renewal when its message is accepted in its totality and with all its demands. It also develops with the sensitivity proper to the Church which is characterized by a disinterested will to serve and by attention to the poorest.

> Finally, it draws upon its rich experience of many centuries which enables it, while continuing its permanent preoccupations, to undertake the daring and creative innovations which the present state of the world requires [OA 42].

The social teaching of the church is therefore not to be understood as an inflexible, almost monolithic body of set doctrines that are universally valid and applicable in the same manner to every situation and in every age. It does not exclude certain choices, for example, the choice of socialism. On the contrary, the social teaching of Paul VI provides criteria for such a choice (cf. OA 31), although naturally it also warns of the serious dangers to faith that may follow from the choice of certain methods of analysis or action (OA 34) or from the influence of atheistic ideologies and conceptions of the human person and society or at least from essentially materialistic philosophies which by their nature promote an exclusive quest of interest and power (OA 26). The teaching of John Paul II likewise admits as legitimate a measure of socialization: "We can speak of socializing only when the subject character of society is ensured, that is to say, when on the basis of his work each person is entitled to consider himself a part-owner of the great workbench at which he is working with everyone else" (LE 14).

THE SOCIAL TEACHING OF JOHN PAUL II

We must not overlook the emphasis that John Paul II puts on the social teaching of the church. At times he refers to the content of this teaching, for example, on private property and the "social mortgage" attached to it (Opening Address at the Puebla Conference [OAPC III, 4]; see also Address to the Indians of Oaxaca and Chiapas [AIOC]); at times he refers to this teaching as such, as when he says that the complete "truth about human beings is the basis of the Church's social teaching" and that this teaching constitutes "a rich and complex heritage" to which we must return (OAPC I, 9; III, 7; see also Address to the Workers in Monterrey [AWM]).

The appeal of John Paul II to this teaching derives its power from the social context in which he directs attention to it: "This voice of the Church [with regard to property in particular] . . . deserves and needs to be heard in our age as well, when the growing affluence of a few people parallels the growing poverty of the masses" (OAPC III, 4). A little later on the pope refers again to this situation of injustice: "When injustices increase and the gap between rich and poor widens distressingly, then the social doctrine of the Church—in a form that is so creative and open to the broad areas of the Church's presence—should be a valuable tool for formation and action" (OAPC III, 7).

The statements of John Paul II and the context with which he is dealing make two points clear: they signify a recognition of the injustices on the Latin American continent, and they reaffirm the value of the church's social teaching precisely in such a situation of injustice. The pope does not offer this social teaching as a "legitimation" or defense of a peaceful social situation that has come about thanks to fidelity to the church's teaching; he presents it rather as a remedy for a seriously anti-Christian situation that is contrary precisely to those values in the social teaching that are called for by our faith itself. In other words, what is happening in Latin America, namely, the growing gap between rich and poor that is a scandal and a contradiction of our very being as Christians, is not the outcome of fidelity to the church's social teaching, but rather its negation and rejection. Consequently legitimacy cannot be claimed for the hermeneutic or interpretation of the church's social teaching that is offered by those who regard themselves as the defenders of a Western and Christian civilization; their interpretation only begets situations of injustice.

John Paul II not only recommends and urges the social teaching of the church; he has also helped make a significant advance in his encyclical on human work, *Laborem exercens*. We may say that for the first time the church has issued its official teaching from within the context of a socialist experience, which it then seeks to modify. The scope of the encyclical is far from being fully appreciated as yet, for this document marks the beginning of a new era in the church's social teaching.

Let us turn now to the way in which the Latin American bishops, gathered at Puebla, see the social context in which the church's social teaching is to serve as the norm for liberating action.

THE LATIN AMERICAN SITUATION
AND THE SOCIAL TEACHING OF THE CHURCH

In the Puebla documents we can see reflection focusing on two poles that represent the two characteristic traits of Latin America: its Christian heritage, and its situation of wretchedness, injustice, and underdevelopment.

The first pole is concerned with the unmerited, loving action of God on behalf of the Latin American peoples in the form of the evangelization that brought us the saving truth of Jesus Christ, and in the form of the grace that enabled this saving truth to become deeply embodied in our culture and popular devotion and to permeate our collective consciousness, especially in the ordinary men and women of our people. Evangelization has been the seed of hope for our peoples. A whole series of reflections at Puebla takes shape around this pole (the doctrinal section, the sections on culture and popular religiosity, and so on).

The second pole is concerned basically with the response given by our society, by individuals and peoples. The Latin American peoples have been evangelized, but they do not meet fully the demands of the faith they have accepted; they have transgressed and are living in a situation of sin, of denial of brotherhood and sisterhood, of denial of peace as a gift of the Lord (see Medellín Document on Peace [Med-P] 14). I am not saying simply that there is wretchedness and underdevelopment; I am saying that there is injustice and the sins that turn persons against their sisters and brothers.

The church sees sin as a reality in the history of Latin America: "The reality of Latin American life forces us to experience this power of sin in all its bitterness and extremes as something in flagrant contradiction with the divine plan" (Final Document of Puebla [DP] 186). Since we are dealing here with a continent that has been evangelized, the sin on our continent is not external to the church, for the church itself asserts that the evangelization of our peoples "was deep enough for the faith to become a constitutive part of Latin America's life and identity" (DP 412).

Sin has in fact marked the church since the beginnings of its evangelizing activity: "In its work of evangelization the Church had to bear the weight of its lapses, its acts of complicity with the earthly powers, its incomplete pastoral vision, and the destructive force of sin" (DP 10).

The church humbly confesses that "the faith of our peoples which implies the originality of love, is not always practiced in its fullness by us Christians" (Message to the Peoples of Latin America [MPLA] 2). "Not all the members of the Church . . . have shown respect for human beings and their culture" (DP 966). "Today's Church is not yet the Church that it is called upon to be" (DP 231). Therefore "the wayfaring Church humbly acknowledges its mistakes and sins, which obscure the visage of God in his children" (DP 209). Puebla says with even greater forthrightness: "On this earth the Church will never succeed in fully living its universal vocation to holiness. It will continue to be composed of just people and sinners. What is more, the dividing line between just person and sinner is one that runs right through the heart of every single Christian" (DP 253). Marked as it is by the sins of its own children, the church is "permanently in need of self-evangelization, greater conversion, and purification" (DP 228). If there are deficiencies in our peoples' faith-life, these are due to an "inadequate proclamation of the Gospel" (DP 173). No other sin received more attention at Puebla than the sin of injustice. Let us therefore turn now to an analysis of the nature and gravity of this sin.

Nature of the Sin of Injustice

A first attempt at an analysis of the reality of injustice in Latin America may leave the impression that we are dealing with a strictly economic problem. In fact, the problem reveals itself as far deeper once it is seen to have its roots in sin, and specifically in the sin of injustice that has taken flesh in the very structures of our Latin American society.

The Growing Gap between Rich and Poor

The bishops point to a "growing gap between rich and poor" (DP 28) that is due to "the appropriation by a privileged minority of a large part of the wealth as well as the benefits created by science and culture" (DP 1208). Side by side with this wealth there is "the poverty of a large majority of our people, who are aware of being left out and of having their growing aspirations for justice and participation blocked" (ibid.). But this situation directly contradicts one of the most evident longings of our peoples, namely, to "close the gap between extravagant luxury and indigence" (DP 133). Echoing this longing, the bishops urge us to see to it "that the distances do not grow greater, that the sins do not multiply, and the Spirit of God does not withdraw from the Latin American family" (MPLA 3). The gap is undeniable; it has even widened since Medellín and produces very concrete effects in the lives of individuals.

"No one can deny the concentration of business ownership in the hands of a few, both in urban and rural areas. . . . Nor can anyone deny the concentration of power in the hands of civilian and military technocracies, which frustrate rightful claims for participation and guarantees in a democratic state" (DP 1263). This undeniable state of affairs has been further aggravated: "The marginalization of the vast majority and the exploitation of the poor has increased" (DP 1260); "Since the Medellín Conference the situation has grown worse and more acute for the vast majority of our population" (DP 487).

It is easy to say that there is a gap. It is difficult, however, to imagine what this means concretely in everyday life for millions of human beings: "The vast majority of our fellow humans continue to live in a situation of poverty and even wretchedness that has grown more acute" (DP 1135). The living conditions under which the majority of families in Latin America labors (see DP 571) add up to a "situation of inhuman poverty in which millions of Latin Americans live," a situation that finds expression in, for example, "a high rate of infant mortality, lack of adequate housing, health problems, starvation wages, unemployment and underemployment, malnutrition, job uncertainty, compulsory migration, etc." (DP 29). And it is not only Latin America but the entire Third World which cries out and lifts its voice through the gathered bishops and which Paul VI heard and brought to the world's attention:

> We know only too well that all the energy and effort of those peoples are invested in the struggle to overcome the things that condemn them to live on the margin of life: hunger, chronic disease, illiteracy, impoverishment, injustice in internal relations and particularly in commercial interchanges, situations of economic and cultural neocolonialism that are sometimes as cruel as political colonialism, etc. [EN 30, cited in DP 26].

We should note that the bishops speak of these problems "in pastoral accents" (ibid.) and that Paul VI had already stated: "The Church . . . has the duty to proclaim the liberation of millions of human beings, among whom are many of the Church's own children; the duty to help bring this liberation forth in the world, to bear witness to it and make sure that it is total. None of this is alien to evangelization" (ibid.).

A Gap That Has Its Roots in Sin

One of the most important assertions of Puebla is that this gap is not a purely economic, political, or social phenomenon, but is intimately connected with sin: "If we view these anxieties and frustrations in the light of faith, we see that they have been caused by sin, which has very broad personal and social dimensions" (DP 73). The social dimension of sin must be thought as being at least a "destructive imprint" left on structures by those who created them (DP 281), so that the term "sinful structures" may be used of them (ibid.). People reject God and God's gift of peace when they live in injustice (Med-P 14); the social world is an arena of sin and grace. "Our social conduct is an integral part of our following of Christ" (DP 476).

How do the bishops conceive the relation between sin and social structures? They see sin as the "root" of the situation of injustice (DP 1258). Through sin "evil, death, violence, hatred, and fear entered the world" (DP 185).

> Sinfulness on the personal level, the break with God that debases the human being, is always mirrored on the level of interpersonal relations in a corresponding egoism, haughtiness, ambition, and envy. These traits produce injustice, domination, violence at every level, and conflicts between individuals, groups, social classes, and peoples. They also produce corruption, hedonism, aggravated sexuality, and superficiality in mutual relations [DP 328].

Sin is, therefore, "the root and source of all oppression, injustice, and discrimination" (DP 517).

By its nature sin destroys communion among persons and with God. It is "a force making for breakdown and rupture" and "will always place obstacles to growth in love and communion . . . both within the hearts of human beings, and within the various structures which they have created" (DP 281). There is

> a crisis in moral values: public and private corruption; greed for exorbitant profit; venality; lack of real effort; the absence of any social sense of practical justice and solidarity; and the flight of capital resources and brain power. All these things prevent or undermine communion with God and brotherhood [DP 69].

This happens when "the human person . . . impregnates the mechanisms of society with materialistic values" (DP 70). Sin is essentially "the destroyer of human dignity" (DP 329).

God alone can forgive sin and free human beings from it (cf. DP 281), but sin also has its concrete seductions and idolatries, and therefore we must "make concrete the liberation that Christ won on the cross" (DP 485) and preach the integral message of Christ, from which "There flows an original anthropology and theology" and which "is a liberating message because it saves us from the bondage of sin" (DP 517). The ultimate source of Christ's liberating action is God's plan, which has for its purpose "to liberate our history from sin" (DP 470).

The Sin of Injustice

Latin America is today "engaged in trying to overcome its situation of underdevelopment and injustice" (DP 864). The injustice becomes clear in view of the real possibilities that exist of changing the situation: "The significant economic progress that has been experienced by our continent proves that it would be possible to root out extreme poverty and improve our people's quality of life" (DP 21). But this real possibility is frustrated because "small groups in our nations, who are often tied in with foreign interests, have taken advantage of the opportunities provided by these older forms of the free market to profit for themselves while the interests of the vast majority of the people suffer" (DP 47). Lay groups "have not adequately undertaken the social dimension of their commitment . . . because they are wedded to their own concerns for economic advantage and power" (DP 824). "Many have demonstrated a faith with little strength to overcome their egoism, their individualism, and their greedy hold on riches. They have acted unjustly and injured the unity of society and the Church itself" (DP 966).

Injustice, born of egotism, finds expression in various choices, be these economic: "development-models that subject workers and their families to cold economic calculation" (DP 37), or political:

> they [governments based on force] look askance at the organizing efforts of laborers, peasants, and the common people; and they adopt repressive measures to prevent such organizing. But this type of control over, or limitation on, activity is not applied to employer organizations, which can exercise their full power to protect their interests [DP 44].

If poverty is "the product of the . . . situations and structures" (DP 30) of society, then love "must become first and foremost a labor of justice on behalf of the oppressed" (DP 327).

Injustice at the Level of Structures

Injustice may be caused by strictly individual decisions. This, however, is not the kind of injustice that concerns us here. There are also decisions made by human beings that leave an impress on the structures of society and produce what Puebla calls "institutionalized injustice" (DP 509, 562). "Analyzing this situation more deeply, we discover that this poverty is not a passing phase. Instead it is the product of economic, social, and political situations, though there are also other causes for the state of misery" (DP 30). The injustice in question here finds expression in, for example, "developmental models that extort a truly inhuman price from those who are poorest. And this is all the more unjust insofar as the price is not shared by all" (DP 50). There is a "grave structural conflict: 'The growing affluence of a few people parallels the growing poverty of the masses' " (DP 1209, citing OAPC III, 4).

Sin, the root of this situation, is a mystery of iniquity that "is at work through deeds and structures that prevent more fraternal participation in the construction of society and in the enjoyment of the goods that God created for all" (DP 267). Nevertheless, it is in the heart of the person that this sin comes to birth; the authors of the structures are those who through their sin leave their "destructive imprint" on structures (see DP 281).

As in the case of all sin, it is the responsibility of human beings to accept the grace of conversion: "This reality calls for personal conversion and profound structural changes" (DP 30). The church "asks all Christians to work together to change unjust structures" (DP 16). "The prayer, work and educational activity of the family as a social cell must be geared to changing unjust structures" (DP 587).

This call for a commitment to structural change has its source in the church's mission of evangelization, because the "dynamism [of evangelization] aims at personal conversion and social transformation" (DP 362).

> The evangelizing activity of our Latin American Church must have as its overall goal the ongoing evangelical renewal and transformation of our culture. In other words, the Gospel must penetrate the values and criteria that inspire our culture, convert the human beings who live by these values, and, insofar as it is necessary, change the structures in which they live and express themselves so that they may be more fully human [DP 395].

The church "urges a rapid and thoroughgoing transformation of structures" (DP 438).

A faithful response to the gospel requires change in the structures for which we are responsible. "Laws and structures will have to be animated by the Spirit, who gives life to human beings and enables the Gospel to be fleshed out in history" (DP 199). "The communion that is to be fashioned between human beings is one that embraces their whole being, right down to the roots of their love. It must also manifest itself in every aspect of life, including economic, social, and political life" (DP 215). The focus is therefore on a liberation that "takes in all the different dimensions of life: the social, the political, the economic, the cultural, and all their interrelationships" (DP 483).

Gravity of the Sin of Injustice

Two approaches will help us grasp the full gravity of this sin of injustice. We may consider the external effect of the injustice, that is, the scandal it causes. We may also consider the internal aspect; I refer to the ideological manipulation that seeks to hide institutionalized injustice behind a religious front.

The Scandal of Injustice

As pastors, the bishops issue warnings designed to make sure "that the distances do not grow greater" (MPLA 3). The present situation frustrates the hopes of people that they may "close the gap between extravagant luxury and indigence" (DP 133).

This situation is a contradiction of the faith: "The contradictions existing between unjust social structures and the demands of the Gospel are quite evident" (DP 1257). "The gap between rich and poor, the menacing situation faced by the weakest, the injustices, the humiliating disregard and subjection endured by them radically contradict the values of personal dignity and solidary brotherhood" (DP 452). The contradiction consists essentially in the fact that by faith we know of Christ's presence in the poor and yet we do not change the situation to their advantage. "This situation of pervasive poverty takes on very concrete faces in real life. In these faces we ought to recognize the suffering features of Christ the Lord, who questions and challenges us" (DP 31). For this reason, this contradiction of Christian existence is described as a "scandal" (DP 28). This scandal of not living up to the faith is partly responsible for many having become estranged from God. "The Church itself cannot be considered blameless in this area" (DP 1113). "What is more, non-belief is a summons and a challenge to the fidelity and authenticity of believers and the Church" (DP 1117).

Once we think of injustice as a scandal, we can understand why Puebla says: "The deep-rooted social differences, the extreme poverty, and the violation of human rights found in many areas pose challenges to evangelization" (DP 90). But we should note that they are not challenges to the *fact* of evangelization, because "we have been evangelized in Latin America for some five centuries" (DP 342). The challenge is rather to the *quality* and *content* of the evangelization. "Situations of injustice and poverty are an indictment in themselves, indicating that the faith was not strong enough to affect the criteria and the decisions of those responsible for ideological leadership and the organization of our people's socio-economic life together" (DP 437).

The evil of scandal affects an external, but nonetheless essential, dimension of the ecclesial community because this community is called to a missionary proclamation of the gospel. Even more serious, however, is the effort to lend religious legitimacy to the scandalous situation; such an attempt is a form of "the sin against the Holy Spirit."

The Evil of Giving Religious Legitimacy to Injustice

Many sins of injustice are committed because of "religious ignorance and indifference" that "prompt many to prescind from moral principles, whether personal or social" (DP 82). I am referring to laypersons (but I might add other sectors of the people of God) who "are deficient in understanding and accepting the Church's social teaching" (DP 824).

Due to their ignorance such people cannot understand why, when confronted with violations of human rights "the Church, by virtue of 'an authentically evangelical commitment,' must raise its voice to denounce and condemn these situations, particularly when the responsible officials or rulers call themselves Christians" (DP 42). In fact, "some governments have come to regard certain features and contents of Christian education as subversive" (DP 1017). Such governments, which generally shelter themselves behind the ideology of national security, "in some instances . . . presume to justify their positions with a subjective profession of Christian faith" (DP 49). For "in some countries of Latin America this doctrine [of national security] justifies itself as the defender of the Christian civilization of the West" (DP 547).

This manipulation of the faith restricts the person of Jesus Christ to the merely private realm (DP 178). There are those "who would restrict the scope of faith to personal or family life; who would exclude the professional, economic, social, and political orders as if sin, love, prayer, and pardon had no relevance in them" (DP 515). This kind of "instrumentalization" may derive "from Christians themselves, and even from priests and religious, when they proclaim a Gospel devoid of economic, social, cultural, and political implications. In practice this mutilation comes down to a kind of complicity with the established order, however unwitting" (DP 558).

Those who manipulate the faith, whether as a veil for injustice or as an instrument in the struggle against injustice, forget the very nature of this faith and abuse the religious spirit of the people. Faith is not an instrument but an encounter with the Lord; it certainly makes demands, but it may not be manipulated or made into a tool.

THE CHURCH'S SOCIAL TEACHING AS NORM
FOR LIBERATING ACTION

What mission does the church's social teaching have in the context of oppression and liberating action? Pope John Paul II assigns it a very important role: its application "guarantees the authenticity of their [the children of the church] involvement in delicate and demanding social tasks, and of their efforts in behalf of the liberation or advancement of their fellow human beings" (OAPC III, 7).

The pope takes up the theme of liberation which Paul VI had discussed in *Evangelii nuntiandi* where he had described all the characteristics which make liberation a proper task of the church. John Paul II takes the same approach and says that "pastoral commitments in this field must be nurtured with a correct Christian conception of liberation. 'The Church . . . has the duty of proclaiming the liberation of millions of human beings, . . . the duty of helping to bring about this liberation' " (OAPC III, 6, citing EN 30).

The pope explains the sense in which the church's social teaching serves as a norm for liberating action:

There are many signs that help us to distinguish when the liberation in question is Christian and when, on the other hand, it is based on ideologies that make it inconsistent with an evangelical view of humanity, of things, and of events (EN 35). These signs derive from the content that the evangelizers proclaim or from the concrete attitudes that they adopt. At the level of content one must consider how faithful they are to the Word of God, to the Church's living tradition, and to its magisterium. As for attitudes, one must consider what sense of communion they feel, with the bishops first of all, and then with the other sectors of God's People. Here one must also consider what contribution they make to the real building up of the community; how they channel their love into caring for the poor, the sick, the dispossessed, the neglected, and the oppressed; and how, discovering in these people the image of the poor and suffering Jesus, they strive to alleviate their needs and to serve Christ in them (LG 8). Let us make no mistake about it: as if by some evangelical instinct, the humble and simple faithful spontaneously sense when the Gospel is being served in the Church and when it is being eviscerated and asphyxiated by other interests [OAPC III, 6].

Pope John Paul II has given a practical example of this evangelical spirit by drawing close to the poor and showing them his desire to serve them: "The pope chooses to be your voice, the voice of those who cannot speak or who have been silenced. He wishes to be the conscience of consciences, an invitation to action, to make up for lost time, which has frequently been a time of prolonged sufferings and unsatisfied hopes" (AIOC).

There can, however, be incorrect interpretations of the church's teaching, and these "call for calm discernment, opportune criticism, and clear-cut stances" (Introduction to OAPC). The mere existence of texts which contain the church's social teaching and are meant to provide norms for liberating action is not enough, unless the texts are correctly interpreted. The hermeneutical problem is how to interpret both the texts and the struggle for liberation, with each of these shedding light on the other. We must know how to judge when liberating action is being undertaken in a Christian spirit and when it is motivated by ideologies that can reduce integral liberation to what is in fact only its economic, political, social, or cultural dimension. Reference to the social teaching of the church enables us to determine the legitimacy of the liberating struggle undertaken by Christians. This teaching is a criterion of interpretation, or a hermeneutical criterion. But the texts themselves likewise require interpretation if their true meaning is to be found, and it is pastoral practice (like that of the pope in his siding with the poor) that assures a correct understanding of the texts.

2

THE HERMENEUTICAL PROBLEM

I have already made a brief reference to the hermeneutical problem. By this is meant the problem of the framework within which, or the key by means of which, the authentic meaning of something is to be determined. We have already seen that fidelity to the magisterium is the hermeneutical key which enables us to decide when liberating action is authentic. In later chapters we shall see that there are hermeneutical criteria which make it possible for us to read the church's social teaching through evangelical and ecclesial eyes. In those chapters we shall be attempting a hermeneutic of this social teaching, one that is analogous to a hermeneutic of the Bible.

Starting with the etymology of the word "hermeneutic," the present chapter will give a short synopsis of the historical development of the hermeneutical problem in philosophy and theology. It will end with a description of the structures of interpretation or understanding.

ETYMOLOGICAL EXPLANATION

The word "hermeneutic" is derived from the Greek verb *hermêneuein* (Latin: *interpretari*), which means to express or set forth one's thoughts in words. The verb also means "to translate" and, finally, "to act as an interpreter." The three meanings have in common that they involve a passage from relative obscurity to relative clarity. In its first meaning *hermêneuein* involves a passage from amorphous and obscure experience to the clarity of linguistic expression. In the act of "translation" there is a passage from the obscurity of a foreign language to the clarity of one's own language. Finally, when one offers a commentary and explanations, that is, when one interprets, one passes from a less clear to a more clear expression of thought.[1]

The Greek verb *hermêneuein* is connected with Hermes, the messenger of the gods, who according to Greek mythology interpreted the divine oracles with the aid of human words. From this point of view, hermeneutic has a numinous dimension, as can be seen in 1 Corinthians 12:10, where it is associated with the gift of tongues. In this context it does not mean simply an ability to give a rational translation; it signifies an interpretation of something given by the Spirit. In Acts 14:12 the people of Lystra called Barnabas "Zeus" and Paul "Hermes," because Paul is the chief speaker.[2] Finally, in Luke 24:27 the risen Lord himself acts as interpreter (*diermêneusen*) of all that the scriptures have to say about him.

Since far back in antiquity there has existed a hermeneutic in the sense of

a sum of concrete guides to right understanding derived from experience, and . . . mostly applied to fixed systems, of an acknowledgedly authoritative character, which aimed at right practice. They aimed at an elaborate "art" or technique of understanding, which is far from what is meant by a "theory of understanding" such as constitutes the modern notion of hermeneutics.[3]

In other words, there has always been an *art* of understanding (norms for correct interpretation) but only in the modern age has a *science* of hermeneutic made its appearance.

In biblical studies a distinction is made between "exegesis" and "hermeneutic" (or interpretation). The goal of hermeneutic is a theory of the principles, general and special, of biblical interpretation. Among the general principles are the following: establish the authentic text; locate the text in its context (with the help of, for example, parallel texts, ancient versions, commentaries); take into account the literary genre, the period and place of composition, the occasion and purpose, the culture and mentality of the author and of the people to which he belonged. The attainment of these goals requires the aid of philology, the comparative history of literatures and religions, history, geography, archaeology, ethnology, and other sciences.

The Catholic church has authoritatively established its own special principles for biblical interpretation, in the form of dogmatic principles which take into account the inspired nature of the texts. There is, for example, the principle that in matters of faith the official interpretation given by the church is to prevail; or the principle that in this area no views may be held which contradict the unanimous patristic interpretation of a passage of scripture. There is also the hermeneutical principle of "the analogy of faith (*analogia fidei*)," which says that any interpretation must be in accordance with the internal harmony of revelation, once the theological meaning of a biblical passage has been determined by the ordinary or extraordinary magisterium of the church or by the unanimous interpretation of the Fathers.[4]

"Hermeneutic" is not limited to the interpretation of religious texts. If "explanation" is understood as the throwing of light on an object that exists independently of the mind, then the "interpretation" (hermeneutic) proper to understanding must be understood as the clarification of an object in the field of intersubjective intellectual experience.[5] It may be said, therefore, that "the basic element in hermeneutic is man's self-understanding, which is inseparable from the historicity of existence."[6]

HERMENEUTIC, A UNIVERSAL PART OF HUMAN EXISTENCE

Hermeneutic is a profoundly human and vital activity. Our everyday talk is a continuous act of interpretation.

Interpretation is a basic part of human existence. When we speak, we continuously interpret both the external world and our own internal experiences, precisely in the measure that we commit these to language, to our common language, to my own personal language. The person who speaks objectivizes his experience in a set of words by means of which he renders this experience communicable. The hearer, who perceives this objectification, accomplishes the corresponding act of subjectivization. This means that hearing and understanding something that has been said is an active process of interpretation which reverses the process that has taken place in the production of linguistic expression. The same can be said of our everyday reading of what has been written. In other words, our everyday dealings in language are already by their nature an interpretative process. Serious difficulties of interpretation usually do not arise in everyday discourse, but this is because we all live in the same world, share the same basic experience of the world and, in addition, have in common a series of basic life-experiences. We also share the same mentality, speak the same concrete language, and have abundant opportunity of asking and obtaining clarification and confirmation.[7]

Everything in our lives requires interpretation. Interpretation is therefore a profoundly human phenomenon; it helps us to become persons to the extent that it enables us to give a meaning to nature, humanize it, and turn it into a framework for human history.

There are various levels of understanding: we have a direct understanding of nature; we understand, next, the tools that human beings and their cultures have created; we understand language and, in an even more radical way, we understand ourselves and our world.

It is a fact, of course, that nature can be regarded as a subject more suited for "explanation" than for "understanding" (two types of knowledge which give rise to two different types of science). Nature is explained when the coherence of its laws is grasped. Nonetheless nature can also be an area for understanding because it not only contains causes and effects but has a meaning insofar as it can be grasped as a totality and in relation to human beings. Then one is concerned with an "anthropological" meaning of the world as distinct from its "cosmological" meaning. In Romans 8:19, for example, Paul sketches an understanding of the world at the theological level.

There is a second range of objects for understanding, and here human persons do not act as passively as they do in dealing with nature. They read and discover a meaning in nature; in the world of tools, however, that is, of objects made by human beings themselves in the context of their culture, there is a meaning which they themselves have put there. A tool, then, is a part of the natural world which persons have transformed in order that they may carry out some purpose. I understand a tool when I understand what it is used for. The more sophisticated the tool, the more charged with meaning it is. To produce the tool we call a hammer is not the same as to produce the tool we call an automobile; the second is an objectification of collective efforts, technical advances, and so on. The "natural object" thus turns not only into an "artificial or cultural object" but also into a "social object," that is, an objectification of human activity which brings meaning with it. But the object that has been turned into an instrument is only halfway to being fully such. In order that a tool may be fully a tool it must be wielded. Only in the moment of actual use is the object fully constituted a tool or instrument of human life.

In their social lives human persons are introduced into an organized "contextual world." A child encounters a world already "ordered" as houses, objects, tools for specific purposes: schools for studying, churches for praying, recreation fields for playing, and so on. The way the contextual world is organized is an expression of the culture. This organization is already in existence, and the child comes upon it as such; there are others who make the organization work effectively. The difference between a dead culture and a living culture is not the existence or nonexistence of objects and tools, but the fact that these are or are not used and incorporated into human life.

Knowledge of the external world, of tools, and of social organization is bound up with language. Language is the most radical of human inventions because it is the instrument of the person's interior and human self-realization. To be a human being is to be able to name things and communicate with others.

Language has its atoms, which are the syllables. Each unit of language has to be integrated into a higher unity, in a continual process of extension of meaning. Various syllables form words; words in turn acquire their meaning in sentences, and sentences in contexts. The same sentence can have a different meaning depending on whether it is enunciated as a straightforward statement or in the ironic mode. Unless therefore we take the various styles into account, we will not understand the real meaning of a sentence or text, even though we may understand all the spoken or written elements of it. The intention of that to which another's interior thought has given objective existence in language will escape us and there will be no communication. Style is thus a kind of "interpersonal atmosphere" in which we must situate ourselves in order to understand the person with whom we are speaking.

Above and beyond the style of a particular work there is the literary genre, which is produced by a kind of historical "accumulation" of similar works. Literary genres give expression to the social need of communicating in a certain way. They bring to light the psychology of peoples, their *Sitz im Leben* (vital or sociological context). The historical dimension of literature establishes the unity and historical embodiment of literary genres, and a literature in its entirety manifests the meaning of a particular human community. The text thus carries us from its own atomic particles to the totality of the culture, rising at every step to new levels of meaning, each of which, if it is to be properly understood, must be understood in terms of the higher levels. There is a "transcendent" dynamism which keeps breaking out of circles of immanence, as though saying that the meaning will not be grasped without going further.

The problem of understanding involves more than "understanding things"; it consists ultimately in knowing ourselves as existent beings. This kind of understanding is radical, fundamental, and ultimate. The proof of this claim is that there are many things ignorance of which causes no anxiety; but we do feel anxious about whether or not our life has meaning, whether or not it "makes sense." We may grasp partial meanings, but the failure to grasp the total meaning of our existence pushes us toward despair.

Once we have raised the question of hermeneutic, we must consider the subject in its full extent and radicality, as a human activity in which everyone engages and in which each individual engages in a highly personal way. If we wish to define a person in hermeneutical terms, we must say that this person is the being who is capable of giving things a meaning. In this understanding, language has an irreplaceable role. We understand to the extent that we can name. New phenomena call for new words. The continued use of old expressions for new contents is a source of many ambiguities, and much potential development of new contents may be limited and lost due to the limitations of trite expressions.

We will best understand the problem of hermeneutic if we follow in its historical trajectory the development of the felt need of human beings to give rational scientific form to their activity of understanding.

HISTORICAL DEVELOPMENT
OF THE HERMENEUTICAL PROBLEM

In studying the development or evolution of hermeneutic we may begin with theology, and this for several reasons. The very etymology of the word brings us back, as we have seen, to a religious phenomenon of the Greek world, namely, the interpretation of the sayings of the gods, the obscurity of which had to be dispelled. But there are deeper reasons than this.

The word of God presents itself to the believer as the ultimate and radical explanation of meaning. The word of God is therefore the original place of a complete hermeneutic of human existence. In the course of history the concern to ensure the correct interpretation of God's message came before the concern to examine the conditions required by mutual understanding among human beings.

The Hermeneutical Problem in Theology

Every revealed religion presents its problems, but Judaism and Christianity are singled out by the fact that they see the word of God as present in and for human history. This word is revelation in the form of promise and of law. The word marks the inception of historical time and gives rise to a communal consciousness that looks for the fulfillment of the promise and thus brings a history into being. In Christianity, theological hermeneutic must explain the divine action that always accompanies the divine word, and vice versa.

The importance of the interpretation of the sacred texts of the Old Testament appears at every step, in the constant reference to the "scribes" or men who devoted themselves to the study and interpretation of the Law. The extent to which a legalistic interpretation can utterly falsify the meaning of relations with God is brought home to us by the daily struggle Christ had to carry on in order to restore a sincerity of heart and a human authenticity to the worship of his people. The prophets for their part engaged in a hermeneutic of true religion when they demanded that worship be accompanied by the practice of justice. Their purpose was to give an authentic religious existence its proper place once again in the Israelite tradition.

In the New Testament too we see a very clear "hermeneutical principle" at work. The entire Old Testament is to be read in the light of its christological meaning. In contrast to Judaism, which continues its own interpretation of the Old Testament, the Christian community reads scripture in the light of the paschal mystery of Jesus. A clear example of this principle in operation is Matthew's application (1:20,23) of the prophecy in Isaiah 7:14 (a young woman shall conceive a son) to Mary and her son Jesus. If we look for a "historical" interpretation, that is, if we try to determine what Isaiah had in mind when he wrote this passage, we will end up with one that differs from the Christian interpretation. This does not mean that we must choose between the two, but rather that we must grasp both of them. Norbert Lohfink writes:

> We are continually faced with the problem of how we are to interpret the Old Testament: in historical terms or in Christian terms? We must interpret it historically because intellectual honesty demands that we search out the original meaning. We must interpret it in Christian terms, because we are dealing with the Bible as the word of God, and we cannot accept that in parts of the Bible God contradicts his own word as expressed fully in Christ.[8]

In the early centuries of the church's life the hermeneutical problem took the form of a controversy between the Antiochene school and the Alexandrian school. The former advocated a literal interpretation of scripture, the latter an allegorical and symbolical interpretation. Origen made the first great Christian hermeneutical effort to synthesize the two views: We are to reach the spiritual meaning through the study of the text as it stands. This Eastern development was repeated in the West where the literalism of Jerome and the spiritualism of Ambrose were synthesized in the work of Augustine.

In the Middle Ages the influence of philosophy led to a concentration on systematic theology. But even this new approach had its corresponding hermeneutical principle: scripture contains dogmatic statements whose implications must be brought to light by dogmatic theology.

In the modern age Christianity is divided precisely by divergent hermeneutical principles. While Protestants cling to the principle of *scriptura sola* (scripture alone), Catholics interpret the Bible in the light of tradition. For the Catholic church the councils have the status of "hermeneutical events."[9]

The Reformation gave the hermeneutical problem a greater urgency. It did so not only by defending new theses based on scripture, but also and more radically by establishing a hermeneutical principle *(scriptura sola)* which, in addition to denying any external rule, asserted the possibility of scripture revealing what Christ is trying to accomplish in the course of history. Quite understandably, then, the Counter-Reformation adopted a polemical stance and defined itself in terms of a different hermeneutical position: the necessity of tradition.

Despite its own hermeneutical position Protestantism developed a whole body of doctrine which defined what "orthodoxy" was. Liberal Protestant theology, relying on the historical critical method, then restored primacy to the hermeneutical principle of *scriptura sola*: the only rule is fidelity to the Bible. This time, however, the questions put to the text did not spring from faith. The reason for this is that the harmony between faith and culture which had characterized previous centuries no longer existed; consequently, the questions which the culture asked of faith were no longer the same. The eighteenth and nineteenth centuries were experiencing the euphoria created by advancing scientific knowledge. Principles were developed that were valid for a science that proceeded by explanation of causes, an interpretative science. But the limits set by a science that focuses on the explanation of nature are extremely narrow. Within Protestantism Martin Kähler objected to the historical critical method; according to him the historical Jesus of modern criticism hides from us the living Christ of the scriptures. Barth agreed with Kähler in this rejection, saying that the historical critical method has but a limited usefulness as one step toward a fuller understanding of the Bible. The interpretation of the Bible must submit to being guided by its object; it must submit to being surprised by the word of God coming to us as something unexpected.

This brings us to Rudolf Bultmann, one of the most important of all writers on the subject of theological hermeneutic. Since theology claims to explain or elucidate and develop the faith of the believer, it must be closely bound up with a hermeneutic, inasmuch as such an explanation is not something fixed once and for all. Theological propositions must be constantly challenged in the light of the definitive and unqualified fact which is Christ. History is an essential factor in theology.

In his interpretation of scripture Bultmann applies the ideas of Martin Heidegger. The latter's existential analytic supplies concepts enabling us to speak in an adequate fashion of how to exist in becoming, and how to choose and form ourselves. Human persons really do not choose other things for themselves; rather each person chooses him or her self as a possibility. If persons decide through their actions what they are to be and if action is not a pure exercise of will but embodies an understanding of reality, then action is the key factor, even in understanding God. "As . . . the actual essence of man is present in action, likewise God is present where He is active. Jesus then does not make known a new conception of God, or revelations of the nature of God; instead, he brings the message of the coming Kingdom and of the will of God."[10]

The encounter between God and persons takes place in history.

> Man, if he rightly understands himself, . . . cannot observe this complex [the living complex of events which make up history and in which persons themselves are essentially involved] objectively as he can observe natural phenomena. . . . Hence there cannot be impersonal observation of history in the same sense that there can be impersonal observation of nature.[11]

Jesus is part of our history, and not someone who stands outside of it; we encounter him when we discover in his words that the meaning of our own existence is that it is in movement and is called upon to decide about itself.

Bultmann's contribution to hermeneutic is of two kinds. He makes a negative or ground-clearing contribution, which consists in rising above myth; scripture must be demythologized. He also makes a positive contribution with his insistence on an existential interpretation.

When we hear the word "demythologization," we tend to think of myth as something false or imaginary. But myth has a different meaning for present-day writers: "Myth is the assignment of meaning to reality as a whole."[12] In this sense, every vision that embraces reality as a whole is mythical or metaphysical.

> Myth is a symbolical expression of reality and an assignment of meaning to it. To this end it makes use of representation, narrative, and image. In this way myth differs from a metaphysical explanation of reality. Both give explanations that go beyond the immediate evidence: metaphysics does it in the rational mode, myth in the figurative mode. In a sense, myth is embodied metaphysics. Precisely for this reason, and despite its transcendent character, myth plays a part in the functioning of reality as such.[13]

Bultmann, too, regards myth as a mode of expression:

> Mythology is the use of imagery to express the other worldly in terms of this world and the divine in terms of human life, the other side in terms of this side. For example, divine transcendence is expressed as spatial distance. It is a mode of expression which makes it easy to understand the cultus as an action in which material means are used to convey immaterial power.[14]

The problem, then, is to get beyond mythological language, for this is meaningless to a person trained in the language of science, which is diametrically opposed to myth and looks upon the world as governed by a coherent set of laws. The point is not to eliminate mythological formulations but rather to understand them. This requires an existential interpretation.

A person is not an object but a being who exists, a being who has a history. An example will show what is meant. The fact that my father is my father can be determined objectively; the reality, however, of his being "my" father can only be grasped by me myself in my personal encounter with him, through his being a father to "me" and through my "making him be" my father.[15] Existence cannot be grasped the way a static phenomenon can; it shows itself as something that happens step by step. An existential interpretation is one in which existent beings feel themselves questioned in their entirety. The sole form taken by this question is the world that opens up for the person a possible self-understanding which has to be won through action. An existential interpretation does not communicate knowledge but calls to a decision. The human person reaches fulfillment through understanding. My response to the question is my decision as to how I want to understand myself. I understand friends without having inquired into the motives for their action; I understand them through the decision which unites me to them in friendship. In this decision I understand myself as one who is a friend.

Bultmann applies to theology Heidegger's idea that every understanding supposes a preapprehension or prior understanding. Only when the matters into which we inquire are a problem for us does a text begin to speak to us. Barth was afraid that to demand such a preapprehension is to set limits in advance on the possibilities of understanding. But Bultmann claims to be calling attention to a universal phenomenon, namely, that every interpretation of a text is controlled by the question asked and by the vantage point from which it is asked (e.g., a cultural interest, an esthetic interest). The more profound the interest with which a text is approached, the more the text will "speak."

It is unacceptable, on the other hand, to turn a preapprehension or prior understanding into a prejudgment, that is, to determine the results of the interpretation in an apriori way or to remain with the preapprehension as though it already provided the definitive understanding. As long as questioners are ready to correct the idea conveyed in their question, they are able to have access to the new and unexpected.

Ebeling, who continues along the line indicated by Bultmann, speaks of human existence as determined by a word that is spoken to it and another which it itself speaks in return: *Wort* and *Antwort* (the English "word" and "answer" loses the word-play here). The word is the place where human existence comes into being, discovers itself, and creates its own universe. The word does not simply convey a content and ideas; it also proposes an end and serves as a guide. If all words do this, much more does God's word do it; God's word alone provides radical meaning. The word makes it possible for the human person to move through history and advance toward the future. The goal of hermeneutic is to turn a past word, crystalized in a document, into a present word that directs the person toward the future. Hermeneutic comes into play when the word is "entangled," that is, when it does not permit a flow from past to future, from the past reality to the spoken word, and from this in turn to the heard word that determines future reality.

I have been citing Protestant authors up to this point because for them the hermeneutical problem has been an especially acute one. Catholics have not felt the problem to be so urgent. An important figure during the Modernist period was Alfred Loisy, whose views approximated those of the historical critical school. Maurice Blondel sought an understanding of the Bible that went beyond the historically verifiable. The debate on the subject was broken off by the condemnation of Modernism, and many years were to pass before Pius XII and Vatican II would display an openness in the discussion of biblical problems.

> The encounter of a Catholic with Jesus Christ, and his initiation into the faith, is not usually the result of merely reading the Bible. Rather, this takes place through baptism and integration into the life of the Church which, by its teaching, by its liturgy, by the witness of its Saints continues to reveal the riches of the "manifold grace" of God and to evoke a more and more personal and total adherence to salvific realities.[16]

Among Catholic theologians Schillebeeckx is perhaps the one who has gone most deeply into this subject. He says that in Catholic theology the problem corresponding to the hermeneutical problem in Protestant theology is the problem of the development of dogma. Catholics need to recognize that "the fifth-century situation enters essentially into the statement of faith itself, without the real content of faith becoming different." The same point can be made in different terms:

> The hermeneutical problem is . . . given a full-length portrait in this: the contemporary scene with its understanding of its own existence is a "hermeneutical" situation, and it is only within this and from this situation (certainly not outside it or from above) that we can understand in faith what the biblical message itself gives us to understand.[17]

Schillebeeckx emphasizes the connection between hermeneutic and practice. The interpretation of the word of God is an operational interpretation because it is new realities that enable us to understand the meaning of God's promises.

The Philosophical Problem of Hermeneutic

An explicit awareness of the hermenutical problem arises as a result of radical spiritual upheavals (the Sophists and Plato; breaks with tradition; the passage from the Old Testament to the New; Reformation and Counter-Reformation; etc.).

On the other hand, a more critical philosophical reflection on hermeneutic was begun by Friedrich Schleiermacher, who is regarded as the father of this discipline in its modern form. He claimed to go beyond the limitations of traditional hermeneutic, in which certain rules of interpretation were applied (yielding a *komparativisches Verstehen*, an understanding through comparison); he emphasized rather the point that an interpretation requires an intuitive appropriation of an author's work (therefore a *divinatorisches Verstehen*, an intuitive understanding).[18] This intuitive appropriation is unmediated, whereas the other type of interpretation supposes the labor of collecting a great deal of detailed grammatical, historical, cultural, and other information. The methods of historical criticism are not able by themselves to get to the bottom of a text; also needed is a kind of imaginative reconstruction of the creative process that produced the work. But it can be objected that this kind of psychological approximation to the author cannot by itself overcome the historical distance separating two different cultural horizons.[19]

Wilhelm Dilthey advanced further along the line initiated by Schleiermacher by distinguishing between the natural sciences (in which explanation is appropriate) and the human, cultural, or moral sciences (*Geisteswissenschaften*) (in which understanding is appropriate).[20] Dilthey went beyond Schleiermacher, whose aim was only to recreate the experience of the author, and pointed out that the historical events of the past must be read as expressions of historical life; hermeneutic therefore expands to take into account the meaning of historical events. A reader today is able to interpret the past because all historical events are effects of the human spirit, and the reader shares the same structures and abilities that men and women of the past had.[21]

Martin Heidegger took a further step by making "understanding" a part of human existence; understanding is an existential, that is, something constitutive of the human person.[22] But Heidegger does not mean simply a psychological understanding of other people nor even an understanding such as is proper to the human and cultural sciences. Understanding, as he uses the term, is even more radical, for it is the understanding of being. The hermeneutical character of human existence finds expression in the understanding human beings have of the world and history. Existence in the world, such as is peculiar to human persons, designates the horizon of their self-understanding. It is therefore possible to speak of a hermeneutical circle, since a new object can make its appearance only within a totality of meaning, while every illumination of a new object takes place within the field of earlier understandings and presupposes these as the conditions of its possibility.[23]

According to Heidegger, all understanding takes place in the medium of language; the historical horizontal level of understanding is established in language. Language is the place of being.[24] Heidegger's thinking has exercised an important influence on theology, both Catholic (Rahner, Welte) and Protestant (Bultmann).

Hans-Georg Gadamer has established a philosophical theory of understanding.[25] He accepts the idea of the hermeneutical circle in the sense given to it by Heidegger and shows the positive value of the "preapprehension" in the sense of a historically transmitted conception of things which, even though not yet made the object of scientific reflection, opens the way to a better understanding. The temporal distance between author and reader should not be thought of negatively, as something to be overcome (that is how Schleiermacher and Dilthey thought of it) but positively, as an encounter of horizons, since the aim, after all, is for us to understand the author. We enrich our own horizon by comparing it with that of others. The possibility of blending different horizons is provided by history; the historical relationship makes it possible to understand, inasmuch as the word spoken in the past enters into history, is developed there, and finally enters into our own horizon. The medium of hermeneutic is language, which conveys, conceals, and then manifests the vision of the world that has been deposited in it, just as it conveys, and so on, the other usual antecedents and conditions for understanding. To a certain extent language also transmits phenomena which are apparently nonlinguistic (power, social interests, etc.) and depend on moral and political action and on public life; in this way language can serve, in a formally universal manner, as a hermeneutic.[26]

Habermas also goes more deeply into the relation between language and practice, as well as between social interests and knowledge.

STRUCTURES OF UNDERSTANDING

At this point I shall bring together various contributions made by philosophers to our subject and point out four structures that are formally present in all understanding, of whatever type it may be.

Horizon

There is no such thing as completely isolated knowledge; the particular always makes its appearance within a horizon. Thus I know something precisely as "some thing"; that is, it appears as what it is only against a comprehensive backdrop, even though the latter is not explicitly present or as clearly perceived as the particular reality which I am now knowing. This totality or horizon within which all knowing is located may be called a "world."

The word "world" may have two meanings. First, there is the cosmological world as it is in itself, independent of human beings. But the world in that sense is an abstraction, since in the concrete the world is the world for human beings, and for the human being the world exists only as the environment of his or her experience and life. We therefore speak, secondly, of "world" as a totality, a reality that is more than the sum of things and of partial knowledges. The meaning of the world is not constituted by the sum of the explanations of things.

How do human persons succeed in grasping the world?

1. To begin with, they put distance between themselves and the world. They are not limited by what is immediately present to their senses, but can distance themselves from this by other kinds of knowing. They are not limited to responding to direct stimuli from the environment but can impose themselves on the environment by conduct that originates in their interior freedom and is not simply a response of a person's organism to stimuli.

2. This distance is accentuated by the fact that human beings are active in regard to the world. They are active even in their knowing. Kant long ago compelled us to recognize that we reorganize the data of experience in accordance with categories. Above all, however, human beings are active through their work: they impose on the world a dynamism, a rhythm, a velocity which they themselves determine.

3. Human beings' grasp of the world is limited. They know that they do not know everything or even every aspect of the things they do know.

4. Persons achieve their grasp of the world in community; they know that it is not the individual but the community that imposes order on the world and organizes it into an "environing world." Individuals can indeed distance themselves from and criticize the order already imposed on the world, but they cannot ignore it; they must start with it.

5. Human beings' grasp of the world is itself captured in language, which perpetuates this grasp and makes it possible to integrate partial experiences into higher units of meaning.

6. Finally, the perception of the horizon is accompanied by a perception of the meaning of existence.

Circularity

When we speak of a "hermeneutical circle," that is, when we say that a preunderstanding is required if we are to understand anything, are we not getting ourselves into a "vicious circle"? We would be, if the preunderstanding functioned as a premise in a deduction, for there would then be no more content in the second act of knowledge than there had been in the first. But the preunderstanding is required not as an explanation but as a condition for the possibility of understanding. Consequently, the circularity consists in the necessary relation between the understanding of meaning and the preunderstanding of the same. By this is meant that not only is there a relation between the objective detail and the objective totality (of this I have already spoken under the heading of "Horizon"), but also that the objective detail is connected with both the objective totality and the subjective totality, although it is not possible to draw very clear lines of demarcation between these two totalities.

It may be objected that the word "circle" is not a very felicitous one for explaining a process which is dynamic. The image of a spiral brings out better the fact that the new understandings we acquire become in turn "preunderstandings" for other future understandings, although at a new level, since the cognitive enrichment meanwhile obtained has carried us beyond the starting point represented by the earlier preunderstanding. An example of the relation between preunderstanding and understanding can be seen in question and answer; a question is not possible unless we already have answers to other, simpler questions that went before. The most difficult thing about the search for truth is the determination of the right questions to be asked.

Dialogue

Because human understanding is bound up with language, it is also dialogical and interpersonal. It is a social event with two dimensions: a theoretical and a practical.

In the first place, there is a theoretical understanding which brings to light human intersubjectivity. In every act of understanding human persons situate themselves in the presence of reality and are conscious of reality. Human consciousness thus has two foci or poles; as I just indicated, in the presence of reality the knower is conscious of this reality, which means that the knower knows him or herself to be a sub-ject, one who perceives, when confronted with an ob-ject. No thinking is possible that does not have this bipolar structure. The object manifests itself only as having meaning for a subject.

The process of abstraction not only defines the object as having an existence in itself; it also makes thematic the consciousness of the "in itself." But the possibility of an "object in itself" can only be grounded in intersubjectivity, that is, in the fact that the object is the same for another speaker as it is for me. In addition, we can speak of "thinking in an objective way" only in the context of intersubjectivity, that is, when the thinking of two subjects is at one with regard to an object, or when one subject knows what another subject also knows.

The possibility of human persons making the world their "object" to a greater extent than as the correlative pole in the object-subject structure is itself rooted in language. Language makes humankind because it establishes a connection with other subjectivities. Language is not simply a naming of an object; it names the object in the presence of, or for, another subject. It not only expresses the subject-object relation, thus explicating what happens in the act of knowledge; it also creates the subject-object relation in the form of a communication of knowledge. To speak is not simply to come to an agreement with regard to something, but also to understand one another. Human understanding is achieved through communication of an understanding of the world, through looking together in the same direction. We may therefore speak of theoretical understanding as "triangular" in its structures: subject—object—subject.

Understanding is also a practical event. Language and dialogue not only express knowledge of the world; they also express the experience of reality-as-desirable, as correlative to the spontaneous movements of appetite. Persons open themselves to reality not only through knowledge but also through freedom and through feeling attracted. Things are "meaning for" but they are also "attraction for." Here again, a process of abstractive reflection enables us to isolate reality with its in-itself and its resultant capacity for attracting others, and to isolate as well the reality of the subject as a self-determining freedom. The relation between subject-as-freedom and reality provokes the self-affirmation of the self, and this self-affirmation, once again, is dialogical; that is, it is posited in the presence of another subjectivity.

When I speak of the dialogical structure of human understanding, I am saying that the *logos* which yields understanding is always a *dia-logos*, that is, a *logos* achieved in, through, and by means of the interaction of subjects who are seeking understanding. Meaning is found only in intersubjectivity. This is not to say that there can be no finding of meaning through the reflection of a subject. But if this discovery is not communicated, it is not meaning for others. The meaning found is really only a seed of meaning; it must undergo a qualitative change if it is to be a fully human meaning.

The dialogical character of understanding reveals at the same time the "linguisticality" and "historicity" of reality. Understanding presupposes the before and after of subjects who are faced with an object; communication is a way of making available repeated experiences of the subject in dealing with the object. Understanding also presupposes that reality is "namable." To give names to things is to introduce them into the space of intercommunication and intersubjectivity; it represents the first and lowest degree of the humanization of nature.

Dialogue should, therefore, be a communication of meaning (theoretical dialogue) and an opening up of possibilities (practice, freedom). History is made through the mutual understanding of human beings in the world.

Mediation

Understanding is not something unmediated, for it is impossible to do away with the subject-object opposition. On the other hand, we must recognize how each conditions the other. Subjects are active in relation to the object known; at the same time, however, subjects are in a certain sense "objects" for their world, since they are molded by their culture and environing milieu. Therefore there cannot be an ahistorical experience of being, but only an experience that is conditioned. In this sense, even metaphysics has its hermeneutical problem.

3

THE SOCIAL TEACHING
OF THE CHURCH

Insofar as interpretation is an act by which meaning is grasped, it is a subjective act of the reader, but it cannot be an arbitrary act. What readers seek is not to "put" meaning "into" the text, but to "find" meaning there, so that in this way they may come in contact with the author. Hermeneutical principles are therefore needed that will help readers to avoid errors in interpretation.

The documents we shall be examining form a body of doctrine called the "social teaching (or doctrine) of the church." Principles must be established that are in keeping with the nature of these texts and will make possible an adequate interpretation of them.

My starting point in this chapter will be a description of what is meant by the church's "social teaching" in the Puebla documents. I shall then go on to inquire how these ideas are rooted in tradition, what kinds of argument are given to validate the existence of this body of teaching, how this social teaching is related to a more general doctrine regarding the teaching office of the church, and finally how we are to go about developing criteria for reading the documents or, in other words, developing a hermeneutic of the church's social teaching.

THE SOCIAL TEACHING OF THE CHURCH
IN THE PUEBLA DOCUMENTS

On the basis of indications given in the teaching of the popes and Vatican Council II, the bishops at Puebla understand the church's "social teaching" to be "the contribution of the Church to liberation and human promotion" as concretized "in a series of doctrinal guidelines and criteria for action." These teachings

> have their source in Sacred Scripture, in the teaching of the Fathers and major theologians of the Church, and in the magisterium (particularly

that of the most recent popes). As is evident from their origin, they contain permanently valid elements that are grounded in an anthropology that derives from the message of Christ and in the perennial values of Christian ethics. But they also contain changing elements that correspond to the particular conditions of each country and each epoch [DP 472].

The bishops stress the active participation of all Christians but especially of the laity: "Thus these social teachings possess a dynamic character. In their elaboration and application lay people are not to be passive executors but rather active collaborators with their pastors, contributing their experience as Christians, and their professional, scientific competence (GS 42)" (DP 473). "Clearly, then, it is the whole Christian community, in communion with its legitimate pastors and guided by them, that is the responsible subject of evangelization, liberation, and human promotion" (DP 474).

The primary object of this social teaching is the personal dignity of the human being, who is the image of God, and the protection of all inalienable human rights (PP 14–21). As the need has arisen, the Church has proceeded to spell out its teachings with regard to other areas of life: social life, economics, politics, and cultural life. But the aim of this doctrine of the Church, which offers its own specific vision of the human being and humanity (PP 13), is always the promotion and integral liberation of human beings in terms of both their earthly and their transcendent dimensions. It is a contribution to the construction of the ultimate and definitive Kingdom, although it does not equate earthly progress with Christ's Kingdom [DP 475].

This social teaching is rooted in a long teaching tradition. John Paul II mentions in this context St. Thomas Aquinas, the teaching of the Fathers of the Church, and, of course, the teaching of sacred scripture, in particular the prophets.

THE CHURCH'S TRADITION OF SOCIAL TEACHING

The church's social teaching has behind it a long tradition. In its modern form it goes back to the encyclical *Rerum novarum* of Leo XIII (1891), but, as just stated, its roots are in ancient biblical and ecclesial tradition.

For the moment, let us see how this social teaching has been understood in more recent documents. In a radio message to Spanish workers (1951) Pius XII speaks of "the social teachings of the popes in the nineteenth and twentieth centuries."[1] He returns to this theme in his Christmas message of 1953: "During the past hundred years and more Christian social doctrine has developed and borne fruit in the practical policies of many nations."[2]

Similar expressions occur in various other addresses of this pope: *Avec une égale sollicitude,*[3] *Mit dem Gefühl,*[4] *Conforto, letizia,*[5] and so on. In *Mit dem Gefühl* Pius XII even refers to the social teaching as "the social program of the Catholic Church."[6] The documents of more recent popes continue to speak of a social teaching; for example, MM 6, 224, 262, 222, 241, 232; PT 160; OA 42. John Paul II, finally has laid an extraordinary emphasis on the relevance of the church's social teaching, particularly in regard to Latin America (OAPC).

As Yves Calvez points out, we must be aware that throughout this long tradition the word "teaching" or "doctrine" has not always been understood in precisely the same sense.[7] In Leo XIII it seems to mean the principles given in the Gospels or, in other words, it refers to one of the two "sources" of social teaching, the latter being based on reason as well as on faith. Pius XII, on the other hand, uses the word "teaching" in the sense that has been standard from then on: the social teaching of the church is the body of teaching proposed by the ecclesiastical magisterium with regard to social problems. Pius XI, for his part, had contrasted social teaching with Catholic "social philosophy," that is, with the thinking of the laity that had not been given a seal of approval by the magisterium. "Teaching" or "doctrine," therefore, even when authoritatively set forth by the popes, represented the thinking of the entire church.

In *Il programma* (1955) Pius XII says: "There exists . . . a Christian social doctrine whose fundamental principles have been determined in the official documents of the Pontiffs" (IP, p. 325). This doctrine cannot, however, be considered in isolation from the work of those "auxiliaries of the Church" who "led especially by the desire that the unchanged and unchangeable teaching of the Church should meet new demands and needs more effectively, have zealously undertaken to develop, with the Church as their guide and teacher, a social and economic science in accord with the conditions of our time" (QA 19–20).

The same kind of universal cooperation and responsibility on the part of the church is emphasized in *Gaudium et spes* 63, where reference is made to our contemporaries who are daily becoming more aware of these discrepancies as a result of growing economic and social imbalances. John XXIII also speaks of "the assistance of learned priests and laymen, specialists in the field," who have helped the magisterium "arrive at clear social teachings" (MM 220). It is Paul VI, however, who places the greatest stress on the cooperation of the entire Christian community in discerning "the options and commitments which are called for in order to bring about the social, political, and economic changes seen in many cases to be urgently needed" (OA 4).

The active role of the Christian community as "the responsible subject of evangelization, liberation, and human promotion" (DP 474) is also emphasized, as was stated above, in the Puebla documents, which ask for the cooperation of the laity in the development of social teaching, that is, in its "elaboration and application" (DP 473).

Along with a growing awareness of ecclesial coresponsibility, based on the fact that in carrying out the task of building a fraternal society under the inspiration of the gospel the entire church must respond to the world and to history, there has also developed a more critically cautious awareness with regard to the nature and meaning of the church's social teaching. The aim of this critical reflection is to keep the teaching free of any "ideology" that would turn it for practical purposes into a program or model binding on all Christians and thus place the church's teaching on the same level as the political doctrines of the various social systems. Signs of this sensitivity, which have been manifested even in the teaching activity of the church, have been: the sobriety of the discussion at Vatican II on the social teaching of the church; the use there of "doctrine" and "teaching" as equivalent terms in order to underscore a basic difference between this and other (dogmatic) doctrines of the church; the recognition of the dynamic character of social teaching, since the latter is by its nature connected with the findings of the social sciences, an area in which the bishops have no technical competence (e.g., MPLA 3; DP 70, 1211) although they do have a pastoral vision for human society (DP 14, 15, 16, 70, 163, 682, 1255).

JUSTIFICATION OF THE CHURCH'S SOCIAL TEACHING

The need to justify the church's social teaching seems to indicate that this teaching does not appear self-evident, at least as perceived at the various historical moments when the church's proper mission obliges it to intervene and promulgate a teaching on society and its problems.

It is beyond doubt that the church's proper mission is one of evangelization[8] and that it is not for the church to propose temporal programs "in matters of technique for which she is neither suitably equipped nor endowed by office"; the church's mission extends rather to "all things that are connected with the moral law" (QA 41). This statement represents also the clear consciousness of the bishops at Puebla, who reflect on the Latin American world as pastors and not as technical experts. At the same time, however, the church does claim "the right and duty to pronounce with supreme authority upon social and economic matters."[9] It considers such interventions to be fully legitimate,[10] and it bases the right of intervention on the following arguments.

1. Social problems cannot be defined solely in terms of the technical aspects of social, economic, and political realities. There is also a moral or ethical aspect.[11] Faith helps to enlighten consciences and enables human beings to fulfill their responsibilities on the historical scene while also retaining their openness to the transcendent. Faith is thus able to lend solid support to the social order.[12]

2. Social problems very often have their origin in human selfishness and sin. The popes speak of the de-Christianization of society,[13] the forgetting of spiritual values,[14] and the organization of economic life in such a way as to ignore or even contradict ethical requirements.[15] The Latin American bishops at Medellín had been especially strong in their references to "sinful situations"; John Paul II uses the same expression in his homily at the shrine of Zapopan, and the Final Document of Puebla unequivocally adopts the same outlook.[16]

3. The church is also concerned about the effects of social problems because living conditions unworthy of the human person are an obstacle to salvation.[17] Such situations imply a contempt for human dignity[18] and a materialistic vision of humankind and society; the contempt and the vision alike are unacceptable to a society that draws its inspiration from the gospel.[19]

4. The right of intervention brings with it a correlative duty of Christians to hear and heed the church's social teaching.[20] The teaching and the response to it are part of a Christian conception of life. Especially in the Latin American situation, the communication and practical implementation of this teaching is an urgent pastoral priority, as John Paul II insists (OAPC III, 2–7).

For these various reasons we may assert that the church, with the pope and bishops as its teachers, has something to say with regard to social conflicts. Its message is concerned not with concrete solutions but with the values that ought to prevail in human life. Pierre Bigo explains as follows the twofold relation of the social with the ethical and the technical: social life is not a mere series of behaviors (to be evaluated in terms of their efficacy and their contribution to temporal well-being) but a totality of specifically human forms of conduct that are under the guidance of conscience and are geared to the total good of man.[21] For this reason Bigo emphasizes the point that in the consciousness of the layperson there must be a synthesis of moral principles with elements drawn from scientific knowledge or from experience.[22]

Along the same lines, John Paul II has reaffirmed the right of the church to speak out on social problems, although he also acknowledges that this teaching is limited to a specific field:

> It is not for the Church to analyze scientifically the consequences which these changes may have on human society. But the Church considers it its task always to call attention to the dignity and rights of those who work, to condemn situations in which that dignity and those rights are violated, and to help to guide the above-mentioned changes so as to ensure authentic progress by man and society [LE 1].

The social teaching of the church rests upon two pillars or, to use a different image, derives from two sources: human reason, which interprets a concrete historical situation, and revelation, which in this same situation calls for a response of faith. The concrete location of this teaching within the framework of a European industrial and capitalist society must not be forgotten. It is necessary, therefore, to distinguish between propositions which are of universal validity, and others that are relative to the situation in which the teaching developed and grew. This distinction is especially important when we are trying to read the statements of the magisterium from within the Latin American context. In the Latin American situation, reason generates particular socioanalytic mediations that must then be confronted with the demands of faith.

SOCIAL PROBLEMS AND THE TEACHING AUTHORITY
OF THE CHURCH

Up to this point I have been considering various statements of the magisterium which deal with social matters and explain what (in general terms) the social teaching of the church is and how its existence is justified.

This teaching is considered an exercise of the church's doctrinal or teaching authority: "There exists . . . a Christian social doctrine whose fundamental principles have been determined in the official documents of the Pontiffs" (IP, p. 325). Such teaching, proposed to us as church doctrine, is in conformity with the church's authentic mission of evangelization; the church has a duty and a right to promulgate such teaching. We have seen the arguments on which this claim is based. The right of the church to intervene in matters of the social order is matched by a duty on the part of Christians to listen to this teaching respectfully and give their assent to it.

Fidelity to the magisterium obliges me to set down all the nuances and qualifications needed in this sensitive area, and to point out any ambiguities. This is, after all, an area in which one may behave lightmindedly and indifferently toward the magisterium or, at the other extreme, indulge in narrow and inflexible interpretations that stick to the letter of the text but are incapable of grasping the spirit which the teaching church is trying to communicate.

The teaching authority of the church is in the service of the faith and must be understood in terms of the faith. This authority belongs to the church's pastors. It is necessary, however, to take into account the level of teaching and the formal authority with which the popes intend to speak, since the teaching of the magisterium is not always presented as infallible.

The Magisterium Is in the Service of the Faith

In view of the danger that exists of looking upon faith as the acceptance of a "catalogue" of doctrinal propositions, it is necessary at this point to insist that in fact faith is first and foremost the attitude by which the person accepts Christ and his mystery. The International Theological Commission, at its 1972 meeting, expressed this truth as follows:

> The truth of the faith is linked to its journey through history from Abraham to Christ and from Christ to the parousia. Orthodoxy is therefore not a matter of assenting to a system; it is a participation in the journey of faith and thus in the "I" of the Church, which perdures through time and is the real subject that believes.

Around Christ as center of life and fullness of truth all the many assertions, deductions, and explications of the content of faith fall into a harmonious order. And in the measure that a doctrinal statement is more "peripheral," the infallible sureness with which the central mystery is being interpreted becomes as it were more "diluted," since the statements have less and less to do with the essential substance and are increasingly dependent on the other human ways of knowing; by the same token, they are increasingly subject to the weaknesses and uncertainties affecting the human process of knowledge. Thus it is possible to distinguish, with Gregory Baum, three areas of magisterial statement which are quite different in their scope, the degree in which they oblige, and their relation to the center of faith, which is Christ himself. These three areas are: (1) divine revelation and what is connected with it; (2) the natural values of human life, both personal and social; and (3) theological and biblical research.[23]

In all three areas the passage of time brings change, in the form of new and different statements of the same truth or in the form of new and different interpretations of. it. Take, for example, Pius IX's encyclical *Quanta cura* (1864) in which he makes a statement that rejects as erroneous the opinion that "liberty of conscience and worship is each man's personal right, which ought to be legally proclaimed and asserted in every rightly constituted society" (QC I, 382, citing MV). Compare this, now, with what is said in Vatican Council II:

> The Vatican Council declares that the human person has a right to religious freedom. Freedom of this kind means that all men should be immune from coercion on the part of individuals, social groups, and every human power so that, within due limits, nobody is forced to act against his convictions in religious matters in private or in public, alone or in associations with others [DH 2, p. 800].

Teaching Authority Belongs to the Pastors of the Church

In a short article in the encyclopedia *Sacramentum mundi*, Karl Rahner sums up the doctrine of Vatican II on the magisterium[24] of the church, to which I have been referring:

> The history of the doctrine concerning the magisterium is in the concrete almost identical with the history of the self-understanding of the Church itself, which cannot but understand itself essentially except as bearer of the gospel message. To ask about the bearers of the message in the Church and their right to demand faith is always a question about the essence of the Church, and vice versa. . . . The doctrinal authority thus reserved to these bishops [of the monarchical episcopate] was understood as the mandate of handing on the doctrine of the apostles. . . .
>
> The object of the magisterium is the content of Christian revelation and all that is necessary or useful for the preaching and the defence of this revelation. In determining the content of revelation and demarcating it off from matters on which the magisterium is not competent, the magisterium is itself the judge of its own authority. That the magisterium does not go beyond its powers when demanding the absolute assent of faith (at

any rate), is guaranteed, according to the Catholic faith, by the assistance given to the Church by the Spirit.[25]

Infallible and Authentic Magisterium

The power to teach (*potestas docendi*) is exercised in two forms: infallible teaching and authentic but not infallible teaching. The magisterium possesses a superior knowledge of the truth about Christ because it has been granted the help of the Holy Spirit in this regard and because the truth about Christ is necessary for the faithful if they are to be saved. In the case of an infallible exercise of teaching authority we are certain of not falling into error; however, in the (merely) authentic exercise of teaching authority we do not have this certainty. But the authentic magisterium does not thereby lose its authority. In everyday life we acknowledge, for example, the authority of doctors, even though we know that they are fallible in their diagnoses. The possibility of their being mistaken does not strip them of authority, unless they have fallen into error so often that we have no assurance for the future that their diagnoses are at least probably accurate. If we apply this norm of everyday behavior to the authentic magisterium, we must say that the possibility of falling into error does not do away with its authority and therefore that we always owe respect to the magisterium.

Inasmuch as the authentic magisterium owes its authority to the will of Jesus Christ, it differs from every other human authority; but insofar as it is fallible, it does not differ from human authority generally. The duty, therefore, of respectfully pointing out possible errors to the magisterium is a duty flowing from fidelity to Christ and his church. When the doctrine in question is one not guaranteed to be infallible, we are permitted to think that it may be altered and corrected. If alteration were impossible because theologians regarded themselves as lacking competence even in regard to noninfallible doctrines, then it would in fact be difficult to improve doctrines which, because noninfallible, are capable of improvement.[26]

Regarding this problem, Rahner writes as follows:

Though the notion of authentic doctrine as opposed to definitive is not to be rejected or made light of, we may expect a greater "reformability" in Church doctrine than was counted on in modern times, before Vatican II.

Unquestionably, the attitude of Catholics, even in non-theologians to the *per se* authentic pronouncements of the magisterium, the non-defined statements, has become more critical. This is due to the experience of the last hundred years. It cannot be denied that the practical preaching of Church doctrine often unduly blurred the basic and acknowledged differences between doctrinal utterances, as regards their binding force. In the preaching of doctrine in the Church today this distinction must be clearly brought out. The normal duty of inner assent to non-defined doctrinal pronouncements of the magisterium (*Lumen Gentium*, art. 25) is not to be propounded in such a way that in practice an absolute assent is still demanded, or as if there were no instance in which one of the faithful might withhold his assent. Reference may be made to the pastoral letter of the German bishops of 22 September 1967, where this difficult question is frankly and soberly treated.[27]

The document to which Rahner refers reads as follows:

At this point we must soberly discuss a difficult question, which in the case of many Catholics today, much more than in the past, either menaces their faith or their spontaneous confidence in the doctrinal authority of the Church. We are thinking of the fact that in the exercise of its office, the doctrinal authority of the Church can be subject to error and has in fact erred. The Church has always known that something of the sort was possible. It has stated it in its theology and developed rules for such situations. This possibility of error does not affect doctrines which are proclaimed to be held with absolute assent, by a solemn definition of the Pope or of a General Council or by the ordinary magisterium. It is also historically wrong to affirm that errors of the Church have subsequently been discovered in such dogmas. This of course is not to deny that in the case of a dogma growth in understanding is always possible and always necessary, the original sense being maintained while previous possible misunderstandings are eliminated.[28]

Magisterial Teaching about "What Is True" and "What Is Safe"

To the distinction between infallible magisterium and authentic magisterium I must now add another distinction which is to some extent a classical one in the older handbooks of ecclesiology. Salaverri, for example, reminds us that doctrinal decrees may be either formally such (that is, there is an obvious exercise of pontifical authority) or only virtually such (for example, the decrees of the Roman Congregations).[29] We must also distinguish disciplinary decrees from properly doctrinal decrees, the latter being such that they have for their immediate object to propose a doctrine that is backed by the authority of the magisterium. Furthermore, the intention of proposing a doctrine may be "direct" or "indirect." According to Salaverri, direct doctrinal decrees are those that propose a doctrine to the faithful as true or reject one as false; indirect doctrinal decrees are those that aim to protect faith or morals against doctrines that may qualify as "safe" or "unsafe." It is, therefore, by no means the same thing for the magisterium to propose a doctrine as "true" (involving a judgment on truth or falsity) and to propose one as "safe" (a judgment on safety or unsafety).

This distinction is an extremely important one, because doctrines which at a given historical moment may be unsafe can come to be regarded as safe (compatible with faith) due to continued study of them and the introduction of new data. Here is Cardinal Billot's statement of the point: "Strictly speaking, that which presently is not safe, especially given the decision that has been made, can subsequently become safe if competent authorities discuss the matter further and, taking new arguments into account, come to a different decision."[30]

In some cases, the church's intention is less to communicate revealed truth than to show the dangers of a historical or scientific proposition. In such cases it might be more appropriate to speak of the church exercising a "pastoral ministry" rather than its "power to teach" in the strict sense. Especially in the fields of science and history, subsequently acquired information may make it possible, as Billot says, to move from a judgment of unsafety to a judgment of safety. Due to the complexity of the problems and the range of data available it is possible to apply to these areas in particular these more general observations of Karl Rahner:

> It is quite possible, for instance, to think that the magisterium would no longer be morally justified when trying to fulfill its duty of informing itself before making a doctrinal pronouncement, if it simply followed the procedures which were formally the best available and also adequate. One reason for this is that the magisterium must not aim simply at material accuracy, but also at the greatest possible efficacy in its declarations. Hence, in face of the *ecclesia discens*, the Church to which instruction and enlightenment is due, the magisterium cannot just appeal to its formal authority. The faithful must also be able to see clearly in any given step taken by the magisterium that the magisterium sees itself as organ and function of the Church as a whole, that it not merely offers men doctrine that is true in itself but tries to bring them into contact with the very reality of salvation and its salutary force. And since the magisterium receives no new revelation when making its pronouncements, it must make every effort to explain intelligibly to the educated faithful *how* it arrived at its decision in the light of the totality of the one revelation which is the life of the Church. . . . Even when a doctrine is true (in the ultimate sense and when properly interpreted), it can be uttered too hastily, couched too harshly, be of too little use for the real life of Christians or formulated against certain backgrounds of thought which make the obedience of faith unjustifiably difficult.[31]

Oswald von Nell-Breuning voices a similar view when seeking to show that some of the indifference to the social teaching of the church may be due to the theologians, not because these are excessively critical of the magisterium but because, on the contrary, they are not critical enough.[32] In other words, they have not accurately pointed out the different levels of discourse that are operative and have confused authentic and infallible magisterium as well as problems of truth and problems of safety. There is no better service the theologians can render to the magisterium than carefully to show what kind of problems the church is pronouncing upon and what the nature of the church's discourse and subject is.

HERMENEUTICAL NORMS FOR SOCIAL TEACHING

In chapter 1 I showed the contemporary relevance of the church's social teaching: according to the pope it provides a solution to the problem of the ever-widening gap separating the minority who have everything from the marginalized and exploited majorities on our continent. In chapter 2 we became better acquainted with the hermeneutical problem; this was a necessity because the aim of the present book is to provide a hermeneutic of the church's social teaching in the context of Latin America. The present chapter has dealt with the content and justification of the church's social teaching and with some important distinctions that must be made in dealing with it. Let me end by calling attention to hermeneutical norms for applying this teaching.

The nature of the documents which we must interpret demands that we take into account four characteristics which define this social teaching as it takes form in texts produced by the church:

1. These are historical documents that were written in concrete circumstances and were an effort to respond to those circumstances in a Christian way.

2. They are, in addition, texts dealing with ethical problems. They make no claim to offer technical solutions or ideologies in support of economic or political systems; rather, they appeal to human conscience at its ultimate and radical level (that is, before God) to assume responsibility on the historical scene for building a just and fraternal world.

3. Consistently with the point just made, the field of ethics has a quite carefully limited sphere: the sphere of the social, economic, and political. Ethics therefore requires the mediation of other disciplines which do not depend directly on revelation, theology, or faith. It is because of this connection with these other disciplines that I thought it important to recall the distinction between infallible and authentic magisterium and between teaching about what is true and teaching about what is safe. The social teaching of the church provides no dogmatic definitions nor does it call for an unqualified assent as if it were dealing with a revealed truth. It does, however, demand respect, trust, and docility, as well as collaboration in developing and applying it.

4. Finally, in the felicitous words of Paul VI, the social teaching of the church "develops with the sensitivity proper to the Church which is characterized by a disinterested will to serve and by attention to the poorest" (OA 42). It is in this spirit and in this perspective that the church's social teaching must be read and put into practice. This teaching is part of the church's evangelizing mission of proclaiming the good news to the poor, since through the ordering of society according to justice, charity, and love the church tells the poor that exploitation and injustice will cease to exist (although not all the evils that accompany human nature can be eradicated in this world). Puebla gives a very central place in the mission of evangelization to the social teaching by which the

magisterium seeks to transform the world and the culture of our day.

These four characteristics determine the course I shall be following in the search for objective hermeneutical criteria. It seems to me these criteria must emerge not from arbitrary subjective choice but from a consideration of the nature of the texts to be interpreted. Each of the four general norms I have proposed will have a chapter devoted to it; the remaining chapters will constitute an application of these norms to some themes that are important in the Latin American context.

4

PROBLEMS OF HISTORICAL INTERPRETATION

The church's social teaching is linked to history in two ways. First, it has been thought out and formulated on the basis of concrete historical situations. Second, it seeks to influence the transformation of these historical situations; it is set forth in order to guide Christians in creating a different kind of society, one which will overcome the defects of the unjust society that was the starting point.

I shall begin by examining the explicit reference to historical situations that is found in all the documents embodying the church's social teaching. Secondly, I shall discuss the hermeneutical problems peculiar to historical texts. Finally, I shall show how the criterion of a historical interpretation enriches our Latin American reading of this social teaching.

REFERENCE TO CONCRETE HISTORICAL PROBLEMS

The encyclical *Rerum novarum* begins by taking note of

the vast expansion of industrial pursuits and the marvelous discoveries of science; . . . the changed relations between masters and workmen; . . . the enormous fortunes of some few individuals, and the utter poverty of the masses; . . . the increased self-reliance and closer mutual combination of the working classes; and also, finally, . . . the prevailing moral degeneracy [RN 1].

This tragic situation of social conflict is described once again, and with exceptional vigor, by Pius XI:

Toward the close of the nineteenth century, the new kind of economic life that had arisen and the new developments of industry had gone to the point in most countries that society was clearly becoming divided more and more into two classes. One class, very small in number, was enjoying almost all the advantages which modern inventions so abundantly provided; the other, embracing the huge multitude of working people, oppressed by wretched poverty, was vainly seeking escape from the straits wherein it stood [QA 3].

In the face of this situation Pius XI emphasizes the importance of the teaching of Leo XIII, which had been a light for consciences. But not all had welcomed the social teaching of *Rerum novarum*: "and so it happened that the teaching of Leo XIII, so noble and lofty and so utterly new to worldly ears, was held suspect by some, even among Catholics, and to certain ones it even gave offense" [QA 14]. Therefore, in order to "defend" the teaching of Leo "against certain doubts" [QA 15], and "after calling to judgment the economic system now in force and its most bitter accuser, Socialism," Pius XI begins "to search out the root of these many evils and to point out . . . the first and most necessary remedy" [QA 98].

In his *Mater et magistra* John XXIII briefly reviews the important advances made by Leo XIII, Pius XI, and Pius XII, and then says that circumstances "have changed greatly over the past twenty years. This can be seen not only in the internal situation of each country, but also in the mutual relations of countries" [MM 46]. He therefore thinks that it is not enough to deal in the classical manner with the themes of wages for work done, property, economic structures, and so on; he sees it as necessary for the church to extend its teaching to new and broader areas:

The progress of events and of time have made it increasingly evident that the relationships between workers and management in productive enterprises must be readjusted according to norms of justice and charity. But the same is also true of the systems whereby various types of economic activity and the differently endowed regions within a country ought to be linked together. Meanwhile, within the over-all human community, many nations with varied endowments have not made identical progress in their economic and social affairs [MM 122].

John XXIII thus anticipates the broadened vision with which the social problem is approached by Paul VI, who locates it at the level of the whole person and of all human beings. "The social question has become world-wide. . . . Today the peoples in hunger are making a dramatic appeal to the peoples blessed with abundance" [PP 3]. In addition to the magnitude which the social problem has attained, there are also new forms of social conflict and of marginalization, produced by, for example, urbanization; all these set new tasks for Christians (see OA 10, 12, etc.).

All such statements presuppose an examination of the situation. The social teaching of the church is therefore not presented as an abstract list of principles which are deduced from human nature and have no connection with concrete facts and situations. On the contrary, it is presented as a reflection, in the light of faith, on situations which prove to be unjust, problematic, and anti-Christian.

If John Paul II frequently emphasizes this social teaching, it is precisely because "injustices increase and the gap between rich and poor widens distressingly" (OAPC III, 7).

The great gap between social groups, a gap made visible in wretchedness and wealth, is analyzed in the Final Document of Puebla as being a structural problem and a situation of sin, as I pointed out in chapter 1. The situation is all the more serious because it exists in a Christian continent. It is therefore a situation that must be transformed by the power of the gospel, because the existence of injustice is a scandal and a contradiction of the values of the faith of the Latin American peoples.

Because the social teaching is related to changing historical situations, it contains elements which become outdated when the situations change; other elements, on the contrary, spring from the experience of faith and make it possible to face up to new situations and give a Christian response to them. In making this distinction between variable and nonvariable elements we need hermeneutical criteria.

THE INTERPRETATION OF HISTORICAL TEXTS AS A HERMENEUTICAL PROBLEM

If we are correctly to interpret documents that have their origins in particular historical situations, we must bear in mind the problem of the "temporal distance" that separates the horizon of the authors from the horizon of the readers of the texts. All authors and readers have a particular "horizon" that limits their vision and contains factors which are not rendered explicit in their thinking but nonetheless condition their approach. The temporal distance is greater when we are interpreting texts from antiquity, whereas we feel more directly in touch with a text that is close to us in time. In this second kind of text we see our own problems reflected. This is the case with the Puebla documents and the social encyclicals.

Two problems are to be distinguished: (1) What attitude is to be adopted toward "temporal distance"? (2) How is a text to be given its "historical potentiality" so that it becomes fruitful for the future?

Temporal Distance

When we interpret texts of authors who are still alive, the difficulties we encounter in their written communication can be resolved through oral dialogue with the authors themselves for the purpose of gaining clarity on their thought. That kind of dialogue is impossible in dealing with texts from the past, texts written in former ages. Thus the interpretation of such texts is complicated by the "temporal distance" between the author and the reader. This distance brings with it, on the one hand, difficulty in understanding, and, on the other, a potential enrichment.

Temporal distance creates difficulty in understanding because it then becomes necessary to possess a good deal of information about a cultural world that is no longer our own. The preunderstanding that is required for all understanding must here be enriched by prior knowledge about language, culture, history, geography, and so on; this knowledge becomes a basis for grasping the author's message. Schleiermacher and Dilthey therefore emphasized above all the need of achieving an "identification" with the author.

On the other hand, a total identification, in addition to being impossible, is neither necessary nor appropriate. If what is being communicated possesses a historical potentiality for spurring a development of thought, this is because the text is being viewed from the standpoint of our present-day world in which the author must now be read and understood. The important thing is not simply that "the author be understood"; equally important is the fact that it is we who are doing the understanding. From this point of view, temporal distance also means an enrichment because it makes us more acutely aware of the limitations on understanding.

What happens when we do not understand something, or when we experience the limitations of our understanding in the face of something unknown? If what we fail to understand is a word, it is enough to go to the dictionary in order to resolve the difficulty. In other instances, however, we understand all the words and yet fail to grasp the meaning because the subject is not familiar to us. Or we may even come to realize that authors make different presuppositions than we do, so that the same words do not consistently mean the same thing for them as for us. In these instances we experience a clash between our universe of preunderstanding and the understanding of the text. The new object of knowledge takes on an unexpected form, and we do not have the categories with which to grasp it. Since the clash obliges us to step back and examine our preunderstanding, it can have either of two effects: we may cling to our preunderstanding as to an island of security, and this attitude will cause us to reject the new knowledge as incapable of integration into our interior world, our personal synthesis; or else the clash will lead us to question our own preunderstanding and in this way enrich us. The shock of the new knowledge is therefore a stimulus either to openness or to fear, depending on the attitude we adopt toward it.

Because, in dealing with historical texts, the worlds of writers and readers are so different, being so distant from one another, what the authors "say" raises questions about both worlds: that of the readers, thus enriching their preunderstanding; but also that of the authors. What they actually say is connected with a good deal that is "not said," not thematized, and that seems to them so obvious as to be beyond question. These elements which condition the authors' thinking are precisely the ones that may seem nonevident to us and that, when challenged from our point of view, may enable us to disengage an authentic insight from the historically conditioned form in which it was expressed.

Historical Potentiality

From the standpoint of the ability to interpret past texts, the historical potentiality of these texts may be defined as their capacity to suggest new possibilities for the future. In this perspective it is important to distinguish between what is said and what is thought. The task of exegesis is to try to reconstruct the thought through the words. I would suggest that hermeneutic attempts to go a step further and move on to what "should be thought" through an examination of the actual thinking behind what is said.

Things are "said" which "cause us to think" something which the author of what is said could not himself or herself have thought. In these instances, what is said is placed in new situations, new historical contexts, and so on, which suggest new questions to be asked of the text. The text serves as an inspiration; it is rich in virtualities. It takes on its full historical dimensions as we go about explicating these virtualities.

This peculiar characteristic of historical interpretation suggests a difference between history and natural causality. In the natural sciences there must be a proportion between cause and effect. In history there is no such proportion. Small events can have major consequences; on the other hand, great events can quickly lose their importance. The real historical dimensions of an event are determined by the way in which the human community receives it. This reception is an essential constituent of the event itself as a historical event. Many events that had been sunk in the sleep of the centuries have subsequently influenced the course of history because of historical discoveries that made possible a new reception by the community.

I am speaking here of tradition as a human phenomenon, and not of tradition as understood in church doctrine, that is, as a source of faith under the action of the Holy Spirit. Tradition, understood as a phenomenon of human life, gathers up the effects of an action or event and is a reflection of a human community's reception of that event. It is a carrier of content. We always stand within a tradition; we are immersed in it. It is true, however, that we can also distance ourselves from it and even question it, and this even with reference to the very sources whence the tradition flows.

Every tradition represents a selection of elements or facets of the event in question: those that are more important to the community which accepts the event. Even the growth of the New Testament did not escape this law, for the New Testament is an expression of a community which selected for its preaching at that time the aspects of the Savior's life which it regarded as most important. It is possible that had the historical context been different a different selection would have been made.

To the extent that we are immersed in a tradition we can say that we are an "object" of history and are conditioned by this history. But we are also subjects of history, since we are able to pass judgment on the tradition itself. Tradition is therefore carrier of a prejudgment, a preunderstanding. For example, scripture is read quite differently by someone located within the Christian tradition and someone outside it.

When we speak of a "prejudgment," we are speaking of something ambiguous. A tradition can restrict the richness of the original event if it forces us to stay with the meaning which the event had for a particular generation. A prejudgment of that kind amounts to a judgment which turns us into repeaters of an interpretation. But "prejudgment" may also be understood in the sense of a judgment that orients our own judgment, our own interpretation, inasmuch as that prejudgment is a concrete effect of the event on history, an effect which we cannot ignore if we wish to interpret the original event. When prejudgment is understood in this second way, then we may legitimately speak of it as enriching the meaning of the event by way of a new existential effect.

This matter of effects on history compels us to see a hermeneutic not simply as an interpretation of the past but in function of the totality of human life and therefore also of humanity's future. History is not merely the succession of events that have already occurred; it is also, and above all, the creation of the possibilities which those events have left open for the future. It is not enough to interpret the event in itself as a record that is already closed. The event continues to exist in history through the possibilities it has opened up.

Understanding of the historical past in a hermeneutic has three aspects. There is a *consecutive* understanding, to the extent that the past is grasped as history in the positive sense, that is, as determinate facts for which we have more or less fragmentary testimony. There is an *actual* understanding that lays hold of the present; the past, like the future, shows itself to us only in function of the present. Finally, there is an *anticipatory* understanding which seeks to grasp the meaning of the future; this too is history, but not in the positive sense, since there are as yet no determinate facts. If philosophy seeks to grasp reality, it must contemplate the future.

Anticipatory thinking works through extrapolation, that is, by continuing the line of the meaning of events, past and present, into the future. Every science claims somehow to predict the future; it makes its prognosis on the basis of past knowledge. Difficulty arises when the future in question is the future created by human freedom, which involves a very large measure of indeterminacy.

If a hermeneutic is an authentic interpretation of the historical being of the human person, then the present is the point of conjunction of two types of thinking: consecutive and anticipatory. Even though the present is relative and constantly slipping away, it is nonetheless the only absolute point of temporal reference for the human being, just as the latter is, in spatial terms, the center of reference for all movement, with the perception of a person's own body as the starting point.

An essential openness to the human future is thus an element in a correct interpretation of historical texts. This is especially true of Christian texts, since these all participate in the dynamic of promise and hope, that is, in a tension toward the future.

TOWARD A LATIN AMERICAN READING
OF THE CHURCH'S SOCIAL TEACHING

Temporal distance allows us to come up with new data that challenge what used to be taken for granted. This challenge can lead us to a deeper grasp of the meaning of what an author "said," to the end that we may determine what the author "should or might have said" if she or he had the same information now available to us.

Due, therefore, to the passage of time and even to the shift in geographical location, a Latin American reading of the church's social teaching will differ from that of the First World, within whose horizon the teaching was originally thought out and formulated. This Latin American reading offers rich new perspectives which make it possible to move beyond the merely verbal formulation of the texts and to gain a deeper understanding of the demands of the gospel.

Property and Peaceful Existence

In *Rerum novarum* Leo XIII has this to say about private property:

> With reason, then, the common opinion of mankind, little affected by the few dissentients who have contended for the opposite view, has found in the careful study of nature, and in the laws of nature, the foundations of the division of property, and the practice of all ages has consecrated the principle of private ownership, as being pre-eminently in conformity with human nature, and as conducing in an unmistakable manner to the peace and tranquillity of human existence [RN 8].

This statement is radically questionable eighty years later when half of the world has organized its existence on the suppression of private ownership of those material goods which can cause the greatest conflict: the ownership of the means of production. Here it is no longer an isolated group that objects to private ownership. Moreover, the experience of the capitalist countries—at least those in which the capitalism is peripheral and dependent on outsiders—shows that private ownership has not guaranteed "the peace and tranquillity of human existence."

In our desire to gain an honest and faithful understanding of the teaching of Leo XIII we must ask ourselves what the conditions are under which private ownership does guarantee a peaceful existence. Certainly not the situation in which ownership is abused, as is the case among us. The very emphasis of Pope

John Paul II on a return to the church's social teaching in an age when "injustices increase and the gap between rich and poor widens distressingly" makes it quite clear that "the reality of ownership" as concretely experienced in Latin America and defended as "a western and Christian value" has little in common with the "ownership as a value" that is set before us in the church's social teaching. There is need, then, of a critical reading of these texts, one which yields formulas that really embody the value to be presented to our peoples and which will not serve to lend legitimacy to unjust situations.

Property as a Guarantee of Democracy

A second example is provided by John XXIII who writes in his *Mater et magistra:*

Moreover experience and history testify that where political regimes do not allow private individuals the possession also of productive goods, the exercise of human liberty is violated or completely destroyed in matters of primary importance. Thus it becomes clear that in the right of property, the exercise of liberty finds both a safeguard and a stimulus [MM 109].

But the Latin American experience of the last decade, which is likewise part of "experience and history," has brought into the spotlight the depressing reality of authoritarian governments that are inspired by the ideology of national security. In pursuit of their claim to be defending private ownership of productive goods these regimes have ended by producing the identical totalitarian results condemned by John XXIII ("the exercise of human liberty is violated or completely destroyed in matters of primary importance").

These contrasting experiences lead us to ask a deeper question: Under what conditions is private ownership of the means of production a real guarantee of democracy in the face of the totalitarian state? These conditions are not presently verified in Latin America because the existing exercise of ownership is not a defense against totalitarianism but on the contrary seems to require it. It is clear that one and the same phrase—"private ownership of the means of production"—can have meanings that are worlds apart if for John XXIII it represents a defense against totalitarianism while in Latin America it calls for the suppression of freedoms, especially those of the unions and the workers.

5

THE PROBLEM
OF THE INTERPRETATION
OF ETHICAL TEXTS

The historical character of the church's social teaching, or, in other words, the intention of this teaching to provide light so that Christians may act here and now in the social, economic, and political spheres in accordance with the central and abiding truths of the gospel, requires that adequate hermeneutical criteria be applied to this teaching. But, as we have just seen, the historical criteria applied to the documents of the church in this area are the same as are applied to all historical documents, and do not suffice for a correct understanding of the church's social teaching.

The aim of the church's social teaching is not to provide a narrative of events but to construct human history in a Christian spirit. It supplies imperatives for action not by appealing to a political philosophy or ideology nor to experience of a technical program but by making a radical and ultimate appeal to the human conscience. In other words, it appeals to an ethics and to religious values. But it is not easy to interpret religious texts of this kind, as is clear from the Pharisaic legalism of the time of Jesus and of every age, which interprets the letter of the law but not its spirit.

Legalism can vitiate the interpretation of texts that set down norms for our conduct. This is a danger. But we must not on that account overlook the need of such directives for action. This is especially true inasmuch as the originality of the church's contribution to social problems is to be found precisely in its ethical judgments on human life, the person, and society.

In our day, the extraordinary development of technology, combined with humanity's inability to control it so as to make it serve the human race, has produced a situation which John Paul II describes as one of "alienation." "This sums up the bitter state of human existence in our day when seen in its broadest and most comprehensive dimensions" (RH 15). "The progress of technology and of a contemporary civilization that is characterized by the primacy of the technical calls for a comparable development of moral life and ethical discipline. This latter development, unfortunately, always seems to lag behind" (ibid.). "The situation of human beings in our time is out of harmony with the objective requirements of morality and justice and even more with the requirements of social love" (RH 16). The race between technology and morality is acting out on a world scale the parable of the rich man and the poor Lazarus (ibid.).

This widespread phenomenon calls into question the monetary, financial, production and commercial structures and mechanisms which, with support from various political pressure groups, are now controlling the entire world economy. These structures and mechanisms are almost completely incapable of eliminating unjust social conditions inherited from the past or of meeting the pressing moral requirements and needs of the present time [ibid.].

Even though the situation is so serious and even critical, the pope urges us to act: .

Such a task is by no means beyond human powers. The principle of solidarity, in the broad sense of the term, should promote an effective search for appropriate institutions and mechanisms—whether in the area of commerce, where a healthy competition must be allowed to flourish, or through a broader and more direct distribution and control of wealth—in order that the people who are now struggling to achieve economic prosperity may be able not only to satisfy their needs but also to develop gradually but surely. . . . This . . . requires commitment on the part of individuals and peoples who are free and united [ibid.].

My reflections on the problem of interpreting ethical texts will be on two levels. The first will be the more comprehensive level of the meaning of Christian ethical norms. The second will be the level of a specific theme: How are we to interpret the church's teaching on natural law? This teaching has made it possible for the church not only to address itself to Christians in the light of evangelical values but also to carry on a dialogue with all men and women of good will on the basis of a humanistic consensus regarding the dignity and rights of the human race as a whole and of every member of it.

THE MEANING OF CHRISTIAN NORMS

It is worth noting that St. Thomas Aquinas does not appear to use the word "norm" in his moral theology.[1] He speaks rather of a "rule" for the human will, meaning by this human reason insofar as it is conformed to the divine reason. [2] But this Thomist conception was subsequently forgotten and replaced by a rigid view of conduct that at times almost turns into positivism.

Accordingly, when we approach the great ethical systems of the past (e.g., Plato, Aristotle, the Stoa and Thomas Aquinas) with this view of "norm," we approach them with an alien view since neither the Greek *aretê* nor the Latin *virtus* corresponds to "norms" in the modern sense. And so, neither can the biblical commandments be seen as "norms."[3]

Thus, for example, an approach to the New Testament that adopts the "normative" standpoint leads to an incomprehension of what is special about the Sermon on the Mount.

> The Sermon on the Mount must therefore be understood as a "striving," but not in a fundamentalist or legalist way. The attitude it demands is one of nobility of soul, not that of the mean calculations of a spiritual grocer or a security official. It calls forth initiative and imagination and shrewd judgment of a situation. . . . Up until now the attitude toward the Sermon on the Mount hovered between legalism and irrelevance. What is important in it is the presentation of an ethos that binds without law.[4]

For this reason we need to think of the New Testament as presenting not norms but ethical patterns:

> A "pattern," or, as Paul and the Fathers would say, a "type," is at the same time something concrete and capable of adjustment. Insofar as it is definite and part of the historical revelation, the pattern would provide that "compulsion" implied in revelation, as we expect it from scripture; but at the same time, the fact that it is a "pattern" allows us to rethink its implications in a new interpretation for the present time.[5]

"If we try to absolutize the 'letter' of scripture, we shall find ourselves unable to bridge the historical gap between then and now."[6] The author I have been quoting points out that such ethical patterns are given in, for instance, 1 Corinthians 8–10 where in dealing with the problem (irrelevant to our modern industrial society) of eating flesh that had been sacrificed to idols, Paul introduces theological observations on attentiveness to the weak brother or sister, respect for such a person's conscience, and the need of asking ourselves whether we should make use of the rights and freedoms that are legitimately ours (1 Cor. 8:7–13). The point that is important for us here is what Paul says about Christian freedom and about the exercise of this freedom in the context of our brothers and sisters. "This is . . . a characteristic of Christian morality and one of lasting importance."[7]

> In the same way there are very many cases where one has to see whether, beyond the historical circumstances and instructions, there is not a deeper and characteristic point made, with some broader intention which can readily be applied to the present situation and seen to be relevant for

modern problems. This does not eliminate the historical content, but we must examine the meaning which lies buried in what once happened but which points beyond the historical circumstances to future relevance.[8]

Christian ethics has always emphasized the point that while human action in concrete circumstances cannot be based on an arbitrary subjectivism, neither can it be based on a simple and crystal-clear deduction from a moral principle, as though such principles could define proper human conduct in advance. The most reliable Scholastic tradition stresses the importance of prudence, while in the modern age an effort has been made to do justice to the profound insights contained in modern currents of thought and to find an orthodox Catholic form of existential ethics.[9]

Insofar as thought on morality is a theological science, it must be affected by the hermeneutical problems of the latter; it too is characterized by a specific way of interpreting, in the light of faith, the scriptures, the dogmatic tradition, the natural moral law, and the signs of the time, in order that it may, with the help of those sources, reach a knowledge of God's will as the norm of our conduct. The role of the church, which is exercised through the magisterium but as a total reflection of the Christian people, is to interpret the ethical imperatives governing human existence. There is here a new "hermeneutical circle." Theo Beemer writes, "The autonomous—or, rather, 'dialogue'— practice of morality, taking place in the present world under the guidance of the 'law' written on man's heart, serves as a preparation for the Gospel, and so enables us to understand the proclamation of God-with-us, God's saving will."[10]

The documents of the magisterium that assert the right to point out the moral course of action in an area must be understood hermeneutically. Finding and satisfying the requirements of God's will is not a matter of legalistically following the letter of a document; it calls rather for re-encountering the Spirit who is life and calls us to new life.

THE CHURCH'S TEACHING ON NATURAL LAW

Insofar as the church's social teaching has reason as one of its sources, natural law becomes a kind of "bridge" making it possible for the church and its magisterium to conduct a dialogue not only with believers, but with every person of good will. This explains the opening of Paul VI's encyclical *Populorum progressio* and John Paul II's encyclical *Redemptor hominis.*

I shall explain, first, what is meant by natural law; then, how it is formulated; and finally what the church's role is in the area of natural law.

What Is Natural Law?

Human beings regulate their conduct with the aid of a set of norms; this is true in particular of social and public life. We contrast positive law and natural law. Positive law is the set of binding rules which are imposed on a people and which those in authority compel the people to observe. Natural law consists in a series of apriori norms which are prior to and above positive law, which reason renders obligatory in all cases not foreseen by the enactors of positive law, and which removes all juridical value from any positive law opposed to it. We may say, then, that natural law is the set of ethical requirements derived "immediately" from the human person, that is, without the mediation of a positive human law.

These requirements flow from a concrete human nature, the needs and possibilities of which are capable of fulfillment. In the final analysis, natural law has its ground in the creative action of God; and God would be contradicting God's own providence by creating a nature with these requirements, needs, and possibilities and then not providing the means of satisfying them.

Necessity alone, however, does not establish a law. A law is established only when the need is that of a personal being whose relationship to things is human and social. A right exists where there is understanding of the self, of things, of the being's own historical destiny, and of a hierarchy of values; in other words, where there is a perception that certain things are ordered to persons.

There are two presuppositions for natural law as thus understood: (1) that there exists a nature which "grounds" laws; and (2) that this nature is knowable. The two presuppositions represent the ontological and gnoseological levels respectively of the overall problem. The two levels are interconnected because a nature does not manifest itself immediately but through knowledge.

The connection between the two levels or problems confronts us with a difficulty, namely, that knowledge of nature reaches us through a culture. For natural law ought not to depend on a particular way of knowing human nature, but should be linked to primary and undeniable data, such as existence, relations to things and persons, sexuality, desire of knowing truth, personal worth, etc.

These basic experiences should be at the center of all philosophical reflection, even though the experiences as such of these values are greatly conditioned by history and culture. There is a minimal set of perennial experiences which, via the manner in which they are had in a particular time and culture, can found a natural law that is changeless but has changeable—though obligatory—consequences. Knowledge of the human person is thus a lengthy, arduous, and difficult social and historical task.

For this reason, while human persons possess in the form of "first principles" certain basic intuitions regarding truth and goodness, they are nonetheless limited by their historical conditioning when they specify the more concrete applications of these principles. Thus the ethics of Aquinas is based on a static image of humanity (so that casuistry becomes important, involving as it does concrete experiences that are inevitably repeated) and lays its chief emphasis on final causes which are pregiven and to which persons subordinate themselves in an exercise of that rationality that is peculiar to each of them.[11]

Persons experience the difference not only between what is and what can be, but also between what is and what ought to be. They know that they must achieve self-fulfillment in a collective manner. They do not know, however, the potentialities that will be available in the future for achieving a greater human self-fulfillment. The connection between theory and practice, that is, the experimental character of human knowledge is responsible for this not-knowing. The future is unknown, and therefore ethics must remain open.

How Knowledge of Natural Law Is Attained

Historical experience alone is not enough; it is also necessary to impose on this experience a rational, philosophical interpretation. Historical experience remains, however, the point of departure. Now, as our knowledge of cultures increases, natural law becomes increasingly questionable in the light of the vast diversity of historical experiences. This does not mean that the existence of the law is to be denied; it does mean that a critical vigilance is needed lest we fall into unjustified and facile extrapolations or generalizations.

A case that has been much studied is marriage in the various cultures. When marriage is examined from an exclusively anthropological standpoint the only conclusion that can be drawn is that all races and cultures are in agreement that "something" must regulate human conduct in this area if it is to be truly worthy of human beings. But the various cultures are not in agreement on the content of this "something."[12] This factual observation does not entail a relativization of the obligation of the norm, provided we keep in mind that human nature operates *within* a culture.

Human experience must be given a philosophical interpretation. But at this point a new problem arises. In the view of the Catholic church the philosophy which should be used in interpreting human experience is Thomist Aristotelianism (or at least the church has historically given a privileged place to this philosophy). Yet it is not possible to deny to any other philosophy the right and duty of interpreting human nature according to its own categories and premises, since if natural law is a law flowing from human nature it ought to be knowable by any human mind, even one not formed by Thomism. Thus, for example, Wilhelmus A.M. Luijpen has written an essay in which he interprets natural law by using the categories of existential phenomenology.[13] Now when this last-named approach to the consideration of natural law is adopted, certain "essential" concepts become unacceptable, and the question arises whether these conceptions are part of natural law itself or of the interpretation which one or other philosophy makes of universal and irreducible data. For an existentialist philosophy it becomes difficult to understand, for example, the sense in which natural law can be changeless.

It is important to emphasize the way in which historicity affects both human nature and our knowledge of human nature. The Stoic concept of human nature completely ignored this historical dimension. Thomas opens it up to us with his distinction between primary and secondary natural law; for it is in secondary natural law that primary natural law really reveals itself and is constituted, and this within the framework of a culture and of history. Thus, for example, the precept of respecting the belongings of others is defined once it is possible to determine within a culture what is mine and what is yours; this determination is not made directly by human nature but comes to light through the establishment of a particular human world and calls for juridical forms.

In summary, natural law has many problematical facets, and its dangers must be faced. I repeat that there is no question here of doing away with natural law or relegating it to oblivion. The Nazi regime provides a sad example of the extremes into which the human race can fall when it operates solely with positive law (whatever is legal is also just) and therefore acknowledges no higher and prior natural law (what is just must serve as the norm for deciding what is legal).

The problems raised by "natural law" may come from either of the two terms in the name:

The term "law" is ambiguous inasmuch as it is only analogous to positive law. Natural law finds expression in a language and a culture, but in reality it stands in judgment on the culture. Juridical formulations can never give adequate expression to what is just. The moral order is an order that is to be brought into existence; it therefore calls for the activity of reason, free initiative, and attention to historical circumstances. Here is an example: it is possible, in the name of natural law, to call for the freedom to form trade unions; but this demand has meaning only within a particular constellation of historical circumstances with its particular economic regime and organization of labor. To speak of natural law in this and similar cases is to say that within a given set of historical circumstances there is a requirement of conscience that must find expression in social legislation and institutions.

The ambiguity of the term "natural" is even greater because "human nature" has a variety of meanings. Franz Böckle reduces these to four:

1. *Ratio ut natura*: human reason as an expression of nature. What is meant here is natural knowledge of a nondiscursive kind, for example, first principles. In this kind of knowledge the person, making use of reason and will, participates actively in the eternal law. And the person is here not simply reading a given order of things but creating it. In the evidential quality of first principles the person perceives the transcendent call of what ought to be (a call not only to do what is good but to seek the Good for the sake of being oneself good, that is, for the sake of self-fulfillment). First principles have value not as a set of norms that control deductive processes, but as a mediation of the transcendental call of what ought to be for achieving self-fulfillment; they are conditions of possibility for a meaningful human existence; they are a call to carry out a project, since the human person is not a being already complete but a being in a state of potentiality. The development and fulfillment of human existence as such is the ethical natural law, which is the center of all natural law.

2. Metaphysical nature: the emphasis here is on universality and immutabil-

ity. If it is possible to define "clearly" the content of the metaphysical essence of a thing, the natural law can then be deduced from this essence. In practice, however, this deduction requires that we work with empirical data and move beyond these. But if we start with empirical data, we must be very conscious of the influence of history on human self-understanding. These assays that have the empirical as their point of departure will clarify the demands of "what ought to be" in the here-and-now historical situation. We must understand the social existence of human persons as natural and therefore pay heed to their historical projects. Attention to the historical influence exerted by human self-understanding brings us to see the historicity of the natural law itself.

I am not here denying the absolute value of the moral norm, since absolute value is a quality which ethical demands possess that can be present even in particular and concrete cases, whether these refer to an individual or a human group or historical age, and so on. What is characteristic of natural law is not atemporality but the fact that it translates into historical terms the profound requirements of the human person which in a sense transcend the present historical context. Natural law is historical because persons develop themselves in history. Law is law if it expresses the dignity and worth of the person. But this worth comes to be understood through an ongoing historical interpretation. Consequently, the historicity of our existence does not lead to relativism, but it does call for a critical vigilance lest we take that which is conditioned by a particular historical period to be an abiding obligation for the human race.

3. "Metaphysical nature of the human act": according to this meaning of the term "nature," natural law is based on concrete action. This approach is in danger, however, of forgetting the subjective dimensions of the person—intentions, attitudes, and so on—and of focusing on the "nature of the act" in a one-sided objectification of ethics. A further danger is that the nature of the act may be defined on the basis of historically conditioned notions. Sexual morality offers many examples of this danger.

4. "Biological-physiological nature": this represents a mistaken development of the conception discussed in the preceding paragraph. It is true, of course, that the body belongs to the human essence, but it must not be given a primacy of value. We have an ethical duty to understand corporeity properly. Ulpian's definition of natural law ("that which nature teaches to all animals") has exercised a weighty influence, especially in sexual morality and its definitions of "nature," "against nature," and so on. The emphasis on corporeity leads to forgetfulness of the fact that in this area of intimate interpersonal relationships human persons are not merely passive subjects of the laws governing their nature but, like God, exercise a providence with regard to themselves and others.

In Böckle's view, the problem of natural law is to be summed up in this way: the root of natural law is the primordial experience of a call to what ought to be, to self-fulfillment. But the concrete content of this ought-to-be can only be known on the basis of the meaning of human existence in history.[14]

Mission of the Church in the Area of Natural Law

The church has repeatedly asserted its right to explain and propose the natural law; this has been especially true ever since the encyclical *Aeterni patris* of Leo XIII. The church was beginning at that time to have experience of a world increasingly separated from the faith; natural law could serve as a bridge to that world. There are numerous statements of the church's mission in the area of natural law.[15]

The explanation of natural law is one of the church's pastoral responsibilities. The *potestas docendi* or power to teach is based on revelation and the mission of Christ; in virtue of this power the church defines the truths of faith for the sake of believers. In dealing with natural law, however, we find ourselves in a broader realm that includes not only believers but all of the human race. It is therefore by reason of its pastoral ministry rather than of its teaching office that the church offers its teaching on natural law as a way of helping all human beings of good will.

The theological statements the church is able to make concerning natural law are very few: that certain texts of the Old and New Testaments seem to imply the existence of a natural law (although exegetes are not unanimous in their explanation of the various texts, e.g., Rom. 1 and 2). It would therefore contradict the very notion of "natural" law to claim that the specific contents of this law were "revealed." The "naturalness" of this law requires that these contents be knowable by human reason insofar as reason has the inherent capacity to "see" what has become historically "visible."

Does this mean that revelation and the church have nothing to do with natural law? Not at all. Revelation provides us with a "negative norm" by setting before us an image of the human person and of society by comparison with which various situations can be perceived as inhuman. A believer therefore needs a special sensitivity in order to perceive in the "contrast-experiences"—of which I shall speak in the next chapter—the ethical commands to rise above the inhuman and to seek the properly human.

But the conviction that society *ought not* to be what it now is (a conviction arising from a comparison between society as it is and the human vocation as set forth in scripture) will not by itself yield a concrete model of what society *ought* to be. With the gospel as its starting point the church proposes to the world a set of moral attitudes based on love. The content of this love is specified in the light of Christ's example (to love *as he does*). The ethical precepts of the New Testament have their value not in themselves but by reason of their connection with love.[16] Scripture has nothing to say about the essential nature of human institutions; it sees these in their concrete historical context (for example, marriage, slavery). It uses love as the norm by which to appraise these institutions: love is responsible for the other until death, and for this reason marriage must be indissoluble, since it is the place and sign of salvation for the spouses inasmuch as by marriage persons render themselves able to exist permanently for others in love. Christ therefore renews institutions from within, leaving untouched the juridical forms of (for example) marriage. In like manner, Paul accepts the idea of the subordination of woman to man, but this does not mean that he gives a Christian legitimation to this historical concept. Christians come to grips with their own existence within the institutions of the world.

Christian love is therefore learned by contemplating both the Lord and life. The church has an obligation to compare every humanism history offers with the freedom, solidarity, and eschatological vocation that Christ has bestowed on us. Natural law must be of service in this encounter with the truth of Christ, and not hinder it. Yet at times an inflexible conception of natural law as existing unchangeably throughout history has been more of an obstacle than a help. A case in point would be certain interpretations of natural law in the area of private ownership of property, as we shall see in chapter 7.

For the moment I need only add that by its very nature any teaching in the field of ethics must be marked by a profound respect for the freedom and conscience of the person.

The essential task [of the church's teaching in the realm of ethics] is to set forth the teaching of Christ in such a way as to enlighten and help Christians to make their own decisions freely and with full awareness, in the presence of Christ. The magisterium cannot take the place of personal decision, because its sole function is to help this decision be more authentic, though not necessarily easier. The magisterium must not try to exercise an external control over the divine action within consciences. A magisterium that does not respect consciences or claims the right to make decisions for them or that tries to impose these decisions after the manner of an umpire, as though it alone had received the Holy Spirit, will not only go beyond its authority but will deny its very self, since the teaching of the theologians on conscience and on the indwelling of the Spirit is an integral part of the Christian heritage.[17]

6

THE INTERPRETATION OF SOCIOPOLITICAL ETHICS

In the preceding chapter I discussed the difficulties raised by the interpretation of texts dealing with ethics. Insofar as the church's social teaching is concerned with specific areas of ethics (the social and the political), it also has links with other nontheological forms of knowledge, namely, the social sciences which explain and render an account of social phenomena. Here is a new source of problems in addition to those we have been discussing. Not only must we consider the relationship between law and freedom, the directives of the magisterium, and the creative responsibility of Christians themselves, as well as the problem of reaching concrete ethical decisions while taking into account universal norms but without attempting to derive from these norms the ultimate and immediate shape of action. Also to be considered now is the role played by the human and, in particular, the social sciences in reaching a concrete decision.

In the church's social teaching the magisterium is not talking of revelation but rather judging historical realities in the light of revelation. In gaining its knowledge of these situations the church does not count on a new revelation. Therefore in order to know what must be done here and now, the church must turn to the experience of many centuries that has achieved codified form in abstract ethical norms, to the mediation supplied by the human sciences, and to the cultural experience of each people. As Edward Schillebeeckx aptly says, "The past has shown that, long before the Church had analyzed the social problem, there were people who, in their commitment and in a preanalytic dialogue with the world, had already reached the moral decision that fundamental changes were required.[1]

THE PERCEPTION OF ETHICAL CONTRASTS

The advance of the human conscience in the field of social and political ethics has not been achieved by deduction from general moral principles but through the experience of ethical contrasts.

58

When we analyze these contrast-experiences insofar as they may lead to new ethical imperatives, we find that these negative experiences imply an awareness of values that is veiled, positive, though not yet articulate; that they stir the conscience which begins to protest. Here the absence of "what ought to be" is experienced initially, and this leads to a perhaps vague, yet real, perception of "what should be done here and now." This experience is of course but the preliminary stage leading to a proper reflection of both a scientific analysis of the situation and of a new assessment of principles gained from experiences of the past.[2]

A consideration of the history of the church's social teaching will confirm this statement of Schillebeeckx. The encyclical *Rerum novarum* seeks explicitly to bring into focus the situation of workers in an age of "changed relations between masters and workmen; . . . the enormous fortunes of some few individuals, and the utter poverty of the masses" (RN 1), a poverty due to the fact that "the hiring of labor and the conduct of trade are concentrated in the hands of comparatively few; so that a small number of very rich men have been able to lay upon the teeming masses of the laboring a yoke little better than that of slavery itself" (RN 3). The wretched condition of workers, the temptation to resort to violence, the denial of God: this situation, so contrary to the plan of God, led to an assertion of the demand for greater justice, brotherhood, and worship of God.

Contrast-experiences supply the basis for subsequent thematization. The task of theology is to clarify these experiences by rescuing them from the prereflective, intuitive level. But in this thematization, precisely because it is dealing with social facts, theology needs the mediation of the social sciences.

There is thus a twofold articulation. Leonardo Boff offers an analysis of it with reference to the theology of liberation, but this analysis is also applicable to the social teaching of the church. At the first level (which Boff calls sacramental) there is a perception of the contrast-situation within the horizon of faith; this perception is accompanied by an intuitive grasp of the conflict involved, which is understood as a "what ought not to be," along with a first, schematic understanding—not yet scientific or concrete—of what Christian commitment demands.

In addition to this first articulation there is another level of critical articulation in which a more careful thematic reflection is made both on the very faith-horizon within which the contrast-experience is seen and on the use of scientific mediations for a more accurate reading of the situation being analyzed and for a corresponding systematic theological reflection on this reading. Thus the first level—the contrast-experience itself—is clarified and explained at the second level, which is that of critical articulation.[3]

This same process goes on in the social teaching of the church, although, as is evident, without advancing to a rigorous sociological analysis. The demonstration of the negative reality (the exploitation of the workers, in *Rerum novarum*; the development of the economy, in *Quadragesimo anno* and *Mater et magistra*; the challenge of the gap between developed and underdeveloped countries, in *Populorum progressio*) is accompanied by a summary attempt at a causal explanation which looks to the deeper roots of the phenomena in question. It is to this necessary mediation provided by nontheological sources that I am referring when I stress the need of a hermeneutical criterion for reading texts on social problems.

When, for example, Pius XI writes in *Quadragesimo anno* that

> as the situation now stands, hiring and offering for hire in the so-called labor market separate men into two divisions, as into battle lines, and the contest between the two divisions turns the labor market itself almost into a battle-field where, face to face, the opposing lines struggle bitterly [QA 83],

he is not only describing the class struggle but also pointing out its causal explanation, and this in terms very similar to those used in Marxist analysis. This does not mean that he accepts as certain the whole of scientific and philosophical thought on the subject. It does, however, mean that the causal explanation offered by the pope for the conflict arising out of the labor market seems to him to be a plausible one.

In the documents of the Second General Conference of Latin American Bishops (Medellín, 1968) we again find in outline form the mediating role played by the social sciences in understanding the primordial experience of the contrast between reality and God's plan. The Medellín documents not only describe the situation,[4] but also look for its causes, which they find in, for example, marginalization[5] or dependence.[6] Nevertheless, above and beyond any sociological interpretation, these documents are interested in a theological explanation: we are living in a situation of sin.[7]

In like manner, the Final Document of Puebla contains a "sociological minimum" inasmuch as the gap between rich and poor is attributed to structural causes (as we saw above in chap. 1). Since it is not their pastoral task, the bishops refuse to decide which methods or schools offer the best causal explanation. At the same time, however, by asserting this "sociological minimum" they avoid shying away from any and every scientific explanation and being content with a naive vision that considers social facts to be purely natural or accidental phenomena.

Paul VI likewise makes it clear that profound reflection and the study of a wide range of information play a necessary role in the elaboration of documents published by the church's magisterium.

> The magisterium of the Church cannot propose moral norms unless it is sure that it is interpreting God's will. In reaching this certitude, the Church is not excused from carrying out research nor from examining all the many questions proposed for its consideration from every corner of the world. Sometimes these operations take a long time and are anything but easy.[8]

The part played by the sciences will be a fruitful one provided a critical attitude is taken to these sciences themselves.

Of course, each individual scientific discipline will be able, in its own particular sphere, to grasp only a partial—yet true—aspect of man; the complete picture and the full meaning will escape it. But within these limits the human sciences give promise of a positive function that the Church willingly recognizes. They can even widen the horizons of human liberty to a greater extent than the conditioning circumstances perceived enable one to foresee. They could thus assist Christian social morality, which no doubt will see its field restricted when it comes to suggesting certain models of society, while its function of making a critical judgment and taking an overall view will be strengthened by its showing the relative character of the behavior and values presented by such and such a society as definitive and inherent in the very nature of man. These sciences are a condition at once indispensable and inadequate for a better discovery of what is human. They are a language which becomes more and more complex, yet one that deepens rather than solves the mystery of the heart of man, nor does it provide the complete and definitive answer to the desire which springs from his innermost being [OA 40].

THEOLOGICAL JUSTIFICATION
FOR A SOCIOANALYTICAL MEDIATION

The need of a very careful association of two types of knowledge about society—the knowledge provided by faith and the knowledge provided by the sciences—must be given a theological justification. In addition, the association must be monitored by a critical epistemological eye.

In its pastoral constitution, *Gaudium et spes*, Vatican Council II offers some suggestions for such a theological justification. It says that the church is a sacrament of salvation for the human race and that although this church is by nature ordered to a religious mission, from this mission itself come a light and a strength that help guide the human community (GS 42). Taking a step further with its idea of "signs of the times," the council sees human history as more than simply the space within which human beings apply the ethical directives given by the magisterium. History is also a sign and call from God, who governs all peoples and addresses us through signals which we must know how to decode and interpret.

The reciprocal church-world relationship, which is a theological point of reference for the social teaching of the church, may be expressed by the following statements.

The Church, a Sacrament of History

We may assert that the church exists for the sake of the world, inasmuch as it is a sacrament of the salvation of world history.

In God's providence the church has a mission of salvation, which is to continue the redemptive work of Jesus Christ throughout the course of history and to make that work present at every point. Nonetheless the church cannot claim absolute value in and for itself. God's saving work, which consists in the building of the kingdom, is the ultimate horizon for all of history. It is God who saves. The church exists for the sake of this work of salvation, as the sacrament, that is, the sign and instrument, of grace. The church therefore does not have its meaning in itself; rather, like any sign or signal, it points to what is signified, seeking thus to transcend itself and turn the eyes of human beings to God the Savior. In other words, the church exists not for itself but for the world, and in order that the world may attain to salvation, which is God's work.

There is a New Testament figure who can be taken as embodying the same meaning that the church has: John the Baptist. Like John, the church must proclaim Christ and, in a sense, decrease so that Christ may increase. A church that makes an absolute of itself will not be faithful to its Lord nor live his life (see RH 18). The church exists in order that human beings may encounter Christ.

However, I must at the same time make the point that the church is not "only a sign," that is, a kind of "empty" signal or symbol that merely refers to something external to itself. The church is, on the contrary, a sacrament, that is, a "full" sign or one which has intrinsic meaning. The church is the community of those human beings who have encountered Christ and are living the life of Christ; the encounter with Christ in faith and sacraments is constitutive of the church. The church is therefore sign and sacrament of salvation to the extent that the human beings who make up the church live by faith, continually encounter Christ, and obey his commandments.

The church is a sacrament of salvation to the extent that its members live as brothers and sisters and as children of God or, in other words, live in conformity with the Spirit of Jesus. It is such a sacrament to the extent that the men and women who live their encounter with Christ in the bosom of the church recognize that they have been saved, redeemed, and set free.

The Acts of the Apostles tell us that "the company of those who believed were of one heart and soul," that "no one said that any of the things he possessed was his own," and that "they devoted themselves to the apostles' teaching and fellowship, to the breaking of bread and the prayers" (Acts 4:32; 2:42). These texts show us the objective existence of a community of persons who have been transformed by faith, a community that calls attention to itself by reason of the love that reigns in it, and in this way proclaims to others that a new existence in the Spirit of the Lord Jesus is possible for them as well.

The World Finds Its Ultimate Meaning Only in the Church

Human beings, societies, and peoples must have a meaning for their lives, something that defines their identity, their existence, their aspirations. When their efforts are frustrated and their aspirations are crushed, a crisis of meaning arises.

In his encyclical *Redemptor hominis* John Paul II describes the radical crisis of meaning from which the human person is suffering in our time. He sums up the crisis as one of "alienation." Men and women sought to give meaning to their world through scientific knowledge and technological change; now, anxious and fearful, they see the works of their own hands slipping from their control and technology becoming a dehumanizing force. The pope sees this crisis of meaning as flowing from a failure of ethics (RH 15–16).

There are various levels of meaning, ranging from the superficial to the profound. The church offers radical, ultimate, transcendent meaning, for it proclaims that human life has its meaning—its origin and its destiny—in God. Human life is not a chance result of cosmic evolution; it is not something that simply happened due to the interplay of natural forces. Behind human existence there is a free, creative will at work that calls the person into life, invites this person to share the joy of divine life, and prepares for it a future that is absolute, transcendent, and definitive.

The radical question regarding the meaning of person and world is answered through revelation and faith, through the word which God sowed among a people who had experienced God's liberating power and had agreed to be "God's people," and through the definitive Word which made its appearance among us in Jesus Christ when the fullness of time had come.

Without this irruption of God into history, human beings would continue on the road of doubt, hesitation, and anxiety. But in Christ we now have some certainties: the certainty that God loves us, the certainty that this love has manifested itself in the crucified and risen Jesus and will manifest itself in us as well. These are certainties of faith, not of experience or knowledge. They are certainties which intensify as persons abandon themselves to the action of God and do not try to be the unaided builders of their own lives; as they realize that a gift has been given to them and must be received with humility: the gift of being children of God and of being able now to be brothers and sisters to others. The world is thus ordered to the church; it needs the church even if it does not realize it. It is being moved by the Spirit of Jesus Christ when it searches for truth, justice, and love. In its *Message to Humanity* (MH) Vatican Council II said that "the Church is supremely necessary for the modern world if injustices and unworthy inequalities are to be denounced, and if the true order of affairs and of values is to be restored, so that man's life can become more human according to the standards of the gospel" (MH 5).

Signs of the Times and Challenges from God

In its explanation of the church's mission to the world, Vatican Council II inaugurated a fruitful approach with its notion of "signs of the times."

The pastoral constitution *Gaudium et spes* was to some extent a novelty in the conciliar tradition. Here, for the first time, social, economic, and political themes became the subject of a conciliar document (they had long since, of course, been dealt with in the papal magisterium). It was natural that this novelty should be regarded by some with reserve and distrust.

These themes entered into the conciliar discussions thanks to a key concept which makes it possible to understand the problems of society and human history as challenges to the mission of the church. The key concept? "The signs of the times." Thanks to this concept, which comes from the Bible (cf. Matt. 16:1–4 and par.), the temporal concerns of the world came within the purview of the council. They functioned as a "bridge," as Paul VI noted in his opening address to the second session of the council.

It was John XXIII who introduced the expression "the signs of the times." At Christmas 1961 he wrote: "In keeping with the advice of Christ the Lord who urged us to recognize the signs . . . of the times, we can, in the midst of all the hideous clouds and darkness, perceive a number of things that seem to be omens portending a better day for the Church and for mankind."[9]

The expression "signs of the times" did not easily win acceptance, especially in view of the question raised by biblical scholars: If the meaning is that there are "new revelations" in the course of history, what do these add to the full revelation that was completed once and for all in Christ? But the expression does not imply any new revelations. Its aim is rather to call attention to the power which certain events have to challenge us when they are examined in the light of the gospel. The properly understood concept of "signs of the times" did finally become part of conciliar language, occurring several times in *Gaudium et spes* (4, 11, 44) and in other documents such as the decrees *Presbyterorum ordinis* 9, *Unitatis redintegratio* 4, and *Apostolicam actuositatem* 14.[10]

It is clear that the expression "the signs of the times" brings human history, including its temporal dimensions, within the purview of faith and theological reflection. If a fact or event is to be interpreted as a sign of the times, it must be seen in the light of faith and so make possible a better understanding of God's will and plan for history.

Above and beyond the use of this expression, it is a particular spirit that turns *Gaudium et spes* into a new way for the Latin American church. For this document regards the analysis of reality as important: reality is interpreted in the light of faith and the gospel, and this reflection leads in turn to pastoral directives. Neither Medellín nor Puebla would have been possible without Vatican Council II and, in particular, without *Gaudium et spes* and the concept of "signs of the times."

The Signs of the Times at Medellín and Puebla

The interpretation of the signs of the times at their deepest level is a prophetic task. The prophets spoke to their people about the marvelous actions of God and God's work of liberation, but they also denounced the sins of the people, their infidelity to the covenant. A satisfactory reading of the signs of the times requires that we see in historical events the interplay of human action and divine action. Purely temporal situations which can be adequately explained in immanent terms are not signs of the times in the evangelical and conciliar sense of this phrase. The thing that turns a historical event into a sign of the times is the dimension of it that stimulates conversion and openness to the call of God.

We may perhaps say that the most primordial and radical sign of the times in Latin America is the contrast between the faith of our people and the injustice of our society. The combination of these two traits sets us apart from the rest of the human race. There are other continents that belong to the Third World, but they are not Christian; there are other continents that are Christian, but they do not belong to the Third World. Our underdevelopment is not simply the result of technological backwardness; it is the fruit of the injustice and sin that shatter brotherhood and sisterhood as the bishops asserted both at Medellín and at Puebla.[11]

Latin America is thus a continent characterized by both faith and injustice. But the point is not simply to call attention to the wretchedness, the gap between rich and poor, the underdevelopment, the need of economic and political reforms. The bishops are saying that all this is due to the structures of society and that the root of this situation in turn is sin, the violations of personal and social morality, the practical denial of the faith that is theoretically accepted. The bishops thus offer a "sociological minimum" (the problems are due to structures) and an "ethical maximum" (the structures are due to sin and the free human will).

However, the bishops are not simply reminding people of an evangelization already received or trying to adjust this to present conditions. They are talking about reality and about applying a meaningful concrete test to this evangelization.

Sacred scripture, which reveals the origin of our filial love toward God and tells us we must order our lives to God, also tells us that there can be a "false" love of God and a "dead" faith: "If any one says, 'I love God,' and hates his brother, he is a liar; for he who does not love his brother whom he has seen, cannot love God whom he has not seen" (1 John 4:20). "If any one has the world's goods and sees his brother in need, yet closes his heart against him, how does God's love abide in him?" (1 John 3:17). "What does it profit, my brethren, if a man says he has faith but has not works? Can his faith save him? If a brother or sister is ill-clad and in lack of daily food, and one of you says to them, 'Go in peace, be warmed and filled,' without giving them the things needed for the body, what does it profit? So faith by itself, if it has no works, is dead" (James 2:14–17).

When the bishops compare the evangelization that has been accomplished with social reality as it is, they are therefore not inspired by a "horizontalism," as has been slyly claimed. The comparison is necessary if we are to know whether faith is authentic and really alive. We should note that in the doctrinal order the proper response to hunger is to give food and the proper response to cold is to offer warmth. St. James derides those who "know" perfectly well what the remedies are but do not put them into practice. An evangelization with a coherent, orderly, and perfectly orthodox content cannot by itself create a world of justice and solidarity. That content must be lived out, embodied, put into practice.

In this perspective I think it can be said that the combination "faith–injustice" is a sign of our time for Latin America. It is a motive of hope, inasmuch as the faith is real, even if imperfect; and it is a motive for conversion because injustice—the practical negation of the solidarity faith calls for—is likewise a reality. In its effort to interpret this sign of the time, Christian faith sees itself forced to come to grips with the mediation of the social sciences, which offer their own explanation, within the parameters proper to them, of the same reality that is being contemplated with the eyes of faith.

CRITICAL VIGILANCE NEEDED FOR A PROPER ARTICULATION OF THE SOCIAL SCIENCES AND THEOLOGICAL REFLECTION

The relation between church and world of which I have been speaking must be the object of a rational, critical analysis of a scientific kind.

There is an initial level of "consciousness" in the perception of relations between church and world. But a step has to be taken to a further level at which this consciousness, which is intuitive and close to reality itself, becomes "scientific," that is, turns into a rational, critical, exact knowledge.

The scientific and critical mediation by which we look at the world may take the form either of philosophy or of the sciences and in particular the social sciences. The scientific mediation which renders an account of the reality called "church" is theology.

Critical rationality represents an important level of our thinking. It must not, however, be turned into an absolute. The thing that is truly important in the sphere of salvation history is that the church and the world should be actually interrelated and correctly interrelated; salvation does not come solely from a (theoretical) knowledge of how church and world are to be correctly related to each other.

On the other hand, unless a strictly critical approach is taken, misleading relations can be established which will hinder rather than help the church in its proper mission to the world. The church may turn itself into an absolute and fail to respect the world and the autonomy of the temporal, but the world, too, may turn itself into an absolute and reject the meaning which the church brings to it. In the former case, the result will be a tendency to an improper sacralization of the temporal; in the latter, the result will be secularism. In the former case, the church will arrogate to itself an exclusive right to pronounce upon the world; it will understand revelation as the source not only of the knowledge of faith but of all science, that is, of every explanation of the origin of the cosmos and the human person. In the latter case, the world will claim to speak the only valid word about the meaning of the human person, thus absolutizing scientific knowledge and divinizing technical progress.

The correct theoretical interrelation of the various disciplines that seek to render an account of "world" and "church" is decisive if we are to attain to a correct practice of the church-world relationship.

This necessity of interrelating church and world brings theology face to face with the sciences and philosophy as mediations for an adequate understanding of the world. In this way, the understanding which theology has of the world from its own proper perspective is enriched.

The knowledge which the church has of the world comes from a special source via revelation. But revelation, though responding to ultimate questions, does not give answers to all the questions raised by the world. In order to harmonize its own knowledge through faith with rational knowledge and to proclaim the faith to those possessing rational knowledge, theology must enter into a dialogue with the other rational and scientific disciplines. The themes that are most crucially important to human beings are: the meaning of their freedom, the building of their history, the nature and essentials of their coexistence and of their action on the universe. All these are philosophical problems, but ones which theology has confronted from antiquity.

The thing that is new in the modern age is the conviction that philosophy is not the sole source of rational knowledge of the world. New disciplines are being developed, scientific disciplines with rigorous methodologies, and notable advances are being made in knowledge of the human psyche, in the laws that govern economic and political relations, and in the understanding of cultures. Unless theology takes these sciences seriously, its message regarding the world will seem hostile, superfluous, and unnecessary in the face of what critical reason has to tell us.

In traditional moral thought, which did not have to take the social sciences into account as we do today, social and political problems were considered almost exclusively from the philosophical angle, that is, at the level of essences (to characterize that approach in broad terms). Today, however, as a result of the new perspectives adopted, the more recent documents of the magisterium have been engaging in a more critical analysis of reality in its concrete dimensions (that is, in its actual existence), as well as of the mechanisms and forces which constitute, determine, and condition this reality.

This new encounter of theology and the social sciences is not without its risks. Theological reflection that is dazzled by the contribution of the empirical sciences can lose its originality and drift into "empiricism" by making political and social practice its exclusive source of knowledge, or into "pragmatism" by taking its bearings from action and looking upon itself as a mere appendage to action. In fact, theological reflection possesses its own autonomy, its own rules of logic which must be respected, and its own sources of knowledge, such as revelation.

Nonetheless, the new matter of "temporal distance," of which I spoke in chapter 6, raises questions even for theology, which in the past was never criticized in terms of its "function" and its "social location." The questioning can lead theologians to retreat into unyielding positions and to be contemptuous of the social sciences from which the challenges issue. But it may cause them also to adopt more balanced and less polemical positions which, without betraying the proper character of theology, acknowledge the necessary connection of thought with reality and the power thought has both of transforming and of immobilizing reality.[12]

We may recall here Rahner's statement, which I cited in chapter 3, that propositions which are true can be uttered too hastily or in an unloving manner or be of little use for the real life of Christians. The obligation of paying heed both to the internal logic of a line of thought and to its fruitfulness in engendering freedom seems incumbent on the discipline of Jesus who wishes to reach the "truth that makes us free."

When that which we seek to know is society and its problems, we must take as our starting point not an unsophisticated knowledge of society (that of "the man in the street"), which often represents a thought already permeated by the prevailing ideology, but a critical, analytical thinking that is capable of explaining the causalities, dynamisms, and forces at work in society. However, this or that socioanalytic mediation that may be adequate for a social scientist is not yet adequate for the theologian or for the church's social teaching inasmuch as theology and social teaching add the vision of faith to a socioanalytic vision of things, and the vision of faith depends not on the human sciences or human knowledge but on revelation. Nonetheless, theologians must accept the information provided and integrate it into their thinking.

Conversely, the vision of faith in turn corrects the ideological elements in the social sciences. The magisterium will exercise this function all the more successfully to the extent that it not only communicates to us truth which is objectively orthodox, but also enables us, in and through this truth, to draw near to the Christian mystery of the life, the abundant life, which Christ brings us. To this end the magisterium will have to get rid of those ideological affiliations that may be conditioning its own teaching.

Deideologization as a critical function of faith becomes necessary whenever the sociology of knowledge tells us that a certain degree of group or class interests colors all our knowledge of society and thus ideologizes it to some extent. A social teaching of the church that is developed with sensitivity to the poorest must supplement this "sympathy" (in the original meaning of the word) with both a theological reflection that grasps the privileged place of the poor in revelation and in the building of the kingdom, and a method of social analysis that penetrates to the real causes of the oppression of the poor and offers possible solutions. Such a vision of faith is incompatible with certain scientific methodologies that look exclusively to the accumulation of capital as the means of economic effectiveness and have no place for a human hierarchy of values; it is incompatible, too, with other methodologies that overstep the limits of strictly scientific knowledge and turn into philosophies, universal and all-embracing visions of humanity and its destiny and, on this basis, prescind from or deny God.

On the other hand, no less incompatible with a true ecclesial sensitivity to the poor is an interpretation of the faith that hardens itself to the demands of justice and retreats into a religious individualism which in turn slips into easy fellowship with the economic individualism called for by some types of economic thinking. Puebla reminds us that there are Christians who have not sufficiently accepted the social dimension of their commitment as can be seen from their clinging to their economic interests and economic power and from their failure fully to understand and accept the church's social teaching (DP 824). Economic liberalism, which is materialist in practice, has an individualistic vision of the human person according to which the dignity of the person consists in economic effectiveness and individual freedom. Such a vision, which is closed in on itself and in many instances is wedded to a religious conception of salvation as an individual matter, is blind to the demands of social justice (DP 321) and reduces Jesus Christ to a purely private concern (DP 178); it reduces the scope of faith to personal or familial life and excludes the professional, economic, social, and political spheres, as if sin, love, and forgiveness had no relevance in these (DP 515). Such mutilations of faith represent in practice a connivance—however unwitting—with the established order (DP 558).

When theology and the social sciences are interrelated in concrete ways (I am thinking here specifically of the Latin American scene), various theories are applied to uncover the key factors that explain the social facts and make it possible to offer diagnoses and come up with programs for solving the problems.

"Developmentalism," for example, considers underdevelopment to be the central problem, especially in the economic area where there is a lack of adequate industrialization. The theory calls for the use of the same means that speeded up the industrial development of the rich nations (developmentalism defines as "rich" only those nations that achieved development through capitalism). A speedy economic development will lead to political stability, the improvement of education and health services, and so on. Chief among the means in question are the stimulus to investment (from which the savers may expect sizable gains), the development of trade (especially foreign trade, which will be a source of currency), the acquisition of high technology (which enables us to offer competitive prices in the international market), etc.

Critics have pointed out that the industrial development of the now developed countries is not easily repeated among us because circumstances here are quite different. In the Latin American countries the accumulation of the needed capital must be obtained primarily through foreign loans; this fact had no parallel in early industrial capitalism in Europe and therefore did not subject many aspects of national life to the pressures of foreign capital. On the other hand, the importation of high technology from countries in which the labor force is limited but skilled into countries in which, on the contrary, workers are abundant will only aggravate the situation of chronic unemployment, which has no escape valve—as it did in Europe in the early phase of industrialization—in the form of massive emigrations to Australia or North America or South America. Our situation is in fact rendered even more disadvantageous because those who do emigrate are often those with the greatest technical skill and preparation; often they are forced to look outside the country for better opportunities.

A Christian critique will point out in addition that the economy does not represent the supreme value and does not possess total autonomy so that everything else must be at its service. The economy must be at the service of human beings and not human beings at the service of the economy. This critique, which is constructive because it tries to suggest possible alternatives, finds voice especially in the writings of François Lebret, who exercised such an important influence on *Populorum progressio*. A further criticism, which is more recent and more original with Latin American Christians, concentrates on denouncing the conditions of exploitation and injustice on which many developmentalist models are built. This criticism condemns not development as such but the conditions in which development takes place, because in practice development benefits only a few and marginalizes the majority.

A second theory has become widespread in Latin America: the theory of "marginalization." The theory examines the superposition of two strata: that part of the population which is more or less "integrated" into the rhythms of the culture and of modern progress; and that part which is "marginalized" and excluded from the sharing in goods and services and the decision-making that are characteristic of the integrated sector.

This theory too has been criticized as inadequate, despite its good point, which is to emphasize anthropological and cultural aspects that are missing from the previous theory. This theory does not take into account, at least explicitly, the ties between the Latin American world and the outside world. Objection is also raised to its strategies for incorporating the marginalized, inasmuch as society in its present form will inevitably go on producing this kind of marginalization; in fact, the number of the marginalized whom the system produces will always be greater than the number of the marginalized who achieve integration. In addition, the critique regards as insufficient a strategy which simply brings goods and services to those who lack them or which promotes certain levels of decision-making that do not question the system as a whole.

A third theory has been formulated on the basis of CEPAL's (Comisión Económica para América Latina) studies of the center-periphery relation and has been developed on a broad scale so as to include not only the economic but also the political and cultural aspects of the problem. According to the theory, the center-periphery (macro) system is reflected in a comparable (micro) system within each country; the links between the two centers (macro and micro) are greatly strengthened by a common interest in the world market, by options in the political sphere, and by the same manner of living out the same cultural values.

Those who criticize the dependence theory focus chiefly on its general and comprehensive character, inasmuch unlike the previous theory (in which the solution is to incorporate the marginalized into an already existing society) there is question here of creating a new and different society that does not exist as yet. Others are suspicious of what they see as a close and even necessary connection between this theory and those of Lenin on imperialism (relations between the micro and macro centers) and of Marx on the class struggle (relations between the micro-center and the micro-periphery). In fact, however, imperialism and the class struggle represent possible but not necessary ways of interpreting undeniable elements of dependency such as foreign neocolonialism and domestic colonialism. We would be going too far were we to attribute a link with or dependence on Marxist analyses to the bishops of Medellín or to Paul VI when he criticizes free trade at the international level as leading to an economic dictatorship because of the power of the rich countries over the weak poor countries (PP 58–61).

In choosing an interpretative theory two perspectives may be adopted: one, scientific and technical, adopts as its norm the greatest possible approximation to reality itself, seeking to explain reality as exactly as possible and to render a coherent and radical account of it; the other, ethical in character, looks for a theory that will be in harmony with basic Christian values.

In ending this chapter I wish to emphasize the point that a hermeneutic of the texts of the church's social teaching must come to grips with an aspect which these texts do not share with other magisterial texts. I refer to the fact that texts embodying social teaching depend on nontheological information and deal with realities that are secular, provisional, and changing. Statements of this type have value only to the extent that they satisfy a condition: they must reflect the concrete historical situation of society and the conditions this society supposes. This is why Schillebeeckx speaks of a statement of the social magisterium as "a non-doctrinal, somewhat 'hypothetical' pronouncement";[13] he is referring precisely to the dependence of such statements on nontheological information. I think he is correct when he warns that "given the pace of development in today's society, these official documents may . . . be soon out of date, so that to keep on appealing to such concrete historical indications might soon become reactionary in the future."[14]

My intention is certainly not to play down the value of the church's social teaching but simply to recognize its true nature and the proper criteria for correctly interpreting it. By reason of its specific character the social teaching of the church will be more subject to change, adaptation, and nuancing than the other documents of the magisterium. This is the reason for Paul VI's unambiguous statements in *Octogesima adveniens* 4, where he declines to set down universal norms and calls upon the concrete communities to exercise discernment in their options.

7

THE PERSPECTIVE OF THE POOR

The preceding three chapters have dealt with three hermeneutical criteria. I turn now to a fourth which is of special importance since it prevents an ideological use of the church's social teaching in order to protect and defend the interests of the established order. Under the pretext of defending Western and Christian civilization, this order denies in practice the demands expressed in this social teaching by reducing it to a set of abstract statements of formal rights and not linking it in any way with social, economic, and political reality.

I shall begin by presenting the justification for this hermeneutical principle and shall then show that its application is necessary if the Latin American church is to act consistently with the preferential option for the poor that was made at Puebla.

SENSITIVITY TO THE POOR AS A HERMENEUTICAL CRITERION IN THE PAPAL MAGISTERIUM

As we saw in chapter 1, Pope John Paul II posits a relation between two poles: liberating action and social teaching. The latter must be the criterion for deciding the Christian quality of the former. But can we convert this proposition and assert, in accordance with the principle of hermeneutical circularity, that liberating action must in turn serve as a criterion in reading and understanding the social teaching? If the answer is yes, then not every reading, undertaken from any social vantage point whatsoever, does justice to the meaning and intentions of the magisterium. Of course, it is also possible to read the social teaching from the vantage point of a situation of oppression and repression and then selectively choose arguments to defend positions already taken!

The following arguments help to establish the validity of the hermeneutical criterion that is the subject of this chapter.

Negative Arguments

It is evident that the popes have disqualified a reading or understanding that would be to the disadvantage of the poor. This fact provides us with a clear criterion of how the social teaching is *not* to be read.

Pius XI in *Quadragesimo anno* and John XXIII in *Mater et magistra* reject an interpretation of the church's social teaching that would be unfavorable to the poor or appear to show partiality to the rich.

Forty years after the publication of *Rerum novarum* Pius XI said that the teaching of Leo XIII on poverty had been misinterpreted, with the result that the church had been slandered:

> Yet since there are some who calumniate the Supreme Pontiff, and the Church herself, as if she had taken and were still taking the part of the rich against the non-owning workers—certainly no accusation is more unjust than that—and since Catholics are at variance with one another concerning the true and exact mind of Leo, it has seemed best to vindicate this, that is, the Catholic teaching on this matter from calumnies and safeguard it from false interpretations [QA 44].

Twenty years after that, John XXIII again referred to an interpretation of the church's social teaching that favored the interests of the rich: "For while some, confronted with the social question, unashamedly attacked the Church as if she did nothing except preach resignation to the poor and exhort the rich to generosity, Leo XIII did not hesitate to proclaim and defend quite openly the sacred rights of workers" (MM 16).

We must observe that these two passages are intended as an authentic hermeneutical key to the entire body of social teaching. It is illegitimate to manipulate this social teaching in order to consolidate, defend, and legitimize an order or situation that is detrimental to the sacred rights of workers.

> It is certainly most lamentable, Venerable Brethren [said Pius XI] that there have been, nay, that even now there are men who, although professing to be Catholics, are almost completely unmindful of that sublime law of justice and charity that binds us not only to render to everyone what is his but to succor brothers in need as Christ the Lord Himself, and—what is worse—out of greed for gain do not scruple to exploit the workers. Even more, there are men who abuse religion itself, and under its name try to hide their unjust exactions in order to protect themselves from the manifestly just demands of the workers. The conduct of such We shall never cease to censure gravely. For they are the reason why the Church could, even though undeservedly, have the appearance of and be charged with taking the part of the rich and with being quite unmoved by the necessities and hardships of those who have been deprived, as it were, of their natural inheritance [QA 125].

In addition, does not John Paul II, in his address to the bishops of Puebla, make a cautious reference to the situation of the many Latin American Christians who abuse their wealth? "Permit me, then, to commend to your special pastoral attention the urgency of making your faithful aware of the Church's social doctrine" (OAPC III, 7).

Positive Arguments

Paul VI expressly states that the church's social teaching "develops with the sensitivity proper to the Church which is characterized by a disinterested will to serve and by attention to the poorest" (OA 42). If sensitivity to the poor must direct the process of formulating and extending the church's social teaching, it is logical to conclude that the same sensitivity must be a criterion in reading and interpreting this social teaching, since the latter should be read in the same spirit in which it was developed.

The church's social teaching must, therefore, not betray the evangelical spirit of poverty. In *Rerum novarum* Leo XIII reminds us that Jesus Christ

> being the Son of God, and God Himself, chose to seem and to be considered the son of a carpenter—nay, did not disdain to spend a great part of His life as a carpenter Himself. . . . Nay, God Himself seems to incline rather to those who suffer misfortune; for Jesus Christ calls the poor "blessed"; He lovingly invites those in labor and grief to come to Him for solace; and He displays the tenderest charity towards the lowly and the oppressed [RN 23].

In his first encyclical, *Ecclesiam suam,* Paul VI emphasizes the value of poverty in this fine passage which deserves to be reread and meditated on:

> The first of them [two points of importance for renewal] is the spirit of poverty, or rather, the zeal for preserving this spirit. We presume to mention it explicitly in this encyclical letter because of Our conviction of the prominence which this precept receives in Christ's holy Gospel. It is a fundamental element of that divine plan by which we are destined to win the kingdom of God, and yet it is greatly jeopardized by the modern trend to set so much store by wealth.
>
> The zeal for the spirit of poverty is vitally necessary if we are to realize the many failures and mistakes we have made in the past, and learn the principle on which we must now base our way of life and how best to proclaim the religion of Christ.
>
> One further reason for Our mentioning it here is the difficulty we all find in practicing it. It is not Our intention to issue special canonical regulations on this subject, but We do ask you, Venerable Brethren, for the support of your agreement, your counsel and your example. It is your

task to interpret with authority the movements and inspirations of the Holy Spirit in the Church, and We rely on you to make clear to pastors and people how the spirit of poverty should regulate everything they do and say. As the Apostle Paul admonished us: "Let this mind be in you, which was also in Christ Jesus." We rely on you to indicate to Us what decisions and regulations we should together make binding on the Church, so that we may base our confidence more on the help of God and on spiritual values, than on fallible, human means. The directives we need are such as will teach us and the men of this era that spiritual goods far outweigh economic goods, the possession and use of which should be regulated and subordinated to the conduct and advantage of our apostolic mission.

The spirit of poverty is a special mark of Christ's Gospel. This passing reference to its necessity and excellence does not, however, relieve Us of Our obligation of pointing out that zeal for poverty is no obstacle to the proper understanding and rightful application of the important laws of economics. This is a subject which has made great strides within recent years. It has been responsible for the progress of civilization, especially in its human and social aspects. But We consider that the inner freedom which results from zeal for evangelical poverty makes us in fact more sensitive to the human aspects of economic questions, and better fitted to understand them. We can pass, where necessary, a calm and often severe judgment on wealth and on the luxuries of life. We can come promptly and generously to the aid of those in need, and do our utmost to ensure that wealth, far from being a source of conflict, selfishness, and pride amongst men, shall be used justly and equitably for the good of all, and distributed with greater foresight.

In all that concerns these external goods—goods which are indeed inferior to those that are spiritual and eternal, but which are nevertheless necessary in this present life—the student of the Gospel can come to a prudent decision. He has a real, human contribution to make in this field. We are most keenly interested in science, technology, and especially in work. The bread which they produce is sacred, whether destined for the table or the altar. This is the Church's traditional social teaching, and it leaves no room for doubt. We readily seize this opportunity of confirming it by Our own authority [ES 54-55].

I shall dwell at greater length on the approach of John Paul II to the subject of poverty, since it will help us to understand the circularity that must exist between social teaching as a criterion of liberation and commitment to liberation as the vantage point from which, and the spirit in which, this teaching must itself be understood.

In the first place, John Paul II points out that we must have a predilection for the poor, and this for evangelical reasons. He develops the concept along the following lines:

• This love is a love that comes into being on the basis of the gospel (ARW) and does not spring from socioeconomic or political motives and inspirations.

• This option for the poor is clearly a "preferential option" for them, although it certainly does not mean excluding anyone from the all-embracing love which every Christian must have (HBG 4). The poor in particular "call for understanding and support" (APR), so that "a certain closeness to the poor as objects of a legitimate priority of attention" is, in the pope's eyes, one of the "reasons for joy and optimism" that he perceives as he reflects on "the manifestations of great vitality in religious life" (ARW).

• The source of this preferential love for the poor is the example of Jesus Christ; therefore priests and religious, "as servants of the people of God, servants of the faith, and stewards and witnesses of Christ's love for human beings" should practice this "love which is not partisan and excludes no one, although it addresses itself with preference to the poorest" (APR).

• The love of Jesus for the poor must be the model of this preferential love. After briefly summarizing the most important characteristics of the work of Jesus, the pope ends this section of his Opening Address at Puebla with this thought: "There can be no doubt that all this imposes exacting demands on the attitude of any Christians who truly wish to serve the least of their brothers and sisters, the poor, the needy, the marginalized" (OAPC I, 4). The church must see the human person as an integral whole; in virtue, therefore, of its own mission it must defend and promote human dignity. And the reason for this, the pope says, is that "in the parable of the Good Samaritan, the Lord outlined the model way of attending to all human needs" (OAPC III, 2).

• But according to John Paul II the reasons thus far given are insufficient. The preferential option for the poor has a still deeper theological foundation: Christ lives in the poor! The least of our brothers and sisters, the poor, the needy, the marginalized, are "those whose lives reflect the suffering countenance of the Lord" (OAPC I, 4). The Lord "said that in the last analysis he will identify himself with the disinherited—the imprisoned, the hungry, and the abandoned—to whom we have offered a helping hand" (OAPC III, 2). For this reason, "if the spirit of Jesus Christ dwells in us, we should feel an overriding concern for those who do not have proper food, clothing, and housing or access to the benefits of the culture" (AWM p. 197).

The most important point about these passages from the pope's messages is that they are reinforced by a personal and pastoral witness of closeness to and predilection for the poorest. The pope embodies this preferential love in himself. That is why he says to the inhabitants of the Barrio Santa Cecilia, as he had said earlier (Feb. 1, 1979) in Santo Domingo:

I feel a solidarity with you, for since you are poor you have a right to my special concern. . . . The pope loves you because you are the beloved of God. When he established his family, the Church, he had present before him the poor and needy human race, and to redeem that race he sent his very own Son, who was born a poor man and lived among the poor in order to enrich us through his poverty. . . . The figure of Christ, hanging on the cross as the price for the redemption of the human race, is a penetrating call to spend our lives in the service of the needy, in accordance with the movement of a love that is disinterested and sides not with injustice but with the truth.

Following the example of Jesus Christ, whose vicar the pope is, this preferential love for the poor finds embodiment in very concrete forms of solidarity. The pope says to the Indians of Oaxaca and Chiapas: "The pope chooses to be your voice, the voice of those who cannot speak or who have been silenced" (AIOC), and then he cries out: "It is not just, it is not human, it is not Christian to continue certain situations that are clearly unjust" (AIOC). He also descends to the concrete level and in behalf of the peasants attacks certain evils:

They have a right to be respected. They have a right not to be deprived of the little they have by maneuvers that sometimes amount to real plunder. They have a right not to be blocked in their desire to take part in their own advancement. They have a right to have the barriers of exploitation removed. These barriers are frequently the product of intolerable forms of egotism, against which their best efforts at advancement are dashed. They have a right to effective help, which is neither a handout nor a few crumbs of justice, so that they may have access to the development that their dignity as human beings and as children of God merits [AIOC].

The pope's personal experience allows him to say in all honesty that he "always feels at home" in the world of the workers (AWG). He addresses workers as "brothers and sisters" (AWG), as "friends and companions" (AWG and AWM), and he can truthfully say: "I have shared the needs of workers, their just demands, their legitimate aspirations" (AWM, p. 196).

For all the reasons given, we may conclude that while John Paul II makes the church's social teaching the hermeneutical criterion of authentically liberating action, he also makes solidarity with the workers the hermeneutical locus for understanding in turn that social teaching itself. It is from within "the church of the poor" that the church's social teaching is to be understood.

In order to achieve social justice in the various parts of the world, in the various countries and in the relationships between them, there is a need for ever new movements of solidarity of the workers and with the workers.

This solidarity must be present whenever it is called for by the social degrading of the subject of work, by exploitation of the workers and by the growing areas of poverty and even hunger. The Church is firmly committed to this cause and considers it its mission, its service, a proof of its fidelity to Christ, so that it can truly be the "church of the poor" [LE 8].

THE OPTION FOR THE POOR AS A PERSPECTIVE
FOR INTERPRETING THE SOCIAL TEACHING

According to the bishops at Puebla, the evangelization of Latin America is characterized by two preferential options: for the poor and for the young; and by three clear doctrinal messages: the truth about Jesus Christ, the truth about the church, and the truth about the human person.

The two pastoral options are really a single option: an option for the evangelization of Latin America, which is a young continent and a continent in which injustice reigns. Evangelization means a call to the young to build a Christian utopia that is defined by service to the most needy because we encounter Christ in them. In this book I shall be dealing basically with the option for the poor, not as though it were opposed to the other option but because it yields the meaning of the new society in which the young are being urged to collaborate.

The objective fact of the gap dividing rich and poor was analyzed in chapter 1 from the standpoint of the subjective consciousness of a church that is discovering its responsibility and is desirous of becoming an agent of liberation. But this intensified subjective consciousness reflects also the subjective consciousness of the oppressed who suffer oppression and make this known by their cry for liberation. This subjective consciousness of the poor is, once again, a fact and will serve as a point of departure for our reflections.

We are dealing with a fact: the cry of the poor. Our aim is to understand who these poor are and why they are crying out. The response of the church when it hears this cry is expressed as a "preferential option for the poor." We must also understand, therefore, the reasons for this option and how it is to be put into practice, both in regard to the evangelical characteristics it ought to have and in regard to the effects it is meant to produce at the historical level.

The Cry

The cry is a fierce cry for justice and faith, and is heard by the church in its pastoral work with the poor.

The bishops at Puebla cite Medellín's statement that "a muted cry wells up from millions of human beings, pleading with their pastors for a liberation that is nowhere to be found in their case" (DP 88). The bishops add: "The cry might well have seemed muted back then. Today it is loud and clear, increasing in volume and intensity, and at times full of menace" (DP 89). The church feels "summoned" by this cry of the people, and "has put much effort into offering them an adequate pastoral response" (DP 93).

What is the object of the cry? "It is the cry of a suffering people who demand justice, freedom, and respect for the basic rights of human beings and peoples" (DP 87). They "ask for the bread of God's Word and demand justice" (DP 93). In other words: "The poor people of Latin America yearn for a society with greater equality, justice, and participation at every level" (DP 1207).

The cry is heard at the pastoral level "in our many pastoral encounters with our people" (DP 24). It is comprehended in the perspective of faith: "From our vision based on faith, we place ourselves in the reality of the Latin American as it finds expression in that human being's hopes, achievements, and frustrations" (DP 15), for "we want to consider carefully [Latin American persons'] aspirations" (DP 131).

The Cry of the Poor

Puebla makes it clear who these poor are: the indigenous peoples (DP 34), the peasants (DP 35, 1266), the workers (DP 29, 36) the marginalized urban dwellers (DP 38), the underemployed and the unemployed (DP 37, 50, 576, 838), the children (DP 32), the elderly (DP 39).

In their cry these poor "ask for the bread of God's Word and demand justice" (DP 93). As far as evangelization is concerned, Puebla points to efforts both past (DP 8) and present (DP 441, 464, 886) to evangelize the indigenous peoples, the peasants, the workers. It calls attention to the importance of evangelizing the marginalized city dwellers (DP 366).

With regard to the cry for justice, the church is endeavoring to be attentive to the aspirations of the poor and to their efforts and struggles, and to be in solidarity with them.

A Cry for the Rights of the Poor

The poor demand many rights, but above all the right to be persons, subjects responsible for history; to begin with, this means the right to be agents in a process whereby groups among the people are liberated. They are conscious of their power in society. Ideologies seek control of the world of the workers (DP 48), which is caught up in a growing industrialization (DP 418); the marginalized are in danger of being looked upon as second-class citizens (DP 1291).

The poor have been acquiring a critical outlook. "Even the peasants, who previously were isolated from contact with civilization to a large extent, are now acquiring this same critical sense" (DP 77). They understand better than ever before what John Paul II expressed very well: "They have a right to have the barriers of exploitation removed, . . . against which their best efforts at advancement are dashed" (DP 28). Their critical awareness has led them to the discovery of their own dignity:

Latin Americans have increasingly taken cognizance of their dignity as human beings and of the desire for political and social participation, despite the fact that in many areas these rights are crushed underfoot. There has been a proliferation of community organizations, such as cooperative movements, especially among the common people [DP 18].

Ours is a young people; and where they have had opportunities to develop their abilities and organize, they have proved that they can win out and regain possession of their just rights and claims [DP 20].

The poor, too, have been encouraged by the Church. They have begun to organize themselves to live their faith in an integral way, and hence to reclaim their rights [DP 1137].

The poor are becoming aware that they constitute a force in society. The workers are seen as "the chief artisans of the prodigious changes which the world is undergoing today" (DP 1244), and the peasants as "a dynamic force in the building of a more participatory society" (DP 1245). This consciousness of power is also a consciousness of responsibility. Latin Americans have "a desire to be truly taken into account as responsible people and subjects of history, who can freely participate in political options, labor-union choices, and the election of rulers" (DP 135). Our peoples are demanding "legitimate self-determination. . . . This will permit them to organize their lives in accordance with their own genius and history and to cooperate in a new international order" (DP 505).

We may say that the fundamental right specified in the cry of the poor is the right to guarantee the rights of the oppressed, that is, the right to be agents of a history of social change and transformation. That is precisely the aim of popular organizations. Nonetheless, "in recent years we have also seen deterioration in the political sphere. Much harm has been done to the participation of citizens in the conduct of their own affairs and destiny" (DP 46). It is especially the poor whose participation is hindered, whereas "employer organizations . . . can exercise their full power to protect their interests" (DP 44). For this reason the bishops energetically defend the right of workers and peasants "to freely create organizations to defend and promote their interests, and to make a responsible contribution to the common good" (DP 1163). In addition, the church claims the right to a mission of consciousness-raising, in regard, for example, to the peasants (see DP 77) and to popular organizations generally:

The mission of the Church is not restricted to exhorting the various social groups and professional categories to fashion a new society for all and with the common people. Nor is it solely to motivate each group to make its specific contribution in an honest, competent way. The Church must also urge them to serve as agents of a general consciousness-raising about the common responsibility, in the face of a challenge that requires the participation of all [DP 1220].

Response of the Church to the Cry of the Poor: A Preferential Option

It can be said that the church has always been present among the poor and the needy (see DP 965); nonetheless in recent years it has especially intensified its commitment to the dispossessed segments of the population, pleading for their integral development (DP 147), dissociating itself from those who hold economic or political power, freeing itself from forms of dependency, and divesting itself of privileges (see DP 623).

The church perhaps best expresses its option for the poor and its love for the common people through the base-level ecclesial communities (see DP 643). These enable Christians to lead an evangelical life in the midst of the people (DP 642); they manifest a greater commitment to justice in the social milieu that surrounds them (DP 640).

Characteristics of the Option for the Poor

Two types may be distinguished: characteristics internal to the option itself and springing from the motivation behind the option; and characteristics having to do with the effects to be sought through the option.

Motives for the Option

It is, above all, the exigencies of Christian love that lead to this option, since among us Christian love must become a labor of justice in behalf of the oppressed (see DP 327). The poor deserve preferential attention no matter what the moral or personal situation of the individual poor person. The poor are created in the image and likeness of God, but this image is dimmed and mocked by the wretched conditions in which they live (see DP 1142).

There is a close connection between the church's mission of evangelization and its option for the poor. The poor majorities of the continent are receptive to the Beatitudes and to God's predilection for them (DP 1129). Like Jesus Christ, the church in each of its members is consecrated and sent to preach the good news to the poor (DP 361), and the authenticity of its evangelizing work will be measured in large part by its preferential love and concern for the poorest and most needy (DP 382). The poor intuit the values of the kingdom in a privileged and forceful way (DP 132); they have an evangelical instinct (DP 448). Moreover, in the church's eyes they are the first ones to whom the mission of Jesus is directed, and their evangelization is the supreme sign and proof of his mission (DP 1142). The poor also have an evangelizing potential which challenges the church itself and calls it to conversion (DP 1147).

Perhaps the most profound link among the church, evangelization, and the poor is the presence of Jesus himself in the poor and his identification of himself with them. Jesus was born and lived a poor man (DP 190). With special tenderness he chose to identify himself with the weakest and most needy (DP 196). The church must constantly bear witness to this predilection of the Lord for those who suffer most (DP 268), and must imitate Jesus Christ in committing itself to the most needy (DP 1141), since he did not refuse to live among the most abandoned and neglected of his day (DP 316). Jesus lives today in the poor (DP 330), and he will pass judgment on us in terms of our service to the poor (DP 339). Service to the poor is the privileged, though not the exclusive, gauge of our following of Jesus Christ (DP 1145).

To opt for the poor means to take up the cause of the poor (MPLA 3). The option has as its objective to proclaim Christ the Savior who enlightens human beings regarding their dignity, helps them to achieve liberation, and leads them to communion and participation (DP 1153). Solidarity with the poor and the option for the poor evangelize the poor themselves by freeing them from individualism and the attraction of riches; but it also evangelizes the rich whose hearts are attached to wealth and enslaved by selfishness (DP 1156).

Because the option for the poor is an evangelical one, it is compatible with a universal love for all human beings. All those who exclude even a single person from their hearts do not possess the Spirit of Christ (DP 205); and the preferential love for the poor must be kept in harmony with the mission of proclaiming the gospel to all human beings without distinction (DP 270).

Historical Effectiveness of the Option for the Poor

If the poor perceive that their basic rights are being violated and if the cry which they address to the human race and which the church hears with a pastoral heart is concerned above all with the right of active participation in history as responsible agents, then the option for the poor must lead the church to effective historical action that will really benefit the "cause" of the poor. In other words, the option is also a decision to back organizations of the people and their efforts for justice (see DP 1162, 1163, 1220), as I pointed out above.

John Paul II must have been putting his seal of approval on this teaching of the Latin American episcopate when in *Laborem exercens* he emphasized the need of solidarity among the workers and with the workers and when he defended the right of workers to unionize.

The historical influence of the option for the poor is tested and proved by the resultant social conflicts into which the church is drawn. The image of the church (the bishops say) has been changing because it is dissociating itself from the powerful and drawing closer to the people (DP 83); it is seeking to become increasingly independent of the powers of this world (DP 144). This new attitude has met with reserve in certain sectors that show little social sensitivity (DP 160); groups that possess economic power and that believed themselves to be leaders of Catholicism even feel abandoned now by the church which, as they see it, has forsaken its "spiritual" mission (DP 79). The church is experiencing internal tensions (DP 90) and even persecutions (DP 1138).

CONCLUSION

The special sensitivity of the church to the poor, a sensitivity that determined the attitude and perspective in which the social teaching was developed, led Leo XIII "with great courage to defend 'the cause of the workers' " (QA 10). The bishops at Puebla urge all "without distinction of classes, to accept and make their own the cause of the poor as if they were accepting and making their own the cause of Christ himself." This summons means returning to the original intention of the church's social teaching and rejecting the reading or interpretation of this teaching due to which the church "could, even though undeservedly, have the appearance of and be charged with taking the part of the rich" (QA 125). For even today there are those who "abuse religion itself, and under its name try to hide their unjust exactions in order to protect themselves from the manifestly just demands of the workers" (ibid.).

The perspective of the cause of the poor is therefore perhaps the most important hermeneutical criterion to be applied in reading the church's social teaching in the context of our continent.

8

PRIVATE PROPERTY

In the preceding chapters I have tried to establish the hermeneutical criteria which make possible an adequate reading of the church's social teaching, one that takes into account its ethical, sociopolitical or economic, and historical character. I have also sought to establish the basic perspective in which this message is to be understood. This and the following chapters will attempt an application of these hermeneutical principles.

I shall begin this work of applying principles by turning to a subject of vital importance: property. It is a striking fact that the church has constantly defended the right of ownership, even though by doing so it has seemed to promote the interests of the rich and thereby to alienate itself from laborers, other workers, and peasants. There can be no doubt that the church sees property as an important value.

Ownership is not simply a relation between a human being and the goods of this world (a relation which goes beyond simple use and becomes one of control); it is also a relation among human beings because it represents a right. Disputes over the precise meaning and scope of this right not only affect the classes of society within a country, but divide the human race into two great property systems (private and social) which give expression to two political outlooks, two ideologies, and provoke the present international tensions of which we are all aware.

The church, which exists in the midst of this conflict of international forces, proposes its teaching on property as encumbered by a "social mortgage." With this teaching it distances itself both from the out-and-out collectivism that often turns totalitarian and from the individualistic self-centeredness that characterizes the geopolitical world of which our Latin American continent is a part.

If, then, we are to grasp the exact meaning of the church's position, we must compare its thinking with that of the two camps just mentioned, which often revile the position of the magisterium or seek to manipulate it because they regard it as either alien or close to their own positions.

Although socialism did not manifest any direct opposition to Christian thinking in the first stages of its historical development, the transition from a "utopian" to a more "scientific" socialism in the work of Karl Marx did generate strong opposition to the church. The point of departure for this opposition was the personal and collective experiences of the founder of Marxism and of his age generally. Marx was born into a Jewish family but saw his father convert to Protestantism in order that he might exercise the civil rights which had previously been denied to him. Under the influence of the atheistic humanism of Feuerbach (who denied God in order that he might assert man) Marx looked upon religion as an opiate and a form of alienation. He could not deny that religion was an important social force in his day, but he was far from persuaded that this force was being used to promote the rights of the poor; on the contrary, for he saw the bourgeoisie constantly appealing to the "sacred right of private property" and the Christian churches seemingly giving their blessing to this view. The encyclical *Rerum novarum* appeared only in 1891 when Marx's ideas had already spread far and wide (Marx wrote his *Economic and Philosophic Manuscripts* in 1844, the *Communist Manifesto* in 1848, and the *Critique of Political Economy* in 1859).

In summary, we can say that in the judgment of Marxism a defense of the "natural right of private property" is purely and simply a defense of the privileged position of the bourgeoisie in industrial capitalism. Paradoxical though it may be, the capitalist system accepts this interpretation of itself and therefore regards itself as defended by the church and identified with the church, as though forming with it a single bloc known as "Western and Christian civilization." But if we are to do justice to the thinking of the church we must not stop at the simple formula "natural right of private property," but must go on to study its significance, limits, and meaning as found in the documents of the church itself. The present study will lead to the surprising conclusion that what the church is defending first and foremost is the right of the workers (to access to property) and that it rather severely restricts the rights of those who have already acquired property. In no way does the church accept the abuses of individualistic self-centeredness.

The capitalist system claims, in fact, that its own conceptions of the private ownership of the means of production are identical with those of the church, as if the church could favor a system "which considers profit as the key motive for economic progress, competition as the supreme law of economics, and private ownership of the means of production as an absolute right that has no limits and carries no corresponding social obligation" (PP 26). On the contrary, Paul VI clearly separates himself from this capitalism that "has been the source of excessive suffering, injustices and fratricidal conflicts whose effects still persist," and he reminds us that "this unchecked liberalism leads to dictatorship rightly denounced by Pius XI as producing 'the international imperialism of money.' One cannot condemn such abuses too strongly by solemnly recalling once again that the economy is at the service of man" (ibid.).

For these reasons, liberal capitalism does not understand the position of the church when the latter insists, in keeping with its teaching, on the social function of property and the social mortgage attached to property and when it emphasizes the right to agrarian reform and denounces land left unproductive at a time when so many families lack food. In the eyes of the capitalist system all this represents a camouflaged infiltration of international Marxism that threatens the principles of the church. It is worth reminding ourselves here of the severe judgment which Pius XI passed on liberalism in his day, pointing out that the church's social teaching attacked the errors of liberalism (QA 14) and broke through the confines set by economic liberalism on the duties of the state (QA 25), and of the fact that he denounced the "concentration of power and might, the characteristic mark, as it were, of contemporary economic life," as "the fruit that the unlimited freedom of struggle among competitors has of its own nature produced, and which lets only the strongest survive; and this is often the same as saying, those who fight the most violently, those who give least heed to their conscience" (QA 107). "The ultimate consequences of the individualist spirit in economic life" are, then, that "free competition has destroyed itself; economic dictatorship has supplanted the free market; unbridled ambition for power has likewise succeeded greed for gain; all economic life has become tragically hard, inexorable, and cruel" (QA 109).

It is not surprising, therefore, that the ideology of national security and the interests of capitalism, especially in the age of the multinational corporations, are in conflict with a church that seeks to teach its own social doctrine. They need the church in order to maintain the social order, since the church is a considerable social force, especially in Latin America, but at the same time they want a church that preserves a greater silence on human rights and is less critical of the excesses of capitalist individualism.

Western capitalism does not understand that the denunciation of its excesses does not always come from the other geopolitical camp, but can flow from the demands of the gospel. A simplistic ideology that tends to divide all of humankind into friends and enemies will lump together those who criticize capitalism from the perspective of socioeconomic and political analysis (as Marxism, e.g., does) and those who criticize it in the light of ethical and moral values which are inspired by the gospel and the social teaching of the church. We must be conscious of this risk as well as of the other risk we run when we defend the right of private property (a defense which in the church's social teaching is primarily a defense of this right for workers), namely, the risk of being accused of trying to defend the interests of the powerful rather than evangelical and human values. It is therefore our responsibility to teach the church's social doctrine while avoiding all these ambiguities, in order that the gospel spirit which leads the church to a preferential option for the poor may shine forth in all its purity.

THE CHURCH'S TEACHING ON PROPERTY

Let us not forget that the church has exercised its teaching function in this area basically in response to the situation of conflict that was created by industrial development. Here is how Leo XIII describes the cause of the conflict:

> The elements of the conflict now raging are unmistakable in the vast expansion of industrial pursuits and the marvellous discoveries of science; in the changed relations between masters and workmen; in the enormous fortunes of some few individuals, and the utter poverty of the masses; in the increased self-reliance and closer mutual combination of the working classes; as also, finally, in the prevailing moral degeneracy [RN 1].

In such a struggle, which is ideological, political, and economic, it is difficult to meet the objective demands of justice. "It is no easy matter to define the relative rights and mutual duties of the rich and the poor, of capital and of labor," and yet it is urgently necessary

> that some remedy . . . be found, and found quickly, for the misery and wretchedness pressing so heavily and unjustly at this moment on the vast majority of the working classes.
>
> For the ancient workingmen's guilds were abolished in the last century, and no other organization took their place. Public institutions and the very laws have set aside the ancient religion. Hence by degrees it has come to pass that workingmen have been surrendered, all isolated and helpless, to the hard-heartedness of employers and the greed of unchecked competition [RN 1].

In the midst of the debate there came a socialist proposal for overcoming the evils flowing from capitalism. The proposal analyzed the roots of the situation and came to the conclusion that the "private ownership of the means of production" was the real reason for the growing concentration of wealth in the hands of the bourgeoisie and the gradual impoverishment of the proletariat. In this ideological controversy, then, the point at issue is not "private ownership of consumer goods," that is, goods necessary for life (food, housing, clothing, resources for education, etc.) but only "private ownership of the means of production," that is, of those goods which in turn produce other goods. In studying the question of private property in the teaching of the church it is vitally important to distinguish these two types of private ownership: that of the means of production (MP) and that of consumer goods (CG), these latter being equivalent, in our discussion here, to the means necessary and suitable for a worthy human life. For convenience I shall refer to these two basic concepts by initials: POMP and POCG.

The description given by Leo XIII at the beginning of *Rerum novarum* shows that the poor majorities not only lack POMP but also POCG, even at minimal levels of necessity: "To this must be added the custom of working by contract, and the concentration of so many branches of trade in the hands of a few individuals; so that a small number of very rich men have been able to lay upon the teeming masses of the laboring poor a yoke little better than that of slavery itself" (RN 1).

Confronted with this state of affairs, the two great conflicting ideologies, liberal capitalism and socialism, offer the following alternatives: (1) eliminate all POMP, for this has caused the working classes to lack POCG. If ownership of the means of production is reserved to the state, the municipality, and so on, this will put an end to the privileged position of the bourgeoisie which oppresses the proletariat; (2) maintain the existing situation and capitalist system, while admitting perhaps the need of some reforms which will enable the working classes to improve their living conditions by means of some access to POCG.

The response of Leo XIII is certainly a bold one! He asserts the right of the worker not only to POCG but also to POMP, and he thus moves beyond both alternatives. He judges insufficient the capitalist proposal that the living conditions of the workers be improved through greater enjoyment of the benefits of the system (POCG), and therefore he asks that the workers have access as well to POMP, since this last plays the key role in decision-making in the economy. On the other hand, he does not agree that improvement in living conditions (POCG) requires the suppression of POMP; on the contrary, he thinks the need is to assert POMP as a right of the workers and to facilitate their access to it.

In my view, this position must be thoroughly understood if we are to grasp the church's social teaching in its entirety. The social teaching of the church, at least as found in its first great document, begins with a defense of the right to property (of those who still have no access to it) and not of property (of those who already possess it). In order, then, to grasp clearly the argument of the magisterium, I shall proceed as follows: I shall analyze first the right of access to property, then the natural right to property, and finally the conditions for the legitimate use of private property by those already possessing it.

Access to Property

Leo XIII rejects the socialist proposal that would suppress POMP in order to benefit the workers. He offers a different proposal instead: if the workers are to be benefited, the need is to maintain POMP, because the workers have a right to this by reason of the work they do.

Let us read the text:

It is surely undeniable that, when a man engages in remunerative labor, the impelling reason and motive of his work is to obtain property, and thereafter to hold it as his very own. If one man hires out to another his strength or skill, he does so for the purpose of receiving in return what is necessary for sustenance and education; he therefore expressly intends to acquire a right full and real, not only to the remuneration, but also to the disposal of such remuneration, just as he pleases. Thus, if he lives sparingly, saves money, and, for greater security, invests his savings in land, the land, in such case, is only his wages under another form; and, consequently, a workingman's little estate thus purchased should be as completely at his full disposal as are the wages he receives for his labor. But it is precisely in such power of disposal that ownership obtains, whether the property consist of land or chattels. Socialists, therefore, by endeavoring to transfer the possessions of individuals to the community at large, strike at the interests of every wage earner, since they would deprive him of the liberty of disposing of his wages, and thereby of all hope and possibility of increasing his stock and of bettering his condition in life [RN 3].

Let me analyze each of the three main elements in this statement: (1) the right to private ownership of the means of production (2) is an authentic right of workers (3) because a just remuneration for their work will allow them to acquire the goods necessary for life (POCG) and even to invest in productive goods (POMP).

The Right to Private Ownership of the Means of Production

As I pointed out, the socialist concern is with POMP. If the pope does not refer to this type of ownership but to another (POCG), the reason is not that he is offering a counterproposal to the socialist position, but that he is touching on a different problem, which socialism does not raise or discuss. On the other hand, in the positions maintained by socialism the issue is not simply that workers should have more (POCG) but rather that the root cause of their social, economic, and political marginalization should be done away with; in the socialist view this root cause is POMP, because it leads to the existence of a privileged class that enjoys all the goods and accumulates all the benefits.

At no point does Leo XIII deny the *situation* produced by capitalism (RN 1), as I reminded the reader a moment ago. His objection to socialism is the kind of *solution* it offers. Consequently, in his argument against socialism, the position he defends is nothing less than that the right to POMP is a true and legitimate right of workers, not by reason of the capital they may already possess, but by reason of the work they contribute to a business. It is not difficult to see the revolutionary consequences of such a statement, which, in my view, is the most important of all those made here, since it is a direct refutation of the socialist position as such. At the same time, however, it distances the church's position from that of capitalism, which admits a certain improvement of the working classes but denies them any participation in POMP.

The teaching of Leo XIII on the legitimate right of workers to POMP is both reaffirmed and clarified by John Paul II. It is reaffirmed because John Paul II insists that work and ownership are not to be separated or opposed:

Isolating these means [the means of production] as a separate property in order to set it up in the form of "capital" in opposition to "labor"—and even to practice exploitation of labor—is contrary to the very nature of these means and their possession.

They cannot be possessed against labor, they cannot even be possessed for possession's sake, because the only legitimate title to their possession—whether in the form of private ownership or in the form of public or collective ownership—is that they should serve labor [LE 14].

John Paul II, too, regards a just wage as the means of assuring the rights of the worker. But in addition to reaffirming the traditional teaching, John Paul also opens new perspectives when he says that this right of the worker is not limited to a single social model (that of the private ownership of the means of production, which is proper to liberal capitalism) but must also find expression in the other, that is, the socialized ownership of the means of production. It is precisely from this perspective that he offers a radical critique of the historical forms of socialism, in which the simple withdrawal of the means of production from private ownership has not led to a truly socialized ownership by the workers, since the means of production have only come to be administered and controlled by a different group of persons, namely, the state. The pope's suggestion has a place even in a regime of social ownership of the means of production: "A way toward that goal [an authentic socialization] could be found by associating labor with the ownership of capital, as far as possible, and by producing a wide range of intermediate bodies with economic, social and cultural purposes" (LE 14).

This new perspective evidently continues to be an important one, for it opens the way for possible political and economic changes, while at the same time reasserting the basic principle, namely, that whether in a system of private ownership of the means of production or in a system of social ownership of these means the rights of the worker must be respected.

Value and Dignity of Human Work

By adopting the perspective of the dignity and rights of the worker John Paul II advances the teaching of the magisterium. The social problem does not consist in the conflict of groups as such but rather in the conflict of the values they represent. It is not the intensity of the conflict that should concern us so much as the inversion of values. To give capital priority over labor is to degrade labor and, in the final analysis, the human person who directly provides the labor. It is fitting, therefore, that we should recall the statements regarding the value and dignity of labor that have been made in the church's social teaching. One of the best of these is the following from *Gaudium et spes*:

Human work which is exercised in the production and exchange of goods, or in the provision of economic services, surpasses all other elements of economic life, for the latter are only means to an end.

Human work, whether exercised independently or in subordination to another, proceeds from the human person, who as it were impresses his seal on the things of nature and reduces them to his will. By his work a man ordinarily provides for himself and his family, associates with others as his brothers, and renders them service; he can exercise genuine charity and be a partner in the work of bringing divine creation to perfection. Moreover, we believe by faith that through the homage of work offered to God man is associated with the redemptive work of Jesus Christ, whose labor with his hands at Nazareth greatly ennobled the dignity of work. This is the source of every man's duty to work loyally as well as his right to work; moreover, it is the duty of society to see to it that, according to the prevailing circumstances, all citizens have the opportunity of finding employment. Finally, remuneration for work should guarantee man the opportunity to provide a dignified livelihood for himself and his family on the material, social, cultural, and spiritual level to correspond to the role and productivity of each, the relevant economic factors in his employment, and the common good [GS 67].

Paul VI repeats these ideas in *Populorum progressio:*

Work . . . is for all something willed and blessed by God. Man created to His image "must cooperate with his Creator in the perfecting of creation and communicate to the earth the spiritual imprint he himself has received." . . . Bent over a material that resists his efforts, a man by his work gives his imprint to it, acquiring, as he does so, perseverance, skill, and a spirit of invention. Further, when work is done in common, when hope, hardship, ambition and joy are shared, it brings together and firmly unites the wills, minds and hearts of men: in its accomplishment men find themselves to be brothers [PP 27].

Pope John Paul II, in his turn, says that he shares the concern for the dignity of work, and this not simply in theory but because of his personal experiences: "I have shared the needs of workers, their just demands, their legitimate aspirations" (AWM, p. 196).

This Christian appreciation of work has a long tradition. Leo XIII points out two aspects of work: work is *"personal,* inasmuch as the exertion of individual strength belongs to the person who puts it forth," and it is *"necessary,* for without the result of labor a man cannot live; and self-preservation is a law of nature, which it is wrong to disobey" (RN 32). From this Leo XIII deduces the existence of "a dictate of natural justice more imperious and ancient than any bargain between man and man" (ibid.), in virtue of which the wage contract must not be drawn up in the spirit of economic positivism, as capitalism holds, but in the light of the higher principles of the natural law. To violate these is to do real violence to the worker and therefore to attack the working class, even if all this be done under the protection of law.

When Leo XIII calls attention to work as necessary, he implicitly justifies a right to work. It is Pius XII, however, who explicitly makes this inference: "To the personal duty to labor imposed by nature corresponds and follows the natural right of each individual to make of labor the means to provide for his own life and that of his children."[1] But, then, who guarantees this right? Pius XII answers:

> The duty and the right to organize the labor of the people belongs above all to the people immediately interested; the employers and the workers. If they do not fulfill their functions or cannot because of special extraordinary contingencies fulfill them, then it falls back on the State to intervene in the field of labor and in the division and distribution of work according to the form and measure that the common good properly understood demands.[2]

John XXIII describes the right to work as a "natural" right: "It is clear that human beings have the natural right to free initiative in the economic field and the right to work" (PT 16). A new formulation of this right appears in *Octogesima adveniens*: "Every man has a right to work, to a chance to develop his qualities and his personality in the exercise of his profession, to equitable remuneration . . . and to assistance in case of need arising from sickness or age" (OA 14).

Can the responsible parties mentioned by Pius XII guarantee the right to work? May not new situations arise which will oblige the state to intervene in a much more permanent way and not simply in "special extraordinary contingencies"? Paul VI seems to be referring to such new situations in *Octogesima adveniens*:

> With demographic growth, which is particularly pronounced in the young nations, the number of those failing to find work and driven to misery or parasitism will grow in the coming years unless the conscience of man rouses itself and gives rise to a general movement of solidarity through an effective policy of investment and of organization of production and trade, as well as of education [OA 18].

These principles yield not a few conclusions with regard to our Latin American situation of dependent capitalism, which makes it difficult for the economic structure to ensure steady and worthy employment for all. Puebla calls attention to the situation of the unemployed and the underemployed, who are pushed aside by the harsh exigencies of economic crises and of models of development that subject workers and their families to cold economic calculations (see DP 37), with such consequences as family instability, shifts of residence, and emigration (see DP 576).

To this series of statements about the dignity of work there must now be added, and in a privileged place, the encyclical *Laborem exercens* of John

Paul II. Here the dignity of human work is not simply one theme; it is the focal point of the entire document and provides the perspective in which the social problem is viewed. More than that: work defines human beings (Intro. to LE) and consequently the defense of the worker's rights is a just ethical cause (LE 8) and gives a humanistic meaning to the struggle for justice. Even the recent history of the human race becomes more intelligible in terms of the antagonism of capital and labor, and the pope laments the fact that the splendid teaching of the church on the dignity of work has not inspired Christian efforts at the historical level in ardent defense of this dignity (LE 9).

A Just Wage as Means of Access to Ownership of the Means of Production

The goal that Leo XIII sees being reached through a just wage is certainly an ambitious one: nothing less than access to POMP. The mere advancing of such a goal and the struggle to attain it already makes the Christian view set forth by the magisterium a valid alternative to the socialist proposal that POMP be completely suppressed for the sake of benefiting the working class. If the Christian proposal were not to accomplish the objective set for it by Leo XIII, the arguments of socialism for the elimination of excessive social power (arguments acknowledged and accepted by Pius XI in QA 114) would continue to have their full weight.

Although some documents of the church seem to consider a just wage to be simply such remuneration as gives workers access to POCG, that is, enables workers and their families to live a life worthy of human beings, we must not forget that this goal is still an inadequate one if Christian thinking on labor is to provide a valid alternative to socialism. Let us look, therefore, first at texts which seem to think only of access to POCG and then at those which go further and call for access to POMP.[3]

POCG. Leo XIII warns that when workingmen "consider their wages insufficient," their dissatisfaction leads to disorders. He suggests preventing these by laws which fix wages at an equitable level in accordance with justice (and not simply in accordance with what is legal in positive law, as so often happens).

In the documents of the church a just wage is sometimes defined in terms of the worthy level of life which the worker deserves to have by means of his wages. Thus, for example, John XXIII writes in *Pacem in terris*: "There is the worker's right to a wage determined according to criteria of justice. This means, therefore, one sufficient, in proportion to the available resources, to give the worker and his family a standard of living in keeping with human dignity" (PT 20). A comparable definition is given in *Gaudium et spes 67* and by Paul VI in *Octogesima adveniens* 14.

Nonetheless a consistent effort to offer more concrete norms has also been made, beginning with Pius XI in *Quadragesimo anno* 63–75. Three criteria have been established:

1. "In the first place, the worker must be paid a wage sufficient to support

him and his family" (QA 71). If this is not possible at present, then "social justice demands that changes be introduced as soon as possible whereby such a wage will be assured to every adult workingman" (ibid.).

2. "In determining the amount of the wage, the condition of a business and of the one carrying it on must also be taken into account; for it would be unjust to demand excessive wages which a business cannot withstand without its ruin and consequent calamity to the workers" (QA 72). If the business is being forced by market conditions to sell its product at a price that brings no profit, then there is evidently an overall situation which "deprive[s] workers of their just wage and force[s] them under the pinch of necessity to accept a wage less than fair" (ibid.).

3. Lastly,

the amount of the pay must be adjusted to the public economic good, . . . namely, that the opportunity to work be provided to those who are able and willing to work. This opportunity depends largely on the wage and salary rate, which can help as long as it is kept within proper limits, but which on the other hand can be an obstacle if it exceeds these limits [QA 74].

Justice, therefore, "demands that wages and salaries be so managed, through agreement of plans and wills, insofar as can be done, as to offer the greatest possible number the opportunity of getting work and obtaining suitable means of livelihood" (ibid.).

These criteria are repeated and developed by John XXIII in *Mater et magistra* 71. A further important point is added in this same document:

We must here call attention to the fact that in many countries today, the economic system is such that large and medium size productive enter- prises achieve rapid growth precisely because they finance replacement and plant expansion from their own revenues. Where this is the case, we believe that such companies should grant to workers some share in the enterprise, especially where they are paid no more than the minimum wage [MM 75].

Lest we fall into an "economic positivism" which regards as just the prices that are determined solely by the chances of the marketplace, it is important in handling these norms to emphasize the priority of the first of them: justice for the workers. It is not permissible to say that the good of the business or of the national economy does not allow justice to be done, if in fact this business or this national economy is being built on violence done to the workers. If the concrete functioning of the business or the national economy does not allow the workers a just wage, then the business or the economy must change rather than that the workers' call for their just rights be suppressed.

John XXIII, therefore, emphatically says: "Just as remuneration for work cannot be left entirely to unregulated competition, neither may it be decided arbitrarily at the will of the more powerful. Rather, in this matter, the norms of justice and equity should be strictly observed" (MM 71).

In summary: POCG should certainly be a minimal goal in the determination of wages. *Gaudium et spes* states: "Private property or some form of ownership of external goods assures a person a highly necessary sphere for the exercise of his personal and family autonomy and ought to be considered as an extension of human freedom" (GS 71). There is no reason why workers should be deprived of such ownership; the contribution they make by their work is a sufficient legitimate title to such ownership, provided this title is respected as it should be.

Confirming the traditional teaching on the requirement of a just wage, John Paul II makes the just remuneration of work the privileged criterion for determining whether a society and its economic system are just (LE 19). This raises a key problem of social ethics: how private ownership of consumer goods is to be achieved and how the dignity of the family is to be ensured.

POMP. The goal of justice in the matter of wages must be access to POMP, since only the latter, as I said above, provides a valid alternative to the socialist position. After establishing in *Rerum novarum* 3 the principle that workers have a right to POMP by reason of their work, which ought to bring them enough not only for the consumer goods they need but also for investment, Leo XIII adds that this right to ownership is inviolable and must be defended by the law: "The law, therefore, should favor ownership, and its policy should be to induce as many as possible of the humbler class to become owners" (RN 33).

Leo XIII offers three reasons for this statement: (1) "property will certainly become more equitably divided," thus lessening or doing away with the difference between the class of the wealthy, "which has in its grasp the whole of labor and trade; which manipulates for its own benefit and its own purposes all the sources of supply, and which is even represented in the councils of the State itself," and "the needy and powerless multitude." This goal, which is a social one, will not cause economic harm, for (2) the better distribution of property "will result in the greater abundance of the fruits of the earth," inasmuch as "men always work harder and more readily when they work on that which belongs to them. . . . That such a spirit of willing labor would add to the produce of the earth and to the wealth of the community is self-evident." And, finally, (3) this attachment to one's native soil will foster stability of residence (RN 33).

These ideas have been subsequently repeated in varying forms. According to Pius XI,

> with all our strength and effort we must strive that at least in the future
> the abundant fruits of production will accrue equitably to those who are
> rich and will be distributed in ample sufficiency among the workers . . .
> that they may increase their property by thrift, [and] that they may bear,

by wise management of this increase in property, the burdens of family life with greater ease and security [QA 61].

Pius XII, for his part, was much concerned about the problems of European migration and therefore stressed the third of the three reasons given in *Rerum novarum* 33: "Of all the goods that can be the object of private property, none is more conformable to nature, according to the teaching of *Rerum novarum*, than the land, the holding in which the family lives, and from the products of which it draws all or part of its subsistence."[4]

John XXIII expressly refers to *Quadragesimo anno* 61 when he proposes, as a way of effecting a wider distribution of property, that "workers gradually acquire some share in the enterprise by such methods as seem more appropriate" (MM 77).

The broader distribution of property (remember that we are now speaking of ownership of the means of production) is therefore a requirement of justice. It is defended in *Mater et magistra*:

It is especially appropriate that today, more than ever before, widespread private ownership should prevail, since, as noted above, the number of nations increases wherein the economic systems experience daily growth. Therefore, by prudent use of various devices already proven effective, it will not be difficult for the body politic to modify economic and social life so that the way is made easier for widespread private possession of such things as durable goods, homes, gardens, tools requisite for artisan enterprises and family-type farms, investments in enterprises of medium or large size. All of this has occurred satisfactorily in some nations with developed social and economic systems [MM 115].

The Natural Right to Private Property

Now that we have considered the right to private property for the worker, which Leo XIII defends as an alternative to the socialist position, let me turn now to the subject of the natural right to private property. Before analyzing its characteristics, it is appropriate to relate what I shall say in this section with what I said in the previous section. The connection is this: If this natural right of private property (NRPP) is not found in the workers (who, as we have seen, have a right, by reason of their work, not only to POCG but also to POMP), then an offense is done to them and natural law is violated. This statement is an important one if we are to avoid the evasions so often heard in capitalist society, which speaks only of the NRPP of those who already possess property, even when the manner in which these owners possess their property prevents others from likewise becoming owners and thus violates the right of the latter to possess property. Any time we speak of a natural right, it is something that must apply to every human being, since all have the identical nature which grounds the right, as we saw in chapter 5. The proper perspective, therefore, that is to be adopted in speaking of NRPP is gained by taking the vantage point of the right of the poor. If the rights of which a society speak are not verified in the poor, then such "rights" are simply an ideological ploy for maintaining a status quo that is based on the privileges of one class over the others.

The present section of this chapter must also be connected with the one that follows, inasmuch as the proper exercise of the right to private ownership is to be judged by its harmony with the demands of natural law, over and above the regulations or grants found in positive law.

With these clarifications made, let me list now the three basic characteristics of NRPP: (1) It is a right that is subordinate to the universal ordination, by the Creator's will, of all material goods to all human beings; (2) this ordination of goods to the service of human beings requires on their part a human use of these goods, which implies in turn ownership and control; (3) in order to make use of the goods supplied by nature and to acquire this control over them, persons transform those goods through their work.

Universal Ordination of All Material Goods to All Human Beings

The social teaching of Pius XII is characterized by a strong emphasis on a Thomist perspective, namely, that the primary purpose of all material goods takes priority over private ownership. The pope states:

> Every man, as a living being gifted with reason, has in fact from nature the fundamental right to make use of the material goods of the earth, while it is left to the will of man and to the juridical statutes of nations to regulate in greater detail the actuation of this right. This individual right cannot in any way be suppressed, even by other clear and undisputed rights over material goods. Undoubtedly, the natural order, deriving from God, demands also private property and the free reciprocal commerce of goods by interchange and gift, as well as the functioning of the State as a control over both these institutions. But all this remains subordinated to the natural scope of material goods and cannot emancipate itself from the first and fundamental right which concedes their use to all men; but it should serve rather to make possible the actuation of this right in conformity with its scope. Only thus can we and must we secure that private property and the use of material goods bring to society peace and prosperity and long life, that they no longer set up precarious conditions which will give rise to struggles and jealousies, and which are left to the mercy of the blind interplay of force and weakness.[5]

Especially since Pius XII, the church in its social teaching continues to refer to this right of all to use the goods provided by nature and regards it as a right that is more radical and basic than the right of ownership which is exercised by some. Thus, for example, *Mater et magistra* bases the "social responsibility" attached to private property on the fact that "in the wisdom of God the Creator, the over-all supply of goods is assigned, first of all, that all men may lead a decent life" (MM 119). In *Populorum progressio* Paul VI warns that "private property does not constitute for anyone an absolute and unconditioned right," because it is subordinated to the right of all human beings to all material goods (PP 23; cf. PP 22).

Vatican Council II had a definitely doctrinal purpose when it chose to speak first of earthly goods being destined for all human beings (GS 69) and only then of ownership and private property (GS 71).

> God destined the earth and all it contains for all men and all peoples so that all created things would be shared fairly by all mankind under the guidance of justice tempered by charity. No matter what the structures of property are in different peoples, according to various and changing circumstances and adapted to their lawful institutions, we must never lose sight of this universal destination of earthly goods. In his use of things man should regard the external goods he legitimately owns not merely as exclusive to himself but common to others also, in the sense that they can benefit others as well as himself. Therefore every man has the right to possess a sufficient amount of the earth's goods for himself and his family. This has been the opinion of the Fathers and Doctors of the Church, who taught that men are bound to come to the aid of the poor and to do so not merely out of their superfluous goods. When a person is in extreme necessity he has the right to supply himself with what he needs out of the riches of others. Faced with a world today where so many people are suffering from want, the Council asks individuals and governments to remember the saying of the Fathers: "Feed the man dying of hunger, because if you do not feed him you are killing him," and it urges them according to their ability to share and dispose of their goods to help others, above all by giving them aid which will enable them to help and develop themselves [GS 69].

The council then goes on to offer a very interesting perspective: it relativizes the very idea of private ownership by reminding us, first, that the purpose of property is to ensure the benefits of all goods to all human beings and, second, that this objective can be achieved without the institution of private property, as happens among people with community-centered cultures and in modern societies in which social planning makes future security depend not on present ownership but on services provided by the state. The council says:

> In economically less developed societies it often happens that the common destination of goods is partly achieved by a system of community customs and traditions which guarantee a minimum of necessities to each one. Certain customs must not be considered sacrosanct if they no longer correspond to modern needs; on the other hand one should not rashly do away with respectable customs which if they are brought up to date can still be very useful. In the same way, in economically advanced countries

the common destination of goods is achieved through a system of social institutions dealing with insurance and security [GS 69].

In *Laborem exercens* John Paul II likewise points out the radical difference between the church's concept of private property and the capitalist concept of the same (LE 14): the church has never defended ownership as an absolute and untouchable right, since it must be subordinated to the common good.

In its social doctrine the church has always taught that in virtue of the universal ordination of all material goods to all human beings, private property has a twofold dimension or function: one being individual and the other social. The latter is in fact nothing else than the recognition of the universal ordination or destination of all material goods to all human beings and, consequently, the requirement that private property be used in such a way as not to contradict this universal destination, inasmuch as this last entails a right even more fundamental and radical than the right to private property. That this teaching has not fallen into disuse but remains fully applicable is shown by John Paul II when he speaks of the "social mortgage" on private property in his addresses to the peasants at Oaxaca and to the bishops at Puebla (AIOC and OAPC III, 4).

This social function is given one of its first and clearest formulations in Pius XI, who speaks of "the twofold character of ownership, called usually individual or social according as it regards either separate persons or the common good" (QA 45). The pope sees the social function as operative first of all at the level of the family, but then also as requiring that "the goods which the Creator destined for the entire family of mankind may through this institution truly serve this purpose" (ibid.). In the view of Pius XI it is the simultaneous assertion of both the individual function and the social function that prevents our falling into either socialism or individualism.

An expression of this social function and of the universal ordination of all material goods to all human beings is the requirement and duty of distinguishing, among the goods one possesses, between what is necessary for oneself and what is superfluous and ought to be shared with others. On the basis of this distinction, which is a classical one in Christian moral thinking, Pius XI says:

> Furthermore, a person's superfluous income, that is, income which he does not need to sustain life fittingly and with dignity, is not left wholly to his own free determination. Rather the Sacred Scriptures and the Fathers of the Church constantly declare in the most explicit language that the rich are bound by a very grave precept to practice almsgiving, benefi- cence, and munificence [QA 50].

In order to grasp the seriousness of the precept of almsgiving, we must understand what "almsgiving" meant in the thinking of the Fathers. A study of the patristic sources will lead us to the conclusion that in a preindustrial age the concept of "alms" was an adequate way, at that time, of recognizing the right, in justice and not simply in charity, of all human beings to make use of all material goods. The statements of the holy Fathers are very clear in this regard:

> Are you not a robber? You who make your own the things you have received to distribute? Will not one be called a thief who steals the garment of one already clothed, and is one deserving of any other title who will not clothe the naked if he is able to do so?
>
> The bread which you keep belongs to the hungry; that coat which you preserve in your wardrobe, to the naked; those shoes which are nothing in your possessions, to the shoeless; that gold which you have hidden in the ground, to the needy [St. Basil, PG 31:277].[6]

Pierre Bigo points out that "St. Augustine asserts the right of the poor even more clearly when he gives his well-known definition of justice: 'helping the unfortunate.' " This definition is noteworthy not only because it was adopted by Peter Lombard and commented on by St. Thomas Aquinas, but also because of the clear meaning that attaches to it in its context. St. Augustine is not giving us to understand merely that a gift to the poor justifies us in God's sight; he is speaking rather of justice as a cardinal virtue and associating it conceptually with prudence, fortitude, and temperance. When looked at thus, justice is a recognition of the right of every being: *cuique suum*, "to each what is rightfully his." The poor therefore have rights: "what is given to the poor is a debt owed them."[7]

Another author, for many years professor of church social teaching at the Gregorian University in Rome, expresses himself as follows:

> If we are to understand the teaching of the Church Fathers on the control and ownership of material goods by man, we must bear in mind that the holy Fathers were unable to raise the question of the reform of social structures; that was impossible both historically and culturally in the age in which they lived. We might say they lacked the technical means of posing such a problem. There are matters which require a certain histori-cal maturation if they are to be given concrete form. Consequently a first and superficial reading of patristic teaching may give the impression of what we today would call a paternalistic attitude on the part of the writers. Nothing could be further from the truth. For even though the Fathers constantly speak of "alms," they assign the latter the function of redistributing income, and for them, adopting as they do a moral stand-point, this is an obligation in justice. The holy Fathers were keenly aware that there is serious disorder in the world of economico-juridical rela-tions, that injustice reigns there on a broad scale. . . . The holy Fathers denounced the disorder and injustice that reigned in their world, and they did so with a forcefulness and outspokenness that we have never dared to show. . . .
>
> But since they had no other means except almsgiving for correcting the

injustice and disorder, they naturally speak of alms and only of alms. But with a full consciousness of the moral, religious, and juridical issues (juridical at the basic level of natural law), they add that this alms is simply a means of restitution, a way of re-establishing a balance which is unqualifiedly due in justice. Due to subsequent developments, later thinkers forgot to some extent this conception of the Fathers, for whom almsgiving was a redistribution of income and an obligation in justice. It is clear that nowadays the problem has to be posed with different technical presuppositions of an economic, juridical, and political kind. It must be formulated no longer in terms of almsgiving but in terms of structural reform. . . . The thinking of the liberal period, which was alien to the modern idea of *social* ethics, rights, and politics, was satisfied with a radically inadequate and equivocal position: the social teaching of the Church is concerned with charity; consequently any correction of the imbalances in the world must depend on the generosity and other good qualities of the rich. This formula corresponds verbally to the patristic formulation, but the spirit behind it is radically opposed to that of the Fathers. This is because fundamental to the entire patristic teaching is the assertion that almsgiving is a duty of justice; it is a form of restitution. . . . Today the need is not solely or primarily to give alms, but rather to create sources of employment, redistribute the national income, organize business in a truly human manner, and spread the ownership of property in an equitable way. All these are strict obligations in justice.[8]

Pius XI is therefore entirely right when he points out that a modern way of fulfilling the duty of giving to all what belongs to all is by reinvesting the profits of a business in the creation of new jobs: "Expending larger incomes so that opportunity of gainful work may be abundant, provided, however, that this work is applied to producing really useful goods, ought to be considered . . . an outstanding exemplification of the virtue of munificence and one peculiarly suited to the needs of the time" (QA 51). Since this is clearly a way of practicing the virtue of justice, all consideration of profit—to say nothing of exploitation!—must be left aside. What is called for is justice in the form of a reinvestment with a social purpose, and not a way of extending the employer's exploitative self-enrichment.

The doctrine of "superfluity" has for its purpose to point out that there is a boundary line separating property which is necessary for the owner's sustenance from property which is not necessary. The right to *use* those material goods that one owns does *not extend* to superfluous goods. The owners do, however, have the right to *determine* where the dividing line between the two lies, as they take into account both their own needs and those of others. Note 10 in *Gaudium et spes* 69 cites a passage from John XXIII's radio message of September 11, 1962, in which the pope urges upon the Christian conscience the duty of attending to the needs of others in deciding where the boundary between the necessary and the superfluous lies. If selfishness dictates the drawing of the dividing line between the two types of goods, it is to be feared that the rich will not share their goods with the needy, and we cannot but recognize that the categories used by a consumer society darken the Christian conscience. It is evidently unjust to assert "superfluous necessities" when there are more urgent "necessary necessities." Paul VI denounces a situation in which "while a small restricted group enjoys a refined civilization in certain regions, the remainder of the population, poor and scattered, is 'deprived of nearly all possibility of personal initiative and of responsibility, and oftentimes even its living and working conditions are unworthy of the human person' " (PP 9).

The rule of superfluity, understood as a duty of strict justice, is not only to be applied to the individual; it also extends to human communities, including nations: "We must repeat once more that the superfluous wealth of rich countries should be placed at the service of the poor nations. The rule which up to now held good for those nearest to us, must today be applied to all the needy of this world" (PP 49).

The Human Use of Material Goods

Now that we have clearly established the principle that the universal ordination of all material goods to all human beings is a primary and fundamental right which takes precedence over NRPP, let us see how this right is described in the magisterium.

Human beings depend on the world for their life, and they satisfy their needs through the use of the goods nature provides. This first and absolutely universal principle reflects the experience of all human beings at all times; it is not, however, enough to allow the deduction of any right (the animals, for example, do not have a *right* to *use* the goods nature provides). A right as such can exist only in a being who makes a *rational* use of nature. Leo XIII therefore writes:

On this very account—that man alone among the animal creation is endowed with reason—it must be within his right to possess things not merely for temporary and momentary use, as other living things do, but *to have and to hold* them in stable and permanent possession; he must have not only things that perish in the use of them, but those also which, though they have been reduced into use, remain his own for further use [RN 4; italics added].

The use which human beings make of nature is, then, a human use, that is, rational, attentive to the future.

For man, fathoming by his faculty of reason matters without number, and linking the future with the present, becoming, furthermore, by taking enlightened foresight, master of his own acts, guides his ways under the eternal law and power of God, whose providence governs all things. Wherefore it is in his power to exercise his choice not only as to matters that regard his present welfare, but also about those which he deems may be for his advantage in time yet to come [RN 5].

Property makes life more human. "Private property or some form of ownership of external goods assures a person a highly necessary sphere for the exercise of his personal and family autonomy and ought to be considered as an extension of human freedom" (GS 71).

It is a fact, of course, that if the human being is understood not as an isolated individual but as a social person, the future in question is also that of others. The popes concentrate more particularly on the first and immediate dimension of this sociability, namely, the family, and for this reason they lay greater emphasis on it. The principle, however, is valid for the whole human race. The future which human beings ensure by their work is that of all humanity.

Without denying this dimension of totality, the assertion of the family future is perhaps what makes itself more directly felt in human experience. Human beings are quite helpless during childhood and are unable for a lengthy period to provide for their own needs; for this they need the family. The popes stress this family aspect. Leo XIII says: "That right of property, therefore, which has been proved to belong naturally to individual persons, must in like wise belong to a man in his capacity as head of a family" (RN 9).

The same idea recurs in Pius XI:

Nature, [or] rather the Creator Himself, has given man the right of private ownership not only that individuals may be able to provide for themselves and their families but also that the goods which the Creator destined for the entire family of mankind may through this institution truly serve this purpose. All this can be achieved in no wise except through the maintenance of a certain and definite order [QA 45].

In like manner, Pius XII says:

Nature itself has closely joined private property with the existence of human society and its true civilization, and in a very special manner with the existence and development of the family. Such a link appears more obvious. Should not private property secure for the father of a family the healthy liberty he needs in order to fulfill the duties assigned him by the Creator regarding the physical, spiritual, and religious welfare of the family?[9]

It is clear that these texts seem to refer above all to POCG and not directly to POMP; on the other hand, it is also certain that they defend a universal right of all human beings and not a privilege of some members of the privileged classes. There is no basis, therefore, for excluding the families of workers or peasants from the right to be able to live in a worthy manner with the help of a family patrimony. Moreover, the violation of these rights of such families, even if the violation appear to be the inevitable consequence of defending POMP, is always contrary to the gospel and contrary as well to the social teaching of the church.

So sacrosanct is this right that if a state, a body of laws, or a status quo does not guarantee *all* fathers and mothers (and not just fathers and mothers of a certain social class) this right of providing for their own, this state, body of laws, or status quo "should be held in detestation, rather than be an object of desire" (RN 9).

Work and the Ownership of Property

Finally, we must not forget that the goods meant for human beings and possessed by them as an expression of "human use" must be altered and transformed, because nature does not always present those goods in a final state to human beings. This transformation is achieved through work. Leo XIII therefore sees work as a direct source of ownership:

> When man thus turns the activity of his mind and the strength of his body towards procuring the fruits of nature, by such act he makes his own that portion of nature's field which he cultivates—that portion on which he leaves, as it were, the impress of his individuality; and it cannot but be just that he should possess that portion as his very own, and have a right to hold it without any one being justified in violating that right [RN 7].

With notable firmness Leo XIII asserts the principle that the land belongs to those who cultivate it: "Is it just that the fruit of a man's own sweat and labor should be possessed and enjoyed by any one else? As effects follow their cause, so is it just and right that the results of labor should belong to those who have bestowed their labor" [RN 8].

Lest there be a confusion of work done on what belongs to oneself with work done on what belongs to another, Pius XI makes a distinction: "Only that labor which a man performs in his own name and by virtue of which a new form or increase has been given to a thing grants him title to these fruits. Far different is the nature of work that is hired out to others and expended on the property of others" (QA 52–53).

Despite this, work that is done for a salary and exercised on material and/or with tools not the worker's own in no way excludes the worker from the *use* of goods meant for all. Leo XIII asserts that the earth, though apportioned among private owners, "ceases not thereby to minister to the needs of all. . . . Those who do not possess the soil contribute their labor" (RN 6). But work, as we have seen, bestows not only a right to use but also a right to ownership, and this with regard not only to consumer goods but even to the means of production.

The Proper Exercise of the Right of Property

The teaching of the church on NRPP not only includes the right of those who are already owners but also strongly asserts the same right for those who have not yet acquired property. This teaching is therefore not a tool for defending owners against nonowners but expresses an unqualified demand that all be owners and that all the means be provided for them to become owners. But the teaching on the NRPP also constitutes the ultimate norm for the just and proper exercise of this right, inasmuch as the justice in question does not flow from the legitimacy of certain positive laws but is rather to be acknowledged and expressed in these laws.

With the doctrine of the NRPP as a foundation it is possible to show that the right of property is abused when the manner of its exercise does not respect either the universal destination of material goods (and the social function of, or social mortgage on, property) or the human use of these goods by all human beings (in an integral manner and in solidarity with others) or the value of human work and its just remuneration.

The abuses in question sometimes arise from the concrete exercise which *individual owners* make of the right of ownership without attending to its limitations or to the social obligations it brings with it. At other times, however, the abuses come, and in a more extensive form, from the *very structures of society* which, in violation of natural law, establish positive laws that permit and tolerate abuses by individuals against the common good.

In this regard there is a passage from Pius XI which seems to acquire new relevance in the Latin American context:

For toward the close of the nineteenth century, the new kind of economic life that had arisen and the new developments of industry had gone to the point in most countries that human society was clearly becoming divided more and more into two classes. One class, very small in number, was enjoying almost all the advantages which modern inventions so abundantly provided; the other, embracing the huge multitude of working people, oppressed by wretched poverty, was vainly seeking escape from the straits wherein it stood [QA 3].

Quite agreeable, of course, was this state of things to those who thought it in their abundant riches the result of inevitable economic laws and accordingly, as if it were for charity to veil the violation of justice which lawmakers not only tolerated but at times sanctioned, wanted the whole care of the poor committed to charity alone [QA 4].

It is quite possible that abuses of ownership seek legitimacy on the grounds that they are necessary if the laws governing the economy are to be followed. One abuse which is widespread in our continent is the flight of capital; it is an expression of the "internationalism of finance or international imperialism whose country is where profit is" (QA 109). Paul VI passes a very severe judgment on this practice which is so prevalent among us: "It is unacceptable that citizens with abundant incomes from the resources and activity of their country should transfer a considerable part of this income abroad purely for their own advantage, without care for the manifest wrong they inflict on their country by doing this" (PP24).

When the way in which the NRPP is exercised is irresponsible and alien to the social function of property, the question arises of the legitimate intervention of the state in behalf of the common good. There may seem to be a contradiction between the defense which Pius XI gives of property as an inalienable right that is not lost even by its abuse and more recent teachings, for example on expropriation and agrarian reform, which are to be found in *Gaudium et spes* 71 and *Populorum progressio* 24. But in fact the contradiction proves more apparent than real if we apply the teaching of Pius XI to POCG (where the abuse does not necessarily affect the common good) and not to POMP. Let us look at the text in question:

In order to place definite limits on the controversies that have arisen over ownership and its inherent duties there must first be laid down as a foundation a principle established by Leo XIII: The right of property is distinct from its use. That justice called commutative commands sacred respect for the division of possessions and forbids invasion of others' rights through the exceeding of the limits of one's own property; but the duty of owners to use their property only in a right way does not come under this type of justice, but under other virtues, obligations of which "cannot be enforced by legal action." Therefore, they are in error who assert that ownership and its right use are limited by the same boundaries; and it is much further still from the truth to hold that a right to property is destroyed or lost by reason of abuse or non-use [QA 47].

This sensitive point needs to be examined in the light of other texts. The misuse of consumer goods does not, properly speaking, affect the common good; the same cannot be said of the means of production, the riches of the soil, and so on. Because misuse here is a real offense against the common good, the council defends the timeliness of agrarian reform:

In several economically retarded areas there exist large and sometimes very extensive rural estates which are only slightly cultivated or not cultivated at all for the sake of profit, while the majority of the population have no land or possess only very small holdings. . . . Reforms are called for in these different situations: . . . estates insufficiently cultivated must be divided up and given to those who will be able to make them productive [GS 71].

The teaching of Paul VI on this subject is much more pointed: "If certain landed estates impede the general prosperity because they are extensive, unused or poorly used, or because they bring hardship to people or are detrimental to the interests of the country, the common good sometimes demands their expropriation" (PP 24).

The four reasons given by Paul VI—(1) extensiveness, (2) poor use or lack of use, (3) resultant hardship for the people, (4) considerable harm to the interests of the country—are separated from each other in the Latin text by *vel* ("or") and therefore do not have to be taken cumulatively (if taken cumulatively only the four together could justify agrarian reform); any one of them is enough to justify agrarian reform. This shows that reasons can exist which make expropriation imperative; such expropriation is justified when nonuse or poor use of productive means becomes an injustice against the good of others who are not owners but nonetheless have the right that this means of production serve the collectivity.

John Paul II stands in this tradition when in his address to the peasants of Oaxaca he denounces the serious evil of great estates being uncultivated even though so many families lack bread and when he describes such a practice as inhuman and un-Christian.

The position of Paul VI is so radical that he can speak not only of expropriation (with suitable compensation) but even of outright confiscation. We may not overlook the possibility that the harm caused to the common good by the wrongful use of property should be made one of the criteria for economic compensation for expropriation and that this compensation may be reduced to nothing if the harm has been great enough.[10]

We must take even more seriously the possibility of abuses being created not by individuals and their selfish inclinations but by the *very system* as it has concretely developed. The expansion of the multinational corporations raises increasingly serious questions for the Christian conscience regarding the legitimacy of the system of private property when this is allowed to reach certain extremes. A point constantly made in the church's teaching on property is the *responsibility* of owners to pay heed in their decision-making to the two functions of property: the individual and the social. But the modern evolution of the capitalist economy, especially in the form of the great national corporations and much more the transnational corporations, has led to a separation of ownership and responsibility, so that the owner no longer exercises responsibility for decisions but entrusts his goods to a set of administrators who are indeed highly qualified but whose sole criterion is profit and a maximum return on capital, without taking any other considerations into account.

This phenomenon did not escape the attention of John XXIII: "In recent years, as we are well aware, the role played by the owners of capital in very large productive enterprises has been separated more and more from the role of management" (MM 104). In acknowledging this fact, John XXIII emphasizes the duty of the state to control this type of business so that it does not do harm to the common good: "This has occasioned great difficulties for governments, whose duty it is to make certain that directors of the principal enterprises, especially those of greatest influence in the economic life of the entire country, do not depart from the requirements of the common good" (ibid.).

The situation has worsened rather than improved with time, and ten years after John XXIII had written his encyclical, Paul VI once again called attention to the risks of injustice entailed in the activity of the multinational and transnational corporations, unless the state, especially in the underdeveloped countries, exercises a vigilance truly inspired by the common good.

Under the driving force of new systems of production, national frontiers are breaking down, and we can see new economic powers emerging, the multinational enterprises, which by the concentration and flexibility of their means can conduct autonomous strategies which are largely independent of the national political powers and therefore not subject to control from the point of view of the common good. By extending their activities, these private organizations can lead to a new and abusive form of economic domination on the social, cultural, and even political level. The excessive concentration of means and powers that Pope Pius XI had already condemned on the fortieth anniversary of *Rerum novarum* is taking on a new and very concrete image [OA 44].

These dangers have become sad reality on our continent, as the bishops note at Puebla. They denounce the existence of economic, technological, political, and cultural dependence and the presence of the multinational corporations (DP 66). They reproach the liberalist economic ideology for putting itself at the service of an international imperialism of money (DP 312) and the urban-industrial culture for being controlled by the great powers in possession of science and technology (DP 417). They point out in particular that the very political and economic authorities of our countries are themselves subject to even more powerful centers (DP 501), so that the power of the multinational businesses overrides the exercise of sovereignty by nations and the complete control by the latter of their own natural resources (DP 1264).

If ownership in the form of capital is so dissociated from responsibility that Christians who invest their capital in the multinational corporations can cause serious harm to peoples thousands of miles away, is it possible to go on defending property that is no longer able to exercise responsibility for its social function? Thus the new realities of economic life create new ethical demands on which there has not as yet been sufficient reflection.

The problem raised by the great conglomerates is a serious one, especially in underdeveloped countries that are powerless to control these businesses.

Contemporary studies show that government becomes increasingly helpless in the face of these businesses, since even in the United States it is weaker than the corporative institutions (the huge businesses) which are under its jurisdiction. Even Adolph Berle, a very great authority on this subject and one who cannot be suspected of antipathy to big business, calls our attention to the fact that the directors of a huge stock company derive their authority from no one but themselves; they are a self-perpetuating oligarchy. The vast power which big business presently possesses has not the least legitimating title. Professor Berle tells us that in the United States the view is gaining ground that whenever a stock company has power to affect the lives of many persons . . . it must be subject to the same constitutional restrictions applying to an agency of the federal or state government.[11]

I shall call attention further on to the interesting similarity between this norm and the argument given by Pius XI in *Quadragesimo anno* 114, where he goes so far as to accept even the socialization of the means of production.

Given the new and complex situations which the development of our capitalist economy has created and which raise problems for the Christian ethical conscience, we must make adequate distinctions with regard to the various levels and meanings of "property" if we are to be faithful to the teaching of the church and defend private property as a human value and not as the exclusive privilege of one social class. I find adequate the distinctions suggested by J. M. Díez Alegría, whose views are summarized in the rest of this section:

The impasse reached in the church's social teaching is due to having contrasted an insufficiently nuanced conception of private property with the concept of a totalitarian collectivization. We must therefore distinguish between:

1. The basic relation of dominion which human beings possess as a body over material goods. All human beings together are owners of all goods. The subject of this right is each individual in active solidarity with the others, and this as a person, that is, prior to any consideration of the state or any other institutional group.

2. The fundamental right to a share in the possession of goods (an effective share and one recognized as a right); this right belongs to persons and enables them to: (a) defend their freedom and dignity; (b) ensure a vital space for the family; (c) give security to the person; and (d) engage in personal action, that is, to exercise sufficient initiative, responsibility, and freedom in the use of material goods.

3. Private property in the narrow sense, that is, ownership of consumer goods.

4. Private property in the broad sense, that is, ownership of the means of production.

Concepts 1 and 2 are concerned with a power that is inherent in the person prior to any consideration of the state and that belongs to the human being as such because he or she is a person. It is to these concepts that Pius XII seems to be referring. If we mean 1 and 2 when we speak of "the right of private property," we must be aware that the right thus understood is compatible with its being exercised in a collective and public way.

As far as consumer goods are concerned, it must be said that the personal power over goods which was described just above cannot be exercised in practice without some form of private ownership of consumer goods. The same cannot be said, however, of ownership of the means of production. As a matter of fact, historically and especially in the present age of industrial society, strictly private ownership of the means of production appears to be incompatible with the adequate exercise by all of a personal power whether over productive goods or over consumer goods. The majority of the human race is deprived of even a minimally adequate power of this kind. And private ownership in the strict sense, when exercised in an individualistic manner over the means of production, is clearly a structural obstacle to all of us having adequate access to the personal power in question.[12]

Social Ownership of the Means of Production

I referred earlier to the fact that the teaching of John Paul II confirms that of Leo XIII and subsequent magisterial authorities on the right of the worker to gain private ownership of the means of production. I also pointed out, however, that John Paul II has introduced a new nuance.

The earlier basis given for the principle was the dignity of human work, which generates a right of ownership. The nuance added takes the demand of respect for the right of ownership generated by work and extends it beyond the liberal capitalist system to the socialist system.

This new perspective adds new strength and vigor to the right in question by not linking it necessarily with a particular type of economy. The right transcends systems and must be respected in all of them.

While Leo XIII specified a just wage as a means of access to private property for the worker, John Paul II establishes that dominion over the means of production can be had not only by way of private possession of them but also by way of a right to participate responsibly in the decisions taken with regard to these means. This demand is in fact not new, since the church in its social teaching had already called for a share of the worker in management, that is, in the decisions affecting a business. What is new is that this demand is extended beyond capitalism to the socialist system.

The pope thinks that the way to achieve implementation of this right of participation is to establish autonomous intermediate groups which can express convergent points of view and offer a balanced array of contributions to mature and responsible choices. To a certain extent this solution had already been suggested by Pius XI (QA 79, 80, 87) and Paul VI (OA 47) when they spoke of the function and task of these free and autonomous groups which occupy a middle position between the individual and the state. They would provide a way of developing an authentic democratic socialism.

The important thing for the moment is be clear on how the position of John Paul II reaffirms the traditional principle while at the same time considerably broadening its application and disentangling it from the conditions proper to the liberal system in which it was conceived and formulated.

SOME PROBLEMS IN THE APPLICATION TO LATIN AMERICA
OF THE CHURCH'S TEACHING ON PROPERTY

When we in Latin America read the social encyclicals in our situation of dependent or peripheral capitalism, we become aware of impasses that seem due basically to the fact that the social teaching of the church was elaborated in the framework of the developed countries and therefore presupposes certain situations which are not verified on our continent. I shall discuss two of these impasses.

Access to Private Property

We may begin by recalling some points already considered. *Rerum novarum* established that access to private ownership of the means of production is a right of workers (figure 1). Because of this right, Leo XIII refused to accept the socialist solution, regarding it as a violation of that right.

W[orker]_____POMP

Figure 1

I duly explained that the way of gaining access to ownership was the just wage, the idea being that workers' wages gave them a legitimate right to consume (C), that is, to enjoy a worthy standard of living through private ownership of consumer goods and, through saving (S), to have access to POMP as well (figure 2). This teaching highlights the importance of a just wage, one that meets the norms of justice, as I have already explained.

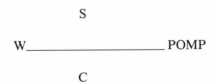

Figure 2

In practice, however, the capitalist system, which ignores the norms of the natural law and is governed exclusively by the market—that is, by supply and demand—frequently determines wages not in function of the worker's right to POMP but in function of the profit which the present owners of the means of production look for from their invested capital. By means of the "legal wage" or wage established by law, the state gives juridical legitimacy to the status quo, and does so all the more unjustly to the extent that the legal wage differs from a "just wage," that is, the wage as it ought to be determined by ethical considerations based on natural law and not simply by economic considerations based on the supply and demand for work.

Two rights to POMP are thus in competition: the right which the workers ought to be able to exercise by means of their work and that of the capitalists, who determine the amount of the wage to be paid. Capitalist practice shows that in this competition of the two rights the worker is at a disadvantage, because the wage actually paid does not permit the worker to have even the minimum of necessary consumer goods, to say nothing of saving, investing, and thus gaining access to the POMP (figure 3, from which S has disappeared).

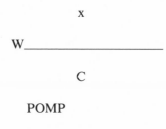

Figure 3

Observe, therefore, the complete difference in content between the two kinds of POMP: that defended by the church as a right of the worker, and that practiced by capitalism, which prevents the worker from exercising his right (figure 4).

In addition to clearly distinguishing between these two conceptions and practices of POMP (the fusion and identification of the two that passes off "capitalist" ownership as "Christian" is simply an insensitive bourgeois manipulation of the church's social teaching), we must ask ourselves:

1. What real capacity does capitalism have for attaining the goal so urgently demanded by the church's social teaching, namely, that the worker be able to acquire POMP by means of work that is properly remunerated?

2. What kind of ownership takes priority and must never be done away with

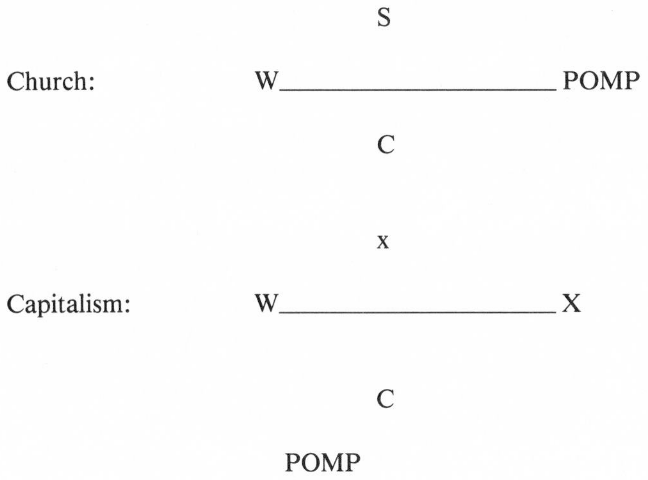

S

Church: W_____ POMP

                                  C

                                  x

Capitalism: W_____ X

                                  C

              POMP

Figure 4

in the case of inevitable and insoluble conflict when not every kind of ownership can be defended?

Capitalism and Remuneration for Work

At least in the beginning, capitalism produced "the enormous fortunes of
some few individuals, and the utter poverty of the masses" (RN 1). This state of
affairs was due to capital's control of the labor contract (ibid.). Forty years
after the promulgation of *Rerum novarum,* Pius XI was still emphasizing the
effect of the accumulation of capital:

> It is obvious that not only is wealth concentrated in our times but an
> immense power and despotic economic dictatorship is consolidated in the
> hands of a few, who are often not owners but only the trustees and
> managing directors of invested funds which they administer according to
> their own arbitrary will and pleasure.
>   This dictatorship is being most forcibly exercised by those who, since
> they hold the money and completely control it, control credit also and
> rule the lending of money. Hence they regulate the flow, so to speak, of
> the life-blood whereby the entire economic system lives, and have so
> firmly in their grasp the soul, as it were, of economic life that no one can
> breathe against their will.
>   This concentration of power and might, the characteristic mark, as it

were, of contemporary economic life, is the fruit that the unlimited freedom of struggle among competitors has of its own nature produced, and which lets only the strongest survive; and this is often the same as saying, those who fight the most violently, those who give least heed to their conscience.

This accumulation of might and of power generates in turn three kinds of conflict. First, there is the struggle for economic supremacy itself; then there is the bitter fight to gain supremacy over the State in order to use in economic struggles its resources and authority; finally there is conflict between States themselves, not only because countries employ their power and shape their policies to promote every economic advantage of their citizens, but also because they seek to decide political controversies that arise among nations through the use of their economic supremacy and strength [QA 105–8].

For this reason an economic dictatorship has supplanted the free market (see QA 109).

When carried along by its inherent dynamism and left free of any control by a watchful state or an organized working class, the capitalist system brings with it the rule of the strongest and therefore a contempt for human work, since the stronger "use human beings as mere instruments of money-making" (RN 31). Pius XI likewise denounces those employers who "treated their workers like mere tools" (QA 135). The weak are abused by the unscrupulous strong (see MM 58). Pius XI describes liberalism as "utterly unable to solve the social problem aright" (QA 10).

The expansion of the capitalist system has as its simultaneous and interconnected byproducts the development of powerful nations and the underdevelopment of the weak nations. Paul VI recalls how the departing colonial powers left "a precarious economy" behind them in the former colonies (PP 7). The resultant situation in these countries has been "manifestly inadequate for facing the hard reality of modern economics. Left to itself it works rather to widen the differences in the world's levels of life, not to diminish them: rich peoples enjoy rapid growth whereas the poor develop slowly" (PP 8).

Capitalism usually points with pride to its accomplishments in the Western countries. But it must be understood that this very achievement is not unrelated to the structure of the world economy. The exploitation which the system produces has been displaced but it has not disappeared. Pius XI recognizes this fact.

Certainly the condition of the workers has been improved and made more equitable especially in the more civilized and wealthy countries where the workers can no longer be considered universally overwhelmed with misery and lacking the necessities of life. But since manufacturing and industry have so rapidly pervaded and occupied countless regions, not only in the countries called new, but also in the realms of the Far

East . . . the number of non-owning working poor has increased enormously and their groans cry to God from the earth [QA 59].

The popes refer to the real situation in the Third World (see GS 63; PP 9). Various aspects of this situation, for example, urbanization (OA 8–10), give clear evidence of the exploitation of person by person that occurs when profit is the moving force in the economy. At the international level exploitation has the same causes as it does in national economies and in businesses; moreover, free trade, which is professed as a principle beyond discussion, is often simply a pretext under cover of which the powerful impose their own conditions.

The rule of free trade, taken by itself, is no longer able to govern international relations. Its advantages are certainly evident when the parties involved are not affected by any excessive inequalities of economic power: it is an incentive to progress and a reward for effort. That is why industrially developed countries see in it a law of justice. But the situation is no longer the same when economic conditions differ too widely from country to country: prices which are "freely" set in the market can produce unfair results. One must recognize that it is the fundamental principle of liberalism, as the rule for commercial exchange, which is questioned here [PP 58].

Populorum progressio goes on to state that "an economy of exchange can no longer be based solely on the law of free competition, a law which, in its turn, too often creates an economic dictatorship" (PP 59).

John XXIII in *Mater et magistra* 171–73 and Paul VI throughout the encyclical *Populorum progressio* speak of international aid for the development of the poor countries. It is clear, however, that the relationship of helper and helped brings with it the possibility of strengthening the bonds of domination and exploitation. The popes are forthright in pointing out this possibility and danger.

Can a dependent and peripheral capitalism guarantee just remuneration for work done? The question must be answered in a scientific way by analyzing the structures of international trade and international investment of money, as well as the concrete experiences of our Latin American countries. There is good reason for the discrepancies in wages that are found in our countries and for the freezing of workers' salaries in order to make exported products cheaper. John XXIII pointed out that

in the economically developed countries, it frequently happens that great, or sometimes very great, remuneration is had for the performance of some task of lesser importance or doubtful utility. Meanwhile, the diligent and profitable work that whole classes of decent and hard-working citizens perform, receives too low a payment and one insufficient for the necessities of life [MM 70].

In our countries, those who service the "public security" receive better pay than those who work in education, even though the latter can more effectively help eradicate social evils than can repressive systems.

Priority of Property Rights

Let us hypothesize—it is only a hypothesis, not a question being answered in the affirmative, for such an answer is for the social sciences to give. The hypothesis is that there is a contradiction between two rights of ownership—the right of capital, which determines the wage to be earned, and the right of workers to have access by means of their wages to POMP—and that as a result of this contradiction the defense of the one right makes it impossible to defend the other right as well. Which of the two rights referred to in this statement takes precedence?

In this hypothesis it could be said that:

1. A POMP (of a present possessor) which for its continuance must deny the POMP of another (the worker) is illegitimate. Under these conditions there would be no question of a right as the church understands it, but rather of a real abuse on the part of the "right" that asserts itself through the denial of another's right. In such a situation some (present) owners do violence to other (future) owners of the means of production.

It is the duty of the state to see to it that the exercise of one right does not entail a violation of another right. As it is a matter of justice to defend property legitimately acquired (RN 28), so too it is a matter of justice to defend the access to property of those who acquire the right to such access through their labor.

2. At least the universal right of all human beings to have a human use of goods through POCG is most certainly a right prior and superior to the right to defend any form of POMP.

If then there were to be a conflict (again, I speak only of a hypothesis and leave its verification to the social sciences) between the POCG as a right of every worker and the POMP as a right of the capitalist, so that the defense of the POMP would prevent access to the POCG, then it must certainly be said that such a defense would not be in conformity with the image of the human person and society which the church possesses through revelation. In such a case the defense of the privileged right of a few would be an obstacle to the good of the entire body, and this in a far more basic and fundamental area than POMP. In other words, when the working populace must live in conditions of wretchedness or relative impoverishment as a result of the concrete way in which the right to POMP is being exercised, there is a substantial violation of the right of ownership as defended by the church. Such a situation is un-

Christian, whatever the verbal claims of those who seek to legitimize it (see figure 5).

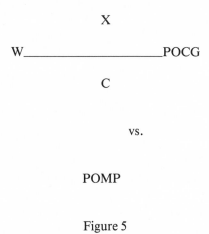

Figure 5

Private Property as Safeguard of Democracy

Another point that causes difficulty for a Latin American reading of the church's social teaching is the following statement of John XXIII in *Mater et magistra*:

> The right of private property, including that pertaining to goods devoted to productive enterprises, is permanently valid. Indeed, it is rooted in the very nature of things, whereby we learn that individual men are prior to civil society, and hence, that civil society is to be directed toward man as its end. Indeed, the right of private individuals to act freely in economic affairs is recognized in vain, unless they are at the same time given an opportunity of freely selecting and using things necessary for the exercise of this right. Moreover, experience and history testify that where political regimes do not allow private individuals the possession also of productive goods, the exercise of human liberty is violated or completely destroyed in matters of primary importance. Thus it becomes clear that in the right of property, the exercise of liberty finds both a safeguard and a stimulus [MM 109].

The pope conceives of property as a safeguard of a democratic state, because when citizens own property they have a degree of responsibility and creativity which makes them independent of the state in some areas of life; as a result, they are not subjected to a statist totalitarianism (figure 6).

POMP_____Democracy

Figure 6

But as a matter of fact, the contemporary proliferation of regimes inspired by the ideology of national security (Puebla refers to these: DP 42, 49, 314, 500, 510, 532, 541, 547, 549, 560, 1262) seems to show the contrary of what the church teaches. For in Latin America the suppression of democracy and the violation and extensive suppression of the exercise of human freedom in the most fundamental matters are regarded as a necessary and inevitable means of safeguarding "the social order" required by the liberal capitalist economy that is based on POMP.

The profound difference between the two kinds of ownership of the means of production is perfectly evident: on the one hand, a POMP whose internal dynamism leads to the promotion of democratic freedoms (this is the POMP defended by the church); and, on the other, a POMP which requires that the voice of the workers be silenced, their right to unionize be restricted, and their right to strike be suppressed (a right constantly defended by the church in its social teaching, as we shall see in the next chapter) in order that a few may continue to have a privileged POMP. Once again, we have here an obvious manipulation of the church's social teaching, as the same name (POMP) is given to two diametrically opposed realities.

POMP_____Democracy

POMP_____Totalitarianism

Figure 7

THE ECCLESIAL SOURCES OF THE CHURCH'S TEACHING ON PROPERTY

By way of confirming the hermeneutical perspective that has led me to assign key importance to the first theme of *Rerum novarum*, namely the right of workers to POMP (a theme which represents the real Christian originality of Leo XIII in response to the evils of his day and the solutions offered for them), I turn now, with the popes in their encyclicals and with the best commentaries on the church's social teaching, to the biblical and patristic sources of this teaching. These sources will demonstrate in an even more radical manner that an interpretation of the church's social teaching which would benefit the powerful is utterly opposed to the entire ecclesial tradition of sensitivity to the poor.

Biblical Sources

On the subject of property we can go back to the earliest roots of Christian thinking. These are to be found in the tradition of the Jewish people as recorded in the Old Testament. Three writings or groups of writings call for our attention: Exodus, Genesis and Deuteronomy, and the prophets.

The Israelite people was groaning under exploitation by the pharaoh (Exod. 1:11-14), and God heard the cry of the people (2:24; 3:7). When Moses asked that his people be allowed time to pray, the pharaoh refused (5:1-2). Prayer, of course, is a powerful raiser of consciousness, because when persons enter into converse with God they become aware of their dignity as persons. The pharaoh not only refused the time asked but became even more repressive (5:6-9) with the aim of turning these human beings into mere tools of production; this is something that all materialist systems, including the capitalist, know well how to do.

The God of the Bible, then, is not a source of alienation but on the contrary raises the consciousness of the poor. Neither is God impartial; God takes the side of the oppressed and through an experience of political liberation leads them out of oppression in order that God may conclude with them a covenant whose ultimate meaning is religious rather than political. This covenant calls for the people to live together in solidarity and justice and so be a sign raised up among the peoples and nations. The chosen people is to remember its own experience of enslavement and never be guilty of such abominable practices but rather live always in freedom.

The religious project we call the covenant finds two kinds of expression. One is metaphysical and emphasizes the identity of the creator God of Genesis with the liberator God of Exodus. The original plan of the Creator was for a human community that would be free of envy such as we find in Cain (Gen. 4:5), would be characterized instead by a sense of mutual responsibility ("Am I my brother's keeper?", 4:9), and would exercise dominion over the earth through work and knowledge (Adam gives things their names, Gen. 1:28-30; 2:20). The second expression is juridical and is found in the laws of the chosen people, especially in Deuteronomy. These laws express a will to live together in justice, under the eyes of the God of the covenant who is constantly offered worship through liturgy and prayer.

In this just coexistence private property has a place, but it is accompanied by a strong social sense. Many texts speak of the right of private property (e.g., Exod. 20:15, 17; Deut. 5:19, 21; Jer. 17:11). Property, however, never becomes something unconditioned, but is seen rather as dependent on God. It is regarded as a sign of blessing from the Lord (Job 42:10ff.; Gen. 13:2; 24:35; 30:43; Deut. 8:7-19). Precisely for this reason God requires that property be available to every member of Israel, and God protects the weak in particular (Deut. 27:19; Exod. 2:20; Isa. 1:23; 3:14; Ezek. 16:49; 22:29; 45:9; Hos. 12:8; Amos 2:6; 4:1; Mic. 2:1; 3:1).

There are concrete juridical mechanisms to protect the rights of the poor: the sabbatical year (whatever can be gleaned from fields not tilled in the seventh year belongs to the poor: Exod. 23:10; Lev. 25:3-7; Deut. 15:1); the jubilee year, which prevents the concentration of property in a few hands (Lev. 25:10); the obligation to help impoverished relatives (Lev. 25:25f.); the rule that the gleanings from the harvest are for the poor (Lev. 19:9; Deut. 14:28; 24:19; the prohibition of interest on loans (Exod. 22:24; Lev. 25:36; Deut. 23:20).

In view of all these provisions it can be said that Israelite legislation establishes a kind of theocratic communism, to the extent that the granting of property rights is severely restricted and made subordinate to the universal use of material goods. That this real use of things by all is not a matter of indifference to God becomes clear in a constant theme of prophetic preaching: There can be no sincere worship of God if relations between the worshipers are marked by injustice. And let us note that in Israelite law "justice" is very restrictive in regard to ownership and the accumulation of goods.

Despite all these precautions the exploitation of person by person made its appearance among the chosen people. An effort was made to hide it behind an outward show of scrupulous worship of God. At this point the prophets came on the scene to explain what the authentic service and worship of God entails. It was not a political or economic zeal of a "horizontalist" kind, but a profoundly religious motivation that led these persons to denounce the show of worship which glossed over the reality of injustice. While the primary concern of the prophets was to watch over the covenant and the worship of the true God, there was a close connection between this mission and the denunciation of injustice concealed by a show of piety. The theological reason for the connection is this: It is no longer the God of the covenant that is being worshiped in these cultic forms; persons are worshiping an idol unless their worship of God is accompanied by justice in dealing with their brothers and sisters.

According to the prophets, "to do justice is to know God." The number of biblical testimonies to this truth is overwhelming: Jer. 22:13-16; Hos. 4:1b-2; 4:3; 6:6; Prov. 21:3; Amos 5:21-25; Isa. 1:11-17; 43:23-24; Mic. 6:6-8; Jer. 6:18-21; 7:4-7.

In the New Testament Jesus reaffirms the same principle: before offering God a sacrifice or a gift, we must be reconciled to our brothers and sisters (Matt. 5:23-24). We should note that this statement occurs precisely in the context of the differences between the old law and the new.

We should note also the similarity of relationships in the exodus situation and the prophetic situation: in both the poor and the lowly are being oppressed. But there is also a difference: in the time of the Exodus the oppressor was a foreign ruler and a foreign people; the prophets, on the other hand, must denounce an oppressor who is located within the chosen people, where all have a knowledge of God's will. To the violation of human rights, of which even the pagan is guilty, there is added a violation of God's express will as made known in God's covenant with the people.

There is a significant analogy here with the situation in Latin America where the violations of human rights and the growing gaps between rich and poor are the work not of atheistic forces but of Christians. All the more reason to cry out with the prophets that in these cases above all others the worship of God is an illusion, a form of idolatry, because faith has been dissociated from justice, and the love of God is no longer joined to love of our brothers and sisters.

The Fathers of the Church

"Anyone who comes to grips with the testimonies of the holy fathers will find it impossible to deny that the poor are not only a constant subject of their thinking as Christians but even occupy the central place in that thinking."[13]

We find various approaches to this subject in the Fathers of the church:

—Faith cannot be separated from charity to the poor. The reason, according to Clement of Rome, is that Christ himself is one of the lowly, and we truly confess our faith in him through our works of love and justice.[14] St. John Chrysostom emphasizes Christian solidarity; in his view almsgiving is of greater value than virginity and fasting because unlike these almsgiving does not remain within the individual but embraces the members of Christ. The final judgment as told by Matthew shows that what will be condemned is not so much wicked actions as failures of solidarity.[15]

—The church must have a predilection for the poor: far from being respecters of persons, Christians must "above all else visit the poor," says Clement of Rome. Polycarp singles out widows, orphans, and the poor as those who must be given primary attention. The Shepherd of Hermas teaches the same. Ambrose insists that even the jewels and treasures of the church must be sold in order to meet the needs of the poor, because then these things turn into useful gold, the gold of Christ.[16]

—Out of love for the rich the church must warn them of the dangers of wealth. Chrysostom says that it is better to lapse into poverty than to adore the golden calf. In the view of Theodoret of Cyr riches come from taking what belongs to others. In addition, riches close the heart to love and bring evils in their train, as Chrysostom points out in a very forceful way. According to Polycarp money is the source of all evils. According to Zeno of Verona the acquisition of wealth by some means suffering for the poor. Chrysostom says that it is not chance that creates the distinction between rich and poor, but theft and the accumulation of riches.[17]

—To care for the poor is to break the yoke that oppresses them; we must therefore look upon the drama being played out in society as including us, says Ambrose. Chrysostom warns us that we cannot practice charity unless we first practice justice.[18]

—The Fathers of the church see society as an arena of conflict: Basil denounces oppression; Chrysostom and Ambrose sternly censure the luxury of the rich as being enjoyed at the cost of the poor; they are even more energetic in their condemnation of the usurer. Chrysostom raises his voice against the exploitation of workers through the kind of wages paid them. Lactantius, Basil, and Gregory of Nyssa denounce inequality and slavery. Asterius of Amaseia and Augustine point out that private property is the source of these inequalities. Basil describes as theft the accumulation of more than is necessary.[19]

—In view of these evils the Fathers of the church maintain that Christian solidarity should be obedient to the following principles:

1. We are not owners but stewards of material goods: Chrysostom, Basil, Asterius, Leo the Great.

2. All created goods are for all human beings. There is a rather broad consensus on this point among the Greek[20] and Latin[21] Fathers.

3. The human person is by nature a social being and is called to live in community: Basil, Lactantius, Augustine.[22]

4. All human beings are basically equal: Gregory of Nazianzus, Chrysostom, Ambrose, Gregory of Nyssa, Lactantius.[23]

5. Private property when unaccompanied by solidarity and a respect for the universal ordination of all goods to all human beings is a source of selfishness, divisions, and exploitation: *Didache*, Tertullian, Lactantius, Basil, Gregory of Nyssa, Chrysostom, Ambrose, Asterius, Zeno of Verona.[24]

6. The sharing of goods is required by justice, so that the destiny of created goods may be fulfilled. In Basil's eyes one who does not alleviate hunger is a murderer; Gregory of Nyssa observes that some people help a single poor person while impoverishing a hundred others; for Chrysostom giving alms is simply giving the poor what belongs to them and is a work of justice; Ambrose says the same. Augustine regards mercy to the poor as a form of justice.[25]

This entire line of patristic thinking is inspired by a real sense of the "right of the poor." The right of the poor springs from their very being; the very reality of the poor is a challenge forcing others to choose between human solidarity and wealth. Those who give alms should do so with the interior intention not simply of practicing asceticism but of being in communion with the poor. The right of the poor does not depend on their being workers, for the right is antecedent to work and is inherent in the life given to us as members of the human family. Is that not how members of a family spontaneously think of one another? Do we ask a newborn child to work if it is to eat?

In addition, the right of the poor here and now is based on the justice that must be accorded their forgotten rights. It is often injustice that has created the present situation of the poor. Natural causes (earthquakes, droughts, etc.) do play a part, but the majority of our marginalized populations are in this condition as a result of economic structures and laws.

In my opinion, Christian tradition has not shown sufficient vigor in proclaiming the message of the Fathers regarding the right of the poor. Historically, the principle of the right of the poor was maintained at the same time as the right of private property.

> The Fathers never tried to develop a coherent theory that would reconcile these two seemingly contradictory rights: the right of the poor and the right to property. At the same time, however, all the elements needed for such a synthesis are present in their discourses. The resources of the earth are meant for (the Fathers say: belong to) those who really need them. The right to property does not do away with the right (the Fathers say: property right) of the poor, and the rich have an obligation in justice to aid the poor. Conversely, the right of the poor does not eliminate the right of property as a form of stewardship. Scholastic theology endeavored to achieve a rational synthesis of these two elements; the effort culminated in the definition of property given in the *Summa theologiae* (II–II, q. 66, a. 2). It must be acknowledged that, as was to be feared, the synthesis unfortunately brought a weakening of one of the two elements, in this case the right of the poor. St. Thomas Aquinas no longer affirms as categorically as before that the superfluous possessions of the rich belong to the poor, and his successors will forget this principle completely. The Fathers did not vacillate at all on this point.[26]

St. Thomas Aquinas

In my opinion, St. Thomas Aquinas still represents a radical position, and we can only be glad that John Paul II mentions him as one of the sources that have inspired the social teaching of the church.

Thomas's thinking on this point is to be found in the *Summa theologiae* (ST) II–II, q. 66, aa. 1–9. Of special interest here are articles 1, 2, and 7.

In the first article, the question asked is whether human beings can possess external goods. The answer given is: "It is natural for man to have dominion over things in the sense of having the power to use them."[27]

The second article raises more directly the question of whether this natural dominion can be expressed in the form of private property. Thomas's answer is as follows:

> Man has a twofold competence in relation to material things. The first is a title to care for and distribute the earth's resources. Understood in this way, it is not merely legitimate for man to possess things as his own, it is even necessary for human life. . . .
>
> Man's other competence is to use and manage the world's resources. Now in regard to this, no man is entitled to manage things merely for himself, he must do so in the interests of all, so that he is ready to share them with others in case of necessity.[28]

The development of thinking on the natural law governing property may be followed with Gratian's Decree as the starting point, because a distinction is made there between the right to use all material things as being a natural right ("there is a natural right to possess all things in common") and the right of property as being a positive right that is maintained by almost all peoples ("positive law makes a distinction between possessions and slaves").

This distinction is also present in Thomas Aquinas, for whom the right to use is of a metaphysical kind, whereas the right of ownership (i.e., the right to dispose of goods) operates on the juridico-sociological level.

Pierre Bigo makes it very clear that the Thomistic concept of property is rather different from ours. In Thomas's view to be an owner means to be able to dispose of a material thing but not necessarily to dispose of it "merely for oneself."

> Ownership is defined as a power. It cannot be defined in terms of use, because as far as their use is concerned things remain in common and as such cannot be possessed in the strict sense. St. Thomas is unwilling to define ownership as the appropriation of a thing for the use of its owner. In his eyes ownership means responsibility and not appropriation. The application of a thing to private use can take place only through a decision of the owner that is based on a judgment regarding distributive justice.[29]

For Thomas the right of private property is a right granted by positive law. This statement is an accurate one and does not contradict another text that might be cited about property (ST II–II, 57, 3c) because it is evident that in Christian thought any and every positive law must be related not only to the law which originates in the Spirit, but also to the higher principles that have their basis in human nature.

It is so evident to Thomas that the authentically natural right is the right to use all material goods that he can say: "In the case of necessity everything is common."[30] That is, in time of need the private ownership of property cannot be used as an objection against the needy person making use of the goods that belong to all or to any individual.

Article 7 of question 66 reads as follows:

> The dictates of human law cannot derogate from natural or divine law. The natural order established by God in his providence is, however, such that lower things are meant to enable man to supply his needs. A man's needs must therefore still be met out of the world's goods even though a certain division and apportionment of them is determined by law. And this is why according to natural law goods that are held in superabundance by some people should be used for the maintenance of the poor. This is the principle enunciated by Ambrose and repeated in the *Decretum: It is the bread of the poor which you are holding back; it is the*

clothes of the naked which you are hoarding; it is the relief and liberation
of the wretched which you are thwarting by burying your money away.[31]

The confusion between the natural right of use and the positive right of ownership, thus making the latter a natural right, was due to Luigi Taparelli (1793–1862), former professor of Leo XIII whom he induced to speak of a "natural right of private property."[32] Properly understood, this expression has a legitimate meaning and has continued in use in the church's social teaching. Ever since Pius XII, however, it has been kept clearly subordinated to another, more radical and primordial, natural right: the right of all human beings to the use of all material goods. This is the present teaching of the popes and of Vatican Council II.

The above cited article 7 of question 66 in St. Thomas is especially enlightening in our situation because it offers an analogy to the conflict of rights of which I spoke earlier in the present chapter: the conflict that arises when the way in which the right of POMP is exercised makes it impossible for workers to have access not only to POMP (to which their work gives them a right) but even to a worthy level of human life as represented by POCG.

In St. Thomas the conflict arises from the existence of owners who have the right to *decide* (that is, to make a distinction between what is necessary for their *own use* and what is superfluous and is to be *shared with others*). But what if the owners decide—as they have a right to do—but they do not make any distinction and therefore decide not to share but to keep all they have for their own use and thus deprive the needy of their right to use material goods?

I shall not digress into the broad area of problems which such a decision raises (if the owners decide to share, how are they to decide on a recipient when there are so many?). In any case, in Thomas's thinking there is one case in which the right to use takes absolute priority. It is the case of poor persons in extreme need; in virtue of this right they can take what they need for life, even if the rich persons have decided not to give them anything. This teaching has been solemnly reconfirmed by Vatican Council II (see GS 69). It is to be observed that Thomas handles this conflict of rights in an article on the subject of theft and that he absolves of any fault poor persons who take goods when they are in extreme need.

By analogy, then, may we not say that if there were, hypothetically, to be an irreconcilable conflict between two property rights, namely POMP and POCG, the latter, as the right which is more universal (the right of all and to the use of all goods) and more fundamental (the issue is human life, and a human life lived in dignity, not in wretchedness), takes precedence over the former (which is the right of a few rather than one universally implemented)? This would allow us to conclude that if a mixed ownership of the means of production (i.e., some businesses run under a system of POMP, and others—those more important and decisive for the national economy—under a system of social ownership of the means of production) would better ensure POCG for all citizens, this would be an ideal more in conformity with the church's social teaching than is a system of pure POMP involving the real and practical denial of POCG to many citizens of the country. In support of this view I may invoke the acknowledgment by Pius XI (QA 114) of the socialist argument for state ownership of the means of production. Pius XI makes the argument his own: "Certain kinds of property, it is rightly contended, ought to be reserved to the State since they carry with them a dominating power so great that [it] cannot without danger to the general welfare be entrusted to private individuals" (QA 114).

The final section of this lengthy chapter has provided an endorsement of the hermeneutic for the teaching on property as developed in the preceding two sections. For this hermeneutic proves to be based not only on the criteria indicated in chapters 4–7 but also to have the support of the entire ecclesial, biblical, patristic, and theological tradition of the church, that is, of the very sources which John Paul II gives as the root of the church's present-day thought and judgment on social matters.

9

THE TEACHING
OF THE CHURCH
ON CONFLICT IN SOCIETY

As in dealing with the subject of private property, so too in dealing with social conflict between classes, a special effort must be made to read the church's teaching from within the framework of Latin American reality, because the forms which social conflict has taken in the industrialized countries are different from those found in our Latin American continent. Industrial progress and the advent of the consumer society seem to have blurred social contrasts in the developed countries to the point where the very harsh descriptions given in the early social encyclicals (esp. RN and QA) seem no longer applicable. But this is far from being the case among us in Latin America, as the bishops at Puebla indicate when they speak of a growing gap between rich and poor as wealth is concentrated in a few hands while the majorities sink deeper into wretchedness (see chap. 1, above). The gap by itself is already evidence of selfishness and a lack of love; but the purely economic phenomenon is accompanied by social and political discrimination so extensive that

> they [the governments] look askance at the organizing efforts of laborers, peasants, and the common people; and they adopt repressive measures to prevent such organizing. But this type of control over, or limitation on, activity is not applied to employer organizations, which can exercise their full power to protect their interests [DP 44].

Because of this discrimination, anyone defending the rights of the poor will incur reprisals and threats. All this is evidence of a conflict between the classes of society, a conflict that is present as an objective fact prior to any ethical evaluation of it and prior to any attempt to extract from it a method or way of solving the problem.

In accordance with the thinking of John Paul II, I want to make a careful distinction between conflict as a social "fact" caused by the economic systems and materialism that the industrial revolution brought in its train, and conflict as a "programmatic class struggle" or social method that is based on the dialectical conception of society, history, and even nature itself which is set forth in Marxist philosophy. Simply to acknowledge the objective fact (as the church does in its social teaching) is not to favor or promote struggle as a method or strategy. After all, it is necessary to determine what the sickness is if a remedy is to be found for it. In the Christian vision of things such a remedy will always be, in the final analysis, some way of making love victorious and of building solidarity and justice.

CONFLICT AS FACT (SITUATION) AND AS METHOD (STRATEGY)

By the "fact of social conflict" I mean here the objective distance existing between social groups because of disparities in those economic resources which determine the extent to which a group is able to exercise other social, economic, political, and cultural rights. In its present form, the objective difference is determined by the prevailing economic model, namely, the "free-market economy," which has widened the gap between rich and poor by giving capital priority over labor and economics priority over social concern (see DP 47) and thus has established a scale of values for appraising (or depreciating) the human person in terms of economic success. Puebla calls attention to a deterministic view of a fatalistic and social kind which is based on the erroneous idea that human beings are not fundamentally equal. In human relationships the objective difference of which I am speaking leads to numerous forms of discrimination and marginalization that are incompatible with the dignity of human persons. This lack of respect for the person shows itself less in a theory than in expressions and attitudes characteristic of those who judge themselves to be better than others. The result is the situation of inequality in which laborers, peasants, native peoples, and domestic servants presently live (DP 309).

The fact of social conflict is explained by John Paul II as due to the capitalist principle that even human work is a kind of merchandise (LE 7) and that human beings and their labor are to be regarded as a means of production (ibid.). The same error infects socialist systems insofar as they maintain the priority of capital (even if in the form of state-owned property) over labor (see LE 8, 11).

I am referring, then, to present-day forms of segregation, marginalization, and exploitation. In other periods of history there were rich and poor, and the laws—and even theology—gave legitimacy to the practice of slavery. St. Thomas put it this way:

From the bare nature of the case there is no reason for this man rather than that man being a slave. It is only when it is looked at pragmatically in its results that, as Aristotle says, it is expedient for him to be ruled by a wiser whom he serves. Servitude, which is part of the *jus gentium*, is natural then in the second sense of our explanation, not the first.[1]

Yet, even after slavery had been abolished, Leo XIII could describe an objective situation as follows: "A small number of very rich men have been able to lay upon the teeming masses of the laboring poor a yoke little better than that of slavery itself" (RN 1).

This objective situation, then, is social conflict as a fact, not as a method. I wish to emphasize the difference between fact and strategy lest the two become confused. "Situations" are realities which precede any choices on our part; they are objectively there, even though they may have been the result of earlier choices, whether our own or others'. "Strategies," on the other hand, are realities that flow from choices which are made with the evident intention either of modifying an existing situation or of supporting and maintaining it. Hunger can be a situation, as when an inadequate wage prevents a person from buying the necessary food to eat; it can also be a strategy, as when persons try by means of a hunger strike to call attention to themselves so that they may claim a right or denounce an unjust situation.

Before Marxism ever urged the strategy of class struggle, capitalism had already produced the conflict between capital and labor and had caused injustice and violence to be inflicted on workers by depriving them of their just wage. Leo XIII refers to this deprivation of a just wage as a form of real "violence" against the worker: "If through necessity or fear of a worse evil the workman accepts harder conditions because an employer or contractor will afford him no better, he is made the victim of force and injustice" (RN 32).

The social encyclicals reject the class struggle as a *strategy* and as a method of analysis, but they are nonetheless aware of the *situation* of social conflict and seek to change it.

The "class struggle" involves an *aversion* between the classes of society. Capitalism tries to conceal the reality without changing it; to this end it resorts to *diversion*; that is, it withdraws people's gaze from the real wretchedness and poverty or explains it by shifting the entire responsibility for it to the poor and marginalized themselves. There are two ways of responding to the *aversion* without lapsing into *diversion*. One way is *subversion*, which starts with revolutionary changes of structures and seeks to affect the hearts of human beings. The other is the way of *conversion*, which starts with the hearts of human beings and seeks to bring about "bold transformations, innovations that go deep," and "urgent reforms" (PP 32) without naively believing that "individual initiative alone and the mere free play of competition" are enough to effect such changes. "One must avoid the risk of increasing still more the wealth of the rich and the dominion of the strong, whilst leaving the poor in their misery and adding to the servitude of the oppressed" (PP 33).

In chapter 8 we saw how one and the same phrase, POMP, can convey two diametrically opposed conceptions: that of the capitalist system and that proper to Christian thought. The challenge is to teach the Christian value of

POMP without falling under the yoke of the POMP urged by capitalism. In like manner we are here looking at the reality of conflict from two points of view: as a situation and as a strategy. The challenge, once again, is to be honest about the situation and to propose a Christian strategy for dealing with it; the call is for a creative response to the situation.

THE FACT OR SITUATION OF SOCIAL CONFLICT

In its authoritative teaching the church takes cognizance of the objective existence of social conflict produced by the labor market, that is, the new economic relationship created by capitalism as, under the latter's influence, the ancient guilds, which secured the rights of workers, disappeared. Leo XIII explains the helplessness of workers by, among other things, the disappearance of the guilds:

> The ancient workingmen's guilds were abolished in the last century, and no other organization took their place. Public institutions and the very laws have set aside the ancient religion. Hence by degrees it has come to pass that workingmen have been surrendered, all isolated and helpless, to the hard-heartedness of employers and the greed of unchecked competition [RN 1].

Capitalism altered the capital-labor relationship by introducing a new principle which was seemingly more beneficial to both parties: the freedom of the marketplace. But the freedom was only apparent, as Leo XIII points out:

> To this must be added the custom of working by contract, and the concentration of so many branches of trade in the hands of a few individuals; so that a small number of very rich men have been able to lay upon the teeming masses of the laboring poor a yoke little better than that of slavery itself [RN 1].

Pius XI makes this same point in even greater detail:

> Labor, as Our Predecessor explained well in his Encyclical, is not a mere commodity. On the contrary, the worker's human dignity in it must be recognized. It therefore cannot be bought and sold like a commodity. Nevertheless, as the situation now stands, hiring and offering for hire in the so-called labor market separate men into two divisions, as into battle lines, and the contest between these divisions turns the labor market itself almost into a battlefield where, face to face, the opposing lines struggle bitterly [QA 83].

It is undoubtedly John Paul II who most clearly brings out the conflictual relationship between capital and labor. He describes the conflicting groups in terms of their numbers, their influence, and their connection with property (LE 11), but he also emphasizes the way in which ownership enables capital to dictate wages by imposing unjust conditions (ibid.). The pope does not make the mistake of claiming that his description is of an ideology or strategy of social conflict; no, prior to any transformation of the conflict into a political instrument it is already a real fact (ibid.).

There is, then, no doubt that in its social teaching the magisterium grasps both the fact and the true nature of the causes of social conflict. There is a breakup "into two divisions, as into battle lines," a "contest," and this is due to something objective that precedes any Marxist ideology or strategy—it is due to the "labor market," which is a technique originating in the most basic principles of liberal capitalism.

We can distinguish different levels of response to this fact or situation: some more timid, others bolder and more consistent.

1. Complementarity of Capital and Labor

The popes see in this conflict not a law of nature but a situation with historical causes. As a matter of fact, the opposition and struggle of social classes is contrary to human nature. The example of the human body, already used in Pauline ecclesiology, is also used by Leo XIII to support the principle of the integration of the various classes into a single organism:

> The great mistake in the matter now under consideration is to take up with the notion that class is naturally hostile to class, and that the wealthy and the workingmen are intended by nature to live in mutual conflict. So irrational and so false is this view, that the direct contrary is the truth. Just as the symmetry of the human frame is the resultant of the disposition of the bodily members, so in a State is it ordained by nature that these two classes should dwell in harmony and agreement, and should, as it were, groove into one another, so as to maintain the balance of the body politic. Each needs the other: Capital cannot do without Labor, nor Labor without Capital [RN 13].

Simply by considering capital and labor as economic factors, we can see how they mutually complement each other. The economic distinction between capital and labor does not necessarily imply the existence of social classes. Even in socialist countries the economy cannot function except with the contributions of both capital (the property of the state) and labor. But even if we suppose private ownership of capital, a system of cooperation maintains the economic complementarity of capital and labor without the existence of antagonistic classes of capitalists and workers. Even in traditional capitalist enterprises it is conceivable that one and the same person could contribute capital to his or her own or another's business and at the same time be a worker in one of those businesses. The problem in all these cases is to establish the rights of capital in an equitable manner, so that there may be no exploitation of surplus value, to which Marxism rightly objects, when the economic contributions of the two factors, capital and labor, become identified with two antagonistic classes, capitalists and workers. At least the early forms of European liberal capitalism, as well as many forms prevailing in our dependent and peripheral capitalism, give evidence of such an identification of capital with the capitalist and labor with the worker. Nor does the *intentio operis* ("intention of the work itself," i.e., the purpose of the business, which necessarily brings the two factors into harmony) coincide with the *intentiones operantium* ("intentions of the agent," i.e., the interests of those who contribute capital and labor respectively; for a higher salary which the worker desires is incompatible with the greater profit which the capitalist desires).

2. Social Inequalities

The social differences between rich and poor have often been justified by religious arguments (e.g., the providence of God). It is undeniable that a prejudiced reading of the church's social teaching which does not look at this teaching as a whole can find in some pontifical statements support for the thesis that social inequality has a basis in nature. For example, one might appeal in support of such a thesis to Leo XIII:

> Let it, then, be taken as granted, in the first place, that the condition of things human must be endured, for it is impossible to reduce civil society to one dead level. Socialists may in that intent do their utmost, but all striving against nature is in vain. There naturally exist among mankind manifold differences of the most important kind; people differ in capacity, skill, health, strength; and unequal fortune is a necessary result of unequal condition. Such inequality is far from being disadvantageous either to individuals or to the community. Social and public life can only be maintained by means of various kinds of capacity for business and the playing of many parts; and each man, as a rule, chooses the part which suits his own peculiar domestic condition [RN 13].

Pius XI even attributes to providence the state of the working person: "And the workers . . . will . . . accept without rancor the place in human society assigned them by Divine Providence . . ." (QA 137).

To remove these texts from their context in the totality of magisterial teaching is to adopt an extremist position that is openly censured by the magisterium itself. Taken in their totality, the statements of the pontifical and conciliar magisterium enable us to understand properly the earlier statements in *Rerum novarum* 13 and *Quadragesimo anno* 137. To begin with, Leo XIII himself pointed out in *Rerum novarum* 1 certain aspects of social inequality that were due to the labor market; Pius XI did the same in *Quadragesimo anno* 83. In addition, Pius XI says "In actual fact, human society now, for the reason that it is founded on classes with divergent aims and hence opposed to one another and therefore inclined to enmity and strife, continues to be in a violent condition and is unstable and uncertain" (QA 82).

John XXIII later made the following very clear assertion:

It is not true that some human beings are by nature superior and others inferior. All men are equal in their natural dignity. Consequently, there are no political communities which are superior by nature, and none which are inferior by nature. All political communities are of equal natural dignity, since they are bodies whose membership is made up of these same human beings [PT 89].

Gaudium et spes confirms this teaching:

All men are endowed with a rational soul and are created in God's image; they have the same nature and origin and, being redeemed by Christ, they enjoy the same divine calling and destiny; there is here a basic equality between all men and it must be given ever greater recognition.

Undoubtedly not all men are alike as regards physical capacity and intellectual and moral powers. But forms of social or cultural discrimination in basic personal rights on the grounds of sex, race, color, social conditions, language or religion, must be curbed and eradicated as incompatible with God's design. It is regrettable that these basic personal rights are not yet being respected everywhere. . . .

Furthermore, while there are rightful differences between people, their equal dignity as persons demands we strive for fairer and more humane conditions. Excessive economic and social disparity between individuals and peoples of the one human race is a source of scandal and militates against social justice, equity, human dignity, as well as social and international peace [GS 29].

The following passage is important in that it points to discrimination as the cause of social differences; that is, social differences are not due to an element of natural inequality but to a social process that creates inequality and does not allow the development of the gifts God has given to every human being.

To fulfill the requirements of justice and equity, every effort must be made to put an end as soon as possible to the immense economic inequalities which exist in the world and increase from day to day, linked with individual and social discrimination, provided, of course, that the rights of individuals and the character of each people are not disturbed [GS 66].

The equality for which human beings struggle, therefore, is not an equality of human aptitudes (no one maintains such a position), but an equality of human possibilities. "Within a country which belongs to each one, all should be equal before the law, find equal admittance to economic, cultural, civic and social life and benefit from a fair sharing of the nation's resources" (OA 16).

Structures are unjust when they do not allow individuals to develop their personal aspirations and aptitudes. They are a hindrance to the call which individuals feel they have. Although *Populorum progressio* explains that individuals are the principal agents of their success or failure and that they are as responsible for carrying out their tasks as they are for their salvation, the encyclical also states that individuals' environments (family, teachers, companions, etc.) aid—or impede—them in carrying out their duties and responsibilities (PP 15).

While not denying the existence of varying aptitudes, we must also pay attention to the data provided by contemporary studies on the nourishment of infants. These make it perfectly clear that the lack of proper food in the first months of a child's life can severely limit its later mental development.

It is therefore not nature (alone) that produces mental differences and differences in human aptitudes; it is rather the fact of there being rich and poor, that is, existing social structures, that produce limitations in the nature which God created. In other words, the poor are not poor because they lack intelligence; on the contrary, they lack intelligence because of their poverty. This is why they are forced to face the labors and difficulties of life under disadvantageous conditions, as compared with those who are born in economic comfort and can benefit from these advantages from the outset.

3. Conversion of the Person

In full agreement with a Christian conception of the person's freedom and responsibility, the church in its social teaching emphasizes the point that the social problem must be attacked from within the heart of the human person. It is just human beings that create just structures. Leo XIII cherished the hope that a Christian education of the consciences of both workers and employers would make clear the demands inherent in duties and rights,

> by reminding each class of its duties to the other, and especially of the obligations of justice. Thus Religion teaches the laboring man and the artisan to carry out honestly and fairly all equitable agreements freely entered into; never to injure the property, nor to outrage the person, of an employer; never to resort to violence in defending their own cause, nor to engage in riot and disorder; and to have nothing to do with men of evil principles, who work upon the people with artful promises. . . . Religion teaches the wealthy owner and the employer that their work-people are not to be accounted their bondsmen; that in every man they must respect his dignity and worth as a man . . . ; that it is sinful and inhuman to treat men like chattels to make money by, or look upon them merely as so

much muscle or physical power. Again, therefore, the Church teaches that . . . the employer is bound to see that the worker has time for his religious duties. . . . Furthermore, the employer must never tax his work-people beyond their strength. . . . His great and principal duty is to give every one a fair wage. Doubtless, before deciding whether wages are adequate, many things have to be considered; but wealthy owners and all masters of labor should be mindful of this—that to exercise pressure upon the indigent and the destitute for the sake of gain, and to gather one's profit out of the need of another, is condemned by all laws, human and divine. To defraud any one of wages that are his due is a crime which cries to the avenging anger of Heaven [see James 5:4]. . . . His [the worker's] slender means should in proportion to their scantiness be accounted sacred [RN 14].

In this area Christianity has its own vision, which refuses to accept the notion that human conduct is the almost mechanical result of psychological drives and social, economic, and political structures. It holds rather that individual human beings are always responsible for their own destiny, their human development, and their salvation (see PP 15).

Puebla rightly calls attention to the extrapolation of scientific knowledge. This knowledge, which is legitimate insofar as it helps to explain human conduct, becomes inadmissible when it turns into a "cognitive imperialism," that is, when it claims to provide the only valid knowledge of the person and to exclude other forms of knowledge such as philosophy and theology.

On the other hand, to identify the Christian position with an idealistic moralism and to believe that the world will take care of itself provided we determine in our hearts that it shall be so is to succumb to another kind of undue extrapolation. The world can only be changed if we pay heed to the objective laws governing it, which have to be known, and to the forces and dynamisms at work in society (and not simply to those of individual psychology), which have to be given direction. For this reason it should come as no surprise that the church in its social teaching should adopt a position on this matter (this represents the fourth of the levels of response to which I referred earlier).

4. Social Mechanisms for the Transformation of Structures

The magisterium recognizes that it is suitable and even necessary for workers to form associations which can take the place of the ancient guilds. Social conflict will not be resolved solely by the conversion of individual persons. Rather an expression of this conversion is, in the case of the worker, solidarity with other workers through organizations, and, in the case of the employer, a respect for the rights and just demands of such organizations. *Rerum novarum* 34 asserts that workers have a full right to form such organizations. Pius XI emphasizes the importance of leaders of the workers:

No less praise must be accorded to the leaders of workers' organizations who disregarding their own personal advantage and concerned solely about the good of their fellow members, are striving prudently to harmonize the just demands of their members with the prosperity of their whole occupation and also to promote these demands, and who do not let themselves be deterred from so noble a service by any obstacle or suspicion [QA 140].

This teaching was repeated by John XXIII; he says that workers have "the right to act freely and on their own initiative within the above-mentioned associations, without hindrance and as their needs dictate" (MM 22).

Vatican Council II in its turn formulated the basic right of workers to organize freely:

Among the fundamental rights of the individual must be reckoned the right of workers to form themselves into associations which truly represent them and are able to cooperate in organizing economic life properly, and the right to play their part in the activities of such organizations without risk of reprisal [GS·68].

The reason the church felt it necessary to assert such a right is suggested by the situation which Pius XI described forty years ago:

At that time [the time of Leo XIII] in many nations those at the helm of State, plainly imbued with Liberalism, were showing little favor to workers' associations of this type; nay, rather they openly opposed them, and while going out of their way to recognize similar organizations of other classes and show favor to them, they were with criminal injustice denying the natural right to form associations to those who needed it most to defend themselves from ill treatment at the hands of the powerful [QA 30].

In certain social and economic contexts the development of the trade unions brought, in addition to the satisfaction of the direct claims made, other gains in the economic and political fields. John XXIII recognizes the truth of this (at least in the developed countries):

As is evident to all, in our day associations of workers have become widespread, and for the most part have been given legal status within individual countries and even across national boundaries. These bodies no longer recruit workers for purposes of strife, but rather for pursuing a common aim. And this is achieved especially by collective bargaining between associations of workers and those of management. But it should be emphasized how necessary, or at least very appropriate, it is to give workers an opportunity to exert influence outside the limits of the individual productive unit, and indeed within all ranks of the common-wealth [MM 97].

The same pope wrote more recently in his encyclical *Pacem in terris*:

We note that the working classes have gradually gained ground in economic and public affairs. They began by claiming their rights in the socio-economic sphere. They extended their action then to claims on the political level. And, finally, they applied themselves to the acquisition of the benefits of a more refined culture. Today, therefore, workers all over the world bluntly refuse ever to be treated as if they were irrational objects without freedom, to be used at the arbitrary disposition of others. They insist that they be regarded as men with a share in every sector of human society: in the socio-economic sphere and in public life and in the fields of learning and culture [PT 40].

In its defense of the rights of workers, the magisterium of the church has not excluded even recourse to social pressures, for it recognizes the fact that in some situations fine words alone do not settle conflicts:

In the event of economic-social disputes all should strive to arrive at peaceful settlements. The first step is to engage in sincere discussion between all sides; but the strike remains even in the circumstances of today a necessary (although an ultimate) means for the defense of workers' rights and the satisfaction of their lawful aspirations. As soon as possible, however, avenues should be explored to resume negotiations and effect reconciliation [GS 68].

Paul VI, too, has explicitly recognized the right to unionize and to strike. In an address to workers on May 22, 1966, in celebration of the seventy-fifth anniversary of *Rerum novarum*, the pope said: "The Church recognized the right to organize into unions. It defended and promoted this right, overcoming a certain theoretical and historical preference for corporative forms and mixed associations."[2]

Precisely because the working class ought to have some social power, Paul VI can speak in *Octogesima adveniens* of the responsible use of such power, especially in regard to strikes:

The important role of union organizations must be admitted: their object is the representation of the various categories of workers, their lawful collaboration in the economic advance of society, and the development of the sense of their responsibility for the realization of the common good. Their activity, however, is not without its difficulties. Here and there the temptation can arise of profiting from a position of force to impose, particularly by strikes—the right to which as a final means of defence remains certainly recognized—conditions which are too burdensome for the overall economy and for the social body, or to obtain in this way demands of a directly political nature. When it is a question of public services, required for the life of an entire nation, it is necessary to be able to assess the limit beyond which the harm caused to society becomes inadmissible [OA 14].

Puebla likewise defends the rights of workers (DP 1163). It recognizes that in a world which is in process of becoming urbanized and industrialized workers play an increasingly important role and have a right freely to create organizations for defending themselves, advancing their interests, and contributing to the common good (DP 1244). The church itself, uniting in a single act of option for the poor, has communicated both the faith and the requirements of justice; as a result, the poor, encouraged by the church, have begun to organize in order to live their faith in an integral way and to claim their rights (DP 1137). It is supremely important that these rights be publicly proclaimed and defended, especially at a time of deterioration in the public sphere (DP 46) and, above all, at a time when unions are being suppressed. In many places labor law is applied in an arbitrary way or simply left out of account. Especially in countries whose regimes are based on force, governments look askance at organizations of workers, peasants, and the common people and take repressive measures to hinder them. The same kind of control and limitation on action is not applied to employer groups which are able to exercise their full power to secure their interests (DP 44). Thus the very situation which Pius XI denounced in *Quadragesimo anno* 30 seems to be recurring.

The encyclical *Laborem exercens* may be described as the Magna Carta of solidarity with and among workers. The pope forcefully emphasizes the ethical character of just social protest against work being degraded to a place within a purely economic and materialistic vision of reality. When solidarity is understood as part of a struggle for justice it embodies an ethical vision of reality as unencumbered by the selfish defense of the rights of capital.

I have described four levels of perception, on the part of the church, of the fact of class struggle. From them we may conclude that there is an awareness of the fact and of its seriousness and causes, and also that ways of active response have been shown. Perhaps the original contribution of Christianity is to combine the last three of the levels into a single explanation without succumbing to one-sided views. The conflict in society is produced by *unjust structures* (4) which make it possible for *selfish individuals* (3) to abuse certain *aptitudes* (2) that in God's plan are meant as means of serving others and not of exploiting them.

THE METHOD OR STRATEGY OF CLASS STRUGGLE

Just as in dealing with POMP a distinction had to be made on the basis of content between the POMP defended in the church's social teaching and the

POMP practiced and made a rule of life by liberal capitalism in Latin America, so now in dealing with class struggle we must make a careful distinction between the (Marxist) method of class struggle, of which I shall now be speaking, and the fact of class struggle (produced by capitalism), of which I spoke in the preceding section of this chapter. The magisterium has admitted the fact of class struggle, without taking refuge in the capitalist form of diversion; but it also rejects a program of structural sub-version and proposes instead a journey of con-version that begins in the person and leads out into a world that needs to be transformed. For this reason, the church has had not only to accept the fact of struggle but also to analyze its nature and causes. The church's response has taken shape on the three levels already described: rejection of every form of discrimination, consciousness-raising and motivation of personal conversion, and support of organizations formed by workers to defend their legitimate rights. These three levels are already implicitly a way of active and constructive response which I would like now to describe more fully by comparing it with other social strategies.

In discussing this sensitive subject we must be clear in our own minds that the church does not condemn the struggle or effort of workers to secure justice and their rights, but that it does condemn a method, namely, violence, and a motivation, namely, hatred, which can be adopted in the struggle. Pius XI, for example, writes as follows:

> If the class struggle abstains from enmities and mutual hatred, it gradually changes into an honest discussion of differences founded on a desire for justice, and if this is not that blessed social peace which we all seek, it can and ought to be the point of departure from which to move forward to the mutual cooperation of the Industries and Professions [QA 114].

The reasons traditionally given by the church for refusing the method of class struggle as a strategy derived from the materialist philosophy and dialectic of Marxism are basically two:

1. Christianity cannot accept hatred as a motivation, since it is intrinsically opposed to the Lord's commandment that we love even our enemies.

2. A Christian cannot agree to the use of violence as supposedly the only possible and appropriate method for changing society. "Class struggle raised to a system harms and hinders social peace," said Paul VI in his address of May 22, 1966.[3]

No to Hatred as a Motive

What is hatred? It is a reaction of human "nature" when the latter is threatened, wounded, or offended. It is an almost instinctive movement that seeks to identify aggressors and then to take vengeance on them. As a psychosocial dynamism it has great power to bind persons together; as a personal psychological motive, it has incredible power to numb all humane feeling.

Hatred of an enemy can unite the citizens of an entire nation with one another in forgetfulness of the differences between them; hatred has caused the most cruel and barbaric tortures and murders. However—and this we must emphasize—hatred never proceeds from human freedom and the sphere of what is authentically personal, but rather from the nonfree and instinctive "nature" of the human being. Individuals can, of course, freely consent to and support the unleashed fury of instinct, but in so doing they abdicate their responsibility as persons to exercise control over their instincts and passions.

The "law of talion" in the Old Testament ("an eye for an eye, a tooth for a tooth") was not, as many people believe, a law ordering vengeance; on the contrary, it was a law that prohibited excessive vengeance and limited the response to the level of the original offense.

The gospel precept of reconciliation and forgiveness goes much further:

> You have heard that it was said, "An eye for an eye and a tooth for a tooth." But I say to you, Do not resist one who is evil. But if any one strikes you on the right cheek, turn to him the other also; and if any one would sue you and take your coat, let him have your cloak as well; and if anyone forces you to go one mile, go with him two miles [Matt. 5:38–41].

Because a Christian has profound respect for the *person* of the other (even if that other be an offender or an enemy), a Christian forgives and looks to respond in ways that are inspired not by natural human instinct but by interior freedom. For this reason, forgiveness must never be misunderstood as cowardice, fear, or passivity. Christian forgiveness is a virtue, that is, power, control, and active movement.

The counsels of Jesus (turn the other cheek, give your cloak, go double the distance) are concerned basically with a psychological orientation of the person: one who is disposed to suffer the actual offense twice over is not moved by instinctive responses but remains free to determine in an objective fashion the best way of helping the other. Christianity is not a morality of individualistic virtues but always has its eye on the community in order to express through *fellowship* the self-offering that pleases God. "Patience" in suffering is not an act of inner wisdom or prudence calculated to avoid further aggression; it is an act of freedom on the part of the sufferer and has the power to lead the aggressor to greater freedom. When Jesus responded as he did after being struck in the face before the tribunal (John 18:22–23), he was not going against his own teaching on turning the other cheek; for the goal of that teaching was interior freedom, and it was in its light that the Lord challenged the offender and incited him (i.e., called him) to freedom.

The teaching of the gospel on forgiveness carries with it an important requirement: Those who preach it must live it, that is, suffer the condition of victim and thereby give their words the consistency proper to a witness. The doctrine of forgiveness is a difficult one which we would never have learned were it not for the example of the Master himself. To teach it without living it is to profane it. There is nothing more sublime than evangelical forgiveness communicated after the manner of Jesus; there is nothing more harmful and alienating than that same forgiveness when its messengers do not suffer privations or mistreatment or oppression or repression by the aggressors toward the poor. For one in cahoots with the powerful to preach forgiveness to the poor is to make the gospel a real opium for the people. If, then, the church bids us not be motivated by hatred, it does so in order that we may make forgiveness a way of life, and this in solidarity and communion with the sufferings of our people, and not in order that we may make the gospel an easy defense of our selfishness. When we turn it into this last, we renew the sad situation of which Pius XI spoke with sorrow and shame: "Even more, there are men who abuse religion itself, and under its name try to hide their unjust exactions in order to protect themselves from the manifestly just demands of the workers" (QA 125).

The only worthy pulpit from which to proclaim evangelical forgiveness is the cross on which the people suffer. This Christian strategy—which does not engage in a capitalist "diversion" in order to deny the suffering, nor make the suffering a reason for "subversion," but instead accepts it through a "conversion"—must be exercised in the solidarity and poverty of the church. All this is difficult to live out, though very easy to say, talk about, and write. This is one more reason to thank God for giving the Latin American church such models as Archbishop Oscar Romero, a true martyr of justice and an example to us on this difficult way.

No to Violence as a Method

I would be unfaithful to the church's teaching were I not to admit honestly that the door has never been closed in an absolute manner to violence, although the use of violence has been limited to exceptional cases and circumstances. When the Bull *Dum diversas* of June 18, 1452, encouraged King Alfonso of Portugal to "oppose Christ's enemies with arms," it did so because the pope judged violence to be licit in these circumstances. Paul VI makes a similar judgment in *Populorum progressio* 31, while clearly specifying the exceptional circumstances.

Allowing for this exception and bearing in mind that violence can never be deliberately chosen (except in the case of greater evil and after having exhausted all peaceful means), I believe the Christian conscience must look for peaceful means of effecting social change and not wait for the situation to become so bad that violence becomes inevitable. This seems to be the line taken at Puebla.

Puebla exhorts us to put all our trust in the civilization of love and its historical fruitfulness (MPLA 8). Christian liberation knows how to use evangelical means which have their own peculiar effectiveness. It does not resort to violence of any kind nor to the dialectic of class struggle, but to the vigorous energy of charity (DP 486). The bishops clearly praise those who renounce violence in demanding their rights and have recourse to methods of defense that are available even to the weakest. They use nonviolent means of re-establishing justice in sociopolitical and economic relations (see DP 522).

Consistency, too, and faithful obedience to the magisterium of the church oblige us here to accept the ultimate consequences of this course of action (see DP 562). The Latin American situation seems to place us in a dilemma:

1. If we act, our action leads to violence. This is the standard argument used by so many Christians who seek to immobilize those who long for justice and who defend the rights of the poor. These people are accused of making themselves useful tools of atheistic ideologies, and so on.

2. Or else, in the name of an evangelical value (nonviolence) we create an even more unevangelical situation: the situation of inaction. Here is an odd reversal of the parable of the Good Samaritan in which the Levite and the priest, having given their example of indifference, now try to persuade the Samaritan to let his wounded neighbor bleed to death, lest he "interfere" in a conflict from which all of them should stand aside.

Christian creativity cannot allow itself to be trapped in this dilemma of violent action or inactive nonviolence. Passivity and self-centeredness are contradictions of the gospel, and God will require an account from us for the people who are forced to suffer due to our passivity, as well as for those who, driven by our passive attitude, ended up convincing themselves that the only way of bringing justice to the poor was the way of violence.

The way of "nonviolent action for justice" is not an easy one. To be effective (and all action seeks to be effective) it must follow a carefully outlined program and be carried out with a total discipline, this last being all the more necessary because an attempt will be made to depict it as in fact violent action, so that it can then be eliminated by force. To this end it must be preceded by a rigorously methodical analysis of society and by training in "nonviolent action." In addition, it requires for maximal effectiveness that it be truly an action of the entire church (see DP 562) which, in profound communion with its pastors, asks of them—and in accordance with the church's social teaching, we may even say: demands of them—that they go before the rest of us with their example, consistent with Medellín and Puebla. A deep sadness would settle on Christian communities if in a matter so central to the gospel pastors were to allow a false prudence to keep them from legitimate action that uses legitimate means in the face of unjustly violated rights, action indeed which they themselves have approved and designated as a Christian response (see DP 533).

There is a special reason why this kind of Christian response is urgent. In Latin America our religious language is shot through with ambiguity, for rich and poor alike claim to be Christians, yet some in the name of their faith demand their unjustly violated rights, while others invoke the faith in order to preserve the structure which violates so many rights and produces such an abyssal difference in the form of an ever-widening gap. At a time when it is unclear what following Jesus Christ means, inasmuch as the oppressed poor follow him and seek liberation on the basis of their faith, while the rich oppressor likewise claims to be following him but is unwilling to change the unjust situation, the church cannot afford the response of complicitous silence. In Latin America there is persecution—real religious persecution—that is being carried on, not, however, by atheists but by selfish Christians who are not responsive to the social teaching of the church. Pastors like Archbishop Romero are murdered for defending the poor, just as six priests of his diocese had already been murdered.

The ambiguity attaching to the following of Jesus can be removed only in the light of the gospel. The situation is such that only a return to the purest sources of the faith can bring the light needed for Christian responses. Our peoples demand of Christians, and especially of their own pastors, the clear and unambiguous witness that consists in giving one's life to defend the poor and oppressed along with their right to organize and achieve justice—to do this by evangelical means, yes, but to do it also by truly active means.

A no to hatred as a motive and a no to violence as a method mean a yes to the gospel call for reconciliation and love. This yes proves its sincerity, however, only if those who speak it suffer with the poor and act in solidarity with them for the attainment of justice. Apart from this twofold commitment, reconciliation and the rejection of violence are worlds apart from the spirit of the gospel. The words of Jesus Christ are indeed repeated, but there is no imitation of him.

Let us believe in the fruitfulness of the gospel. But let us also for that very reason live it in the most radical way possible.

10

IDEOLOGIES

The preceding two chapters have brought to light two key points in the Latin American problematic: POMP and the class struggle. Under both headings we have seen the Christian positions taught by the magisterium and how these differ from capitalist POMP and the Marxist class struggle. But when capitalism and Marxism speak to these two points, they bring to bear broader visions of society, visions to be described as ideologies. In the present chapter I shall discuss the subject of ideologies, especially as it is treated in the Puebla documents. Such a study will then allow us to deal in the next and final chapter with the scope of politics.

The gospel is not an ideology because it is, above all, the proclamation of a salvific *event* which has already taken place and continues to take place. Moreover, instead of providing a defense or justification—as ideologies do—of the interests of groups or individuals, this event criticizes and challenges all interests. The gospel finds acceptance only by way of a conversion, and such a conversion is already, in a way, a deideologization, a questioning of one's own securities and positions as these are challenged by the Other who enters into our lives as something new.

The social teaching of the church serves as a mediation which enables the gospel to stand in judgment on ideologies, for in this teaching the evangelical project (which is fundamental, but does not take the form of a specific model for all places and times) confronts the data of each historical moment, and an effort is made to discover the directives for action in this situation that seem to flow from the project. Hence the necessity of defending this social doctrine against efforts to manipulate it in the service of one or other ideology.

THE IDEOLOGY THEME BEFORE PUEBLA

"Ideology" made its appearance as a word and as a problem in the modern age. The term is said to have been coined by A. Destutt de Tracy who offered it as a key to the understanding of human beings, that is, to the science of ideas.

Napoleon despised the ideologists as charlatans, but this was because they accused him of having destroyed the political program of the French Revolution, while at the same time they called for educational reforms. It can be said that at that time the ideologists gave expression to a bourgeois and liberal movement which aimed at putting an end to Napoleon's absolutist regime. Napoleon for his part saw in religion a means of legitimating his own authority; he used ideology as a justification.

An ideology may be defined as a complex of ideas which are regarded as true, not because of their internal meaning but because of the practical interests which they defend and protect. But special interests are often the cause of distortion in our perception of reality. Alongside this pejorative concept of ideology we may set this other one suggested by Karl Mannheim: ideology is a universal aspect of knowledge (sociology of knowledge) and therefore calls for the constant application of ideological suspicion as a means of correcting our spontaneous way of looking at things.

The problem of ideologies has made its appearance only gradually in the social teaching of the church. True enough, from its very beginnings this social teaching has been involved in ideological confrontation with liberal capitalism and socialist collectivism, but only starting with *Mater et magistra* do we find remarks on ideology as such.

Ideologies in *Mater et Magistra*

The subject is discussed in the fourth part of the encyclical, after the pope has recalled, in the first part, the benefits of the church's social teaching and after he has given an account of earlier teaching in the second part and considered more recent problems in the third part. John XXIII looks at ideologies from the standpoint of those orientations and norms that seek to establish a balance between human relationships and new scientific and technological advances.

Without trying to define ideologies, the pope refers to the disappearance of many of them and suggests the reason for this: they do not "encompass man, whole and entire. . . . They fail to take into account the weakness of human nature, such as sickness and suffering: weaknesses that no economic or social system, no matter how advanced, can completely eliminate" (MM 213).

Over against these ideologies, which present a distorted picture of humankind, the pope sets the church's social teaching, the cardinal point of which is that individual persons are the foundation, cause, and end of all social institutions (MM 219). From this principle are derived social teachings (MM 220) which form a whole that is inseparable from what the church teaches about human life (MM 222). But this theory or teaching is not meant to be simply a collection of theoretical statements. The pope claims that the teaching is "for all time valid" (MM 218), although he acknowledges that the passage from theory to practice is rendered laborious by selfishness, materialism and, above all, the difficulty of determining the demands of justice in a given concrete situation (MM 229). He offers as a practical method for effecting this transition a three-step process: "observe, judge, act" (MM 236). This statement represents an authoritative recognition, at the highest level, of the pedagogy used in the worker movements (the Jocists and others); it also offers a structure for theological reflection that will prove its value in subsequent Latin American thinking at Medellín and Puebla.

Ideologies in *Pacem in Terris*

Pacem in terris 159 plays an extraordinarily important role in discernment with regard to socialism, as practiced, for example, by Paul VI in *Octogesima adveniens* 31. After saying in 158 that a careful distinction must be made between error and the person who errs, John XXIII goes on to make a distinction between, on the one hand, false philosophical theories about the nature, origin, and end of humankind and the world and, on the other, economic, social, cultural, or political movements, even if these have their origin and inspiration in such philosophical theories. The reason is that while a doctrine remains unchanged once it has been developed and defined, the movements necessarily undergo continual change (PT 159). Therefore, the pope adds, contacts which in the past seemed useless may today prove profitable (PT 160).

The concept of ideology may refer to either of the two levels distinguished by John XXIII. As a philosophy, an ideology is static and therefore deserves to be rejected insofar as it is in error regarding the nature and historical destiny of humankind. This way of understanding ideology is more in accord with the thinking expressed in the earlier parts of the encyclical.

But an ideology can also be understood as a coherent body of ideas that accompanies a concrete historical movement and endeavors to explain and justify the why and how of changes. An ideology thus understood (and this sense of the word is perhaps closer to the modern concept of ideology) does not claim to be a complete explanation of a philosophical kind but a more immediate and limited explanation of social activity. If ideology is understood in this sense, it is possible to accept it while always maintaining a critical attitude toward it.

Ideologies in *Gaudium et Spes*

In *Gaudium et spes,* 7 and 19–21, ideologies are again considered as metaphysical and philosophical statements, especially in the context of the problem of God. In general, the more specific problem of ideology as a political and social phenomenon is not raised in *Gaudium et spes*, apart from a few allusions in 12–22 where the subject is the dignity of the human person, and in 73. The criticism has been made that the treatment of the political problem in *Gaudium et spes* is skimpy and certainly inadequate for such a complicated and difficult subject.[1] The short shrift given to ideologies is perhaps indicative of the skimpiness.

Ideologies in *Populorum Progressio*

Paul VI understood by ideology a philosophy or doctrine that offers a complete explanation of human life and a guide for action. Every action implies some doctrine (PP 39). The church has a vision of development (PP 14) which enables it to pass judgment on other visions incompatible with the faith. A Christian cannot accept a materialistic and atheistic doctrine or philosophy that respects neither the orientation of life to its ultimate end nor the freedom and dignity of humankind (PP 39). Paul VI also criticizes the ideological principles of the liberal capitalist system: profit as the key motive, a private ownership of the means of production that accepts no social limitations, and so on. Nonetheless the pope defends the thesis that, providing the basic values a Christian must defend are safeguarded, a pluralism of professional organizations and trade unions is permissible. Such organizations usually manifest a more direct and concrete ideological imprint that sometimes prescinds from any properly philosophical vision and makes no claim to explain the whole of human life and even its trandscendent destiny, but instead is meant to unify the action of its members for the sake of immediate and concrete goals.

Ideologies in *Octogesima Adveniens*

It is in *Octogesima adveniens* 25–37 that we find the most explicit statement of the magisterium on ideologies and the one that supplies the most guidance.

The pope says that all political action, unless it is content to advance blindly, must be based on a plan for society. Since historical movements or trends also need to determine the objectives of their action and for this purpose need some ideological reference point, we may consider two possible levels of ideology. One of these pertains to "ultimate convictions on the nature, origin, and end of man and society" (OA 25).

In order to avoid confusion and make possible a better reading of *Octogesima adveniens* as well as to enable us to refer to the problem earlier hinted at in *Populorum progressio* 39 and *Pacem in terris* 159, I suggest that we make use of two analogous (and not equivocal) concepts of ideology. The first I shall call Ideology 1 (I-1): ideology as a philosophy, a doctrine, a system of thought, a global vision of humankind and its destiny, or, in other words, the "ultimate convictions" referred to a moment ago.

The second concept is Ideology 2 (I-2): the consensus needed by every human group and every historical movement that seeks to act in the social, political, or economic field. An ideology of this second kind does not necessarily raise the ultimate human questions but seeks rather to be a bond of unity for action in a concrete political movement.

It is possible to distinguish four levels of problems in *Octogesima adveniens:* (1) the function of ideologies; (2) the subject who develops ideologies; (3) the relation between Christian faith and ideologies; and (4) the ambiguity of ideologies.

The statement of Paul VI that all political action is based on a plan for society can apply to both I-1 and I-2. The same holds for his remark about the connection between means and aspirations. On the other hand, the statement that an ideology is a plan for society that gives expression to a comprehensive view of the human vocation can apply only to I-1.

If we are speaking, then, of this global plan for society that asserts and translates into social terms the essential values of a people, it is clear that, as the pope says, it is neither the state nor political parties that develop it and impose it on a people. The active subjects in this case are rather cultural and religious groups that live and give expression to these basic values. It is the function of these groups to develop a plan for society within the social body of which they are a part, and to do so in a disinterested manner with the sole aim of expressing the feeling of the people, and in ways proper to them, ways, namely, of communion and the defense of values.

On the other hand, there is no reason why states and political parties cannot impose a more direct and limited ideological stamp on their own activity, although clearly it may not contradict the plan for society which the people wants. In this case we are dealing with I-2.

The distinctions already made enable us to understand better the thinking of John XXIII and Paul VI on the possibility or impossibility of accepting ideological systems and historical movements. We ought to take very much to heart the clear statement that Christians who reflect on their faith and want to live it in an authentic manner cannot adhere to ideological systems (whether socialist or liberal) which radically or substantially go against the Christian faith and concept of life (OA 26). It must be emphasized that at the I-1 level both types of systems must elicit serious objections from a Christian conscience. Not only the Marxist ideology but the liberal as well—and I mean the system itself and not simply the abuses of it (which might be corrected)—call for great caution.

We pass, however, to another and clearly distinct concept of ideology when we pass to the level of historical movements to which Christians may give their allegiance even though those movements were born of ideologies in the previous sense. If the movements are really to be forms of political action, they must be based on a plan for society, but the plan now refers to immediate issues, to questions debated in a particular set of circumstances, and need not imply a global vision of humankind and its destiny, especially its transcendent destiny. In speaking of such movements, then, we are dealing with I-2.

Christianity gives us the elements of a conception of humankind and society that enables us to exercise discernment with regard to I-1 and that also makes it possible—once a judgement on I-1 has been made, and to the extent that a given I-2 is not so closely bound up with an unacceptable I-1 as to be out of bounds for a Christian—to offer guidance to believers with regard to their concrete commitments. As a matter of fact, when the bishops urge political action within the two systems, the socialist and the capitalist, now existing on the Latin American continent, they urge it to the extent that adherence to I-2 does not make it necessary for a Christian to accept unconditionally the I-1 of the system.

Paul VI is strongly critical of the possible instrumentalization of an ideology in the service of action (OA 27–28). Truth should be the goal of thinking, and it is on the basis of truth that a plan for humankind should be based, especially at level I-1. In the political sphere, on the other hand, where the aim must be what is possible, thinking should supply strategy and tactics for action through the development of an I-2. Thought that takes a critical approach will always be able to evaluate action rather than simply to justify it at any cost, even when it proves inhuman.

Here is where the Christian faith offers us considerable help in both our thinking and our action. Faith, too, pays heed to thought, but the thought in this case is that of God: God's project, God's plan of salvation. This project challenges all our human projects; it urges us to critical honesty in our thinking.

It is worth our pointing out these distinctions, since even Puebla continues to show a certain lack of semantic precision when it speaks of "secularism" as an ideology (DP 434, 83). This statement is correct if ideology is understood as I-1, but not when it is taken as I-2, that is, as representing the interests of social groups, as is clear from the definitions given in the Puebla documents themselves. Puebla understands secularism rather as a global vision of society and humankind.[2]

The Ideology Theme in *Laborem Exercens*

In surveying the universal magisterium of the church, as I have been up to now, I must include the ideology theme as treated in *Laborem exercens,* although this comes later than the Puebla document. Obviously, it is not possible to claim that the teaching of this more recent document is included at Puebla; on the other hand, *Laborem exercens* complements the spirit of Puebla.

It is very clear to John Paul II that even in dealing with important ideological conflicts we must not forget that they spring from other more real and basic conflicts. There is a danger of forgetting the situation that gave rise to an ideology and condemning the latter without seeing why it came into existence in the first place. Now, as far as Puebla is concerned, it has a great deal to say about ideologies, but it is only right to point out that it is also unsparing in its prophetic condemnations of injustice, as I have made abundantly clear in these pages.

Laborem exercens, then, confirms the action of the church on two levels: by denouncing injustices that are violations of the Kingdom, and by issuing warnings with regard to problematical ideologies. The same two-level ecclesial action also characterizes Puebla.

THE IDEOLOGY THEME AT PUEBLA

The Experience of Ideologies

According to the bishops at Puebla, Latin America "is tempted by anti-Christian ideologies and coveted by extremist leaders and power centers" (DP

864). Ideologies make their way in especially at centers for the transmission of culture and values. "The ideologies that are in vogue know that universities are an ideal place for them to infiltrate and to gain control over culture and society" (DP 1053). For this reason the bishops state specifically:

> We discern ideological influences in the way that education, even Christian education, is conceived. One conception is utilitarian and individualistic. It views education simply as a means to ensure oneself a good future, an investment in tomorrow. Another view seeks to turn eduction into a tool, not for individualistic ends but for the benefit of a certain kind of sociopolitical project, be it statist or collectivist [DP 1021].

Ideologies attract the young especially, because they are anxious to find a meaning for the world they are to build (see DP 1170).

The Definition of Ideology

The bishops provide a definition of ideology (see DP 535). In the statements made we can distinguish several aspects:

1. An ideology is "any conception that offers a view of the various aspects of life." Included here are concepts, ideas, slogans, characteristic expressions, norms. As an explanatory vision of things an ideology seeks to appear rational and logical.

2. But it is a view "from the standpoint of a specific group in society." By these "groups in society" we are to understand, in the last analysis, the classes in a society. Professional groups may produce specialized forms of ideologies, but these do not claim to explain the whole of life in society. There is no "ideology" for doctors or for engineers. There is, however, such a thing as a bourgeois or proletarian ideology.

These two characteristics make up the constitutive structure of any vision of society, for society will always be seen from the standpoint of a particular group within it. The social location of thought is a fact already demonstrated by the sociology of knowledge.

3. An ideology is a vision of society's life from the standpoint of a particular group, and it expresses the aspirations, justifications, values, and interests of this group. At this point we confront another real fact: the vision in question is not a disinterested one, but a view of society freighted with the value judgments, experiences, and utopian longings of the group.

4. Since an ideology gives expression to interests, values, aspirations, and experiences, it is not reducible to a set of concepts. Rather it incites to action; it calls for solidarity and for the transformation of society as a means of realizing the aspirations. In an ideology, then, ideas are valued not for their truth but for their effectiveness.

The four characteristics thus far described do not require a negative judgment on ideologies, not even insofar as these defend the interests of a group.

The bishops point out that an ideology may be legitimately used to defend interests when the defense is legitimate and respects the rights of other groups.

Insofar as they are mediating factors leading to action, ideologies play a necessary and indeed inevitable part in social life. Without an ideology no human group, party, or movement would be able to act effectively.

Nevertheless, ideologies are ambiguous things. The bishops express reservations on three points:

1. The tendency of an ideology to become "an ultimate explanation of everything." When it yields to this tendency, an ideology excludes every other contribution from reason and rejects all questioning; it becomes a hermeneutical prism through which all knowledge must be reflected.

2. The tendency to become an absolute. We may note two ways in which this process operates. One is to project the special interests of a group as being the complete interests of the nation, the people, and other human groups. The second is to apply the category of "religion" to an ideology, to make it an absolute in the sense that its demands become unconditional. When this happens, an ideology becomes an "idol" (DP 536), a "lay religion" (ibid.).

3. The tendency to pseudoevidentiality. That is, ideologies present themselves as obvious and natural. "Many people live and struggle in practice within the atmosphere of specific ideologies, without ever having taken cognizance of that fact" (DP 537).

The unmasking of ideologies requires that these tendencies or temptations be overcome. When the church proclaims the reign of God as the ultimate and transcendent meaning of the world, it accomplishes in regard to ideologies what it accomplishes in regard to cultures: "the critical denunciation of the various forms of idolatry, that is, of values that have been set up as idols" (DP 405). Discernment enables us to escape "ambiguity and reductionism" (DP 488).

Puebla not only offers principles of discernment but also shows how to practice it. It exercises discernment with regard to the main ideologies presently operative in Latin America.

The Discernment of Ideologies

Puebla examines three ideologies in particular: liberal capitalism, Marxist collectivism, and national security.

The Ideology of Liberal Capitalism

The ideology of liberal capitalism asserts the *value* of private property and of jealously protected individual rights. This ideology possesses a motivating power which the bishops recognize: "We acknowledge that it has given much encouragement to the creative capabilities of human freedom, and that it has been a stimulus to progress" (DP 542). Similarly, before expressing their reservations, the bishops point out that the form of the liberal capitalist ideology has varied:

> In some countries its original historical form of expression has been attenuated by necessary forms of social legislation and specific instances of government intervention. But in other countries capitalism persists in its original form, or has even retrogressed to more primitive forms with even less social sensitivity [ibid.].

In any case this ideology manifests *ambiguities* that must be pointed out. These show themselves in the "explanation" offered of social reality. In order to understand this reality and to energize progress in it, the liberal capitalist ideology "takes for granted the primacy of capital, its power, and its discriminatory utilization in the function of profit-making" (DP 550). The assignment of "priority to capital over labor, economics over the social realm" (DP 47) is therefore a deliberately chosen position, the effects of which widen the distance between the rich and the poor. This is a system that does "not regard the human being as the center of society" (DP 64); it is a form of real "individualistic materialism" (DP 55) that hinders solidarity. The ideology contains an at least implicit anthropology, and it is one the bishops do not accept:

> Operating in the service of consumer society but projecting its vision beyond it, economic liberalism and its materialistic praxis offer us an individualistic view of the human being. According to it, the dignity of human persons lies in economic efficiency and in individual freedom [DP 312].

The liberal capitalist ideology leads not only to discrimination and a wide gap between rich and poor; it also justifies and rationalizes these results. We may apply to it the following statement of Puebla:

> A variant form of this deterministic view, which is more social and fatalistic, is based on the erroneous idea that human beings are not fundamentally equal. This supposed difference gives rise to many forms of discrimination and marginalization that are incompatible with human dignity. . . . Frequently this gives rise to the situation of inequality lived by laborers, peasants, native peoples, domestic workers, and many other segments of the population [DP 309].

This ideology thus embodies a real "philosophy of 'getting to the top' and dominating others" (DP 95) that corrupts and dehumanizes the young.

The ambiguity in liberal capitalism also manifests itself in the area of what I earlier called "absolutization." I pointed out two levels at which this tendency operates: the false supposition that the interests of a minority coincide with those of the people as a whole; and the sacralization of the values of the ideology, to the point of giving these a religious dimension.

The liberal capitalist system defends private property, but it is likely to think of this in an abusive manner as "an absolute right that has no limits and carries no corresponding social obligation" (PP 26). "The illegitimate privileges stemming from the absolute right of ownership give rise to scandalous contrasts, and to a situation of dependence and oppression on both the national and international levels" (DP 542).

From this point of view the liberal ideology provides one of the clearest examples of the absolutization of the interests it defends (see DP 536), which are those of a small minority, and also of the instrumentalization of persons and institutions in the service of the effective attainment of its goals. The whole economy is governed in function of these minority interests, so that society shows a deepening split due to the widening gap between rich and poor (DP 133, 1208, 1209, 1263). This situation has not evolved by chance but in obedience to structural causes (DP 30) and to models consciously chosen and programmed (DP 50) which are justified precisely by the ideology itself (DP 47). Social structures in the economic, political, cultural, and other spheres are located in turn within a broad framework of international relations that are characterized by dependence (DP 47, 66, 312, 501, 1264).

The instrumentalization is even more serious when the manipulation extends to the religious sphere. This is the other side of ideological absolutization. We may distinguish two aspects: the absolutization of a value, which is thus turned into an idol; and the instrumentalization of the Christian sense of our people.

When wealth is turned into an absolute value, it becomes an idol (DP 185). "Earthly goods become an idol and a serious obstacle to the kingdom of God (Matt. 19:23–26) when human beings devote all their attention to possessing them or even coveting them. Then earthly goods turn into an absolute, and 'you cannot give yourself to God and money' (Luke 16:13)" (DP 493). The bishops regard this idolatry not as a remote possibility but as a present reality: "The cruel contrast between luxurious wealth and extreme poverty, which is so visible throughout our continent and which is further aggravated by the corruption that often invades public and professional life, shows the great extent to which our nations are dominated by the idol of wealth" (DP 494).

To worship money as a god is to fall into idolatry. It is even worse, however, to worship money under the cloak of Christianity. Here once again is an example of the instrumentalization of persons and institutions as a means of attaining goals dictated by an ideology.

The idea of the church being turned into an instrument of the liberal ideology is expressly formulated by Puebla. The passage worth citing:

> In propounding an absolutized view of the human being to which everything, including human thought, is subordinated, ideologies and parties try to use the Church or deprive it of its legitimate independence. This manipulation of the Church, always a risk in political life, may derive from Christians themselves, and even from priests and religious, when they proclaim a Gospel devoid of economic, social, cultural, and political

implications. In practice this mutilation comes down to a kind of complicity with the established order, however unwitting [DP 558].

The instrumentalization of the faith that is practiced by the liberal ideology is artful and very dangerous because it corrupts religious life at its root. The bishops recall that "many have shown a faith with little strength to overcome their egotism, their individualism, and their greedy hold on riches. They have acted unjustly and injured the unity of society and the Church itself" (DP 966). This removal of the dimension of solidarity from the faith is typical of the reductionism practiced by the liberal ideology and by the economic anthropology behind it:

> Closed off in themselves and often locked into a religious notion of individual salvation, people of this view are blind to the demands of social justice and place themselves in the service of the international imperialism of money. Associated with them in this service are many rulers, who forget their obligations to the common good [DP 312].

The church offers us a correct interpretation of the gospel. The bishops write:

> Confronted with the realities that are part of our lives today, we must learn from the Gospel that in Latin America we cannot truly love our fellow human beings, and hence God, unless we commit ourselves on the personal level, and in many cases on the structural level as well, to serving and promoting the most dispossessed and downtrodden human groups and social classes, with all the consequences this will entail on the plane of temporal realities [DP 327].

For this reason it is understandable that Puebla should say: "The Church criticizes those who would restrict the scope of faith to personal or family life; who would exclude the professional, economic, social, and political orders as if sin, love, prayer, and pardon had no relevance in them" (DP 515).

Finally, let me recall the third tendency or temptation that betrays the ambiguity of the liberal ideology: its aspect of pseudoevidentiality. The bishops allude to this in passing when they remark that of the various views of the human person "perhaps the least conscious, but the most pervasive is the consumptionist view" which is promoted by this ideology (DP 311). Pseudoevidentiality also implies a distortion of the faith, as we have just seen.

The Ideology of Marxist Collectivism

As in judging liberal capitalism, so in judging Marxist collectivism the bishops first call attention to the positive values of this ideology, those capable of inspiring action, and then they point out its ambiguities.

The values which the Marxist ideology embodies are a concern for social justice (DP 48), the tools for analyzing and the desire for combating the injustices caused by capitalism (DP 313), an esteem of human work (in this respect it is opposed to liberal capitalism which gives capital priority over labor) (DP 543), and a critique of the fetishism or idolatry of commodities (ibid.).

These values and aspirations are powerful sources of motivation, especially for the working classes, which lack capital and the privileges capital bestows in society. Marxism thus has an obvious power to unify the workers, the young who long for justice and the transformation of society, and Christians who wish to live in solidarity with the workers and the young in opposition to the social and religious individualism that is the product of the liberal capitalist ideology.

But Marxist collectivism also has its ambiguities. The bishops link these with what I have called the three tendencies or temptations of every ideology: to provide the ultimate explanation of everything, to turn into an absolute and become an idol, and to pervade the social environment as something obvious and taken for granted.

In the area of *explanation* the bishops single out three points: the collectivist anthropology which underlies the ideology; the close connection between the ideology and an analysis not only of reality but also of every form of thought, including theology; and, finally, some particular results of this explanation.

The collectivist anthropology is characterized by its identification of the goal of human existence with the development of the material forces of production and by its giving so important a role to economic factors in social life that these factors become constitutive of consciousness and impose norms of behavior via the regulations established by those who are in charge of social, political, and economic structures (see DP 313).

Secondly, the bishops point to the close connection between the ideology and a method of analysis (they are here applying the teaching of Paul VI in *Octogesima adveniens*). They remind us, too, that this ideology can invade even the sphere of theological reflection (DP 545). It is worth noting that no parallel observation is made about a danger of having theology ideologized under the influence of the liberal ideology, although the bishops do speak in the context of liberal capitalism about an ideologization or deformation of the Christian faith (religious individualism, etc.).

Finally, Puebla is critical of certain concrete results of this ideology, in particular its principle of revolutionary violence and its utopian unrealism.

In the area of *absolutization* we find once again that a group promotes its own interests by claiming them as the interests of the entire social body. While it is true that there is no real parallelism between the interests of a minority (which are defended by capitalism) and the interests of the majorities (which Marxist collectivism claims to be defending and protecting), we must nonetheless ask whether the means taken by Marxism to defend the rights of the majorities— namely, the dictatorship of the proletariat and the absolute power of a totalitarian state (see DP 313, 544, 550)—are in fact appropriate ways of defending these rights. In other words, we must ask whether the mediation of the party and the state does not lead in its turn to a similar extension of the interests of these limited groups (even though they may intend to express the views of the majorities) and an identification of these with the interests of the people as a whole.

Absolutization does not take the form solely of an extension of group interests and an identification of these with the interests of all. It also manifests itself in pseudoreligious garb. As in the case of the liberal ideology, so here this phenomenon may take either of two forms: either the turning of an absolutized value into an idol or the instrumentalization of the faith.

The bishops point out that Marxism too turns wealth into an idol, although it is now the wealth not of individuals but of the collectivity (DP 543). As scripture reminds us, human beings used to sacrifice human lives and the rights of persons to idols. To the idol of collective wealth (the bishops say) Christian values are now being sacrificed (DP 48) and in particular the sacred value of religious freedom, with which other freedoms are connected (DP 313).

The instrumentalization of religion takes the form here of an identification of the kingdom of God (a religious category) with the building of a socialist society (a political category). This identification is understood as an unqualified one; that is, it does not permit the category of "kingdom" to keep its transcendent and ultimate character, whereby it stands in judgment on whether its historical values are validly incarnated in the socialist model.

Finally, there is also ambiguity in the area of the *pseudoevidentiality* which ideologies tend to engender. In the case of Marxism, an uncritical acceptance of its positive contributions can lead, according to the bishops, to "the total politicization of Christian existence, the disintegration of the language of faith into that of the social sciences, and the draining away of the transcendental dimension of Christian salvation" (DP 545). These developments come to seem natural and inevitable, as people fail to realize that though faith does have a political dimension, Christian existence is not limited to the political order, especially when the latter is understood as nothing but party politics. They fail to see that while Christians accept the language and aid of the social sciences, there are also languages proper to faith and theology which are essential to their lives. Finally, they fail to realize that while the historical embodiments of justice are part of the kingdom, they are not the kingdom in its entirety but only its partial, intrahistorical embodiments.

Before turning from this reflection on these two ideologies, I must point out that Puebla judges them to be "equally sinful system[s]" (DP 92).

The Ideology of National Security

The ideology of national security also contains legitimate motivating values. National security is "certainly necessary for any political organization" (DP 314). The church does not deny the necessity of the functions performed by the modern State. We are talking about a State that respects basic rights and freedoms; a State that is grounded on a broad base of popular participation involving many intermediate groups; a State that promotes autonomous development of an equitable and rapid sort, so that the life of the nation can withstand undue pressure and interference on both the domestic and international fronts; a State that is capable of adopting a position of active cooperation with the forces of integration into both the continental and the international community; and, finally, a State that avoids the abuse of monolithic power concentrated in the hands of a few [DP 541].

The bishops add that "fraternal coexistence requires a security system to inculcate respect for a social order that will permit all to carry out their mission with regard to the common good" (DP 548).

In the area of *explanation* the bishops make several points: the ambiguity in the anthropology behind the ideology of national security; the basic presupposition that war must be permanent; and the weakness of an ideology that must use force to maintain itself while at the same time it justifies clear abuses of power and violations of human rights.

The concept of humankind on which this ideology is based does not show the traits of dignity, freedom, and autonomy which the Christian tradition bestows on the person. On the contrary, "the Doctrine of National Security, understood as an absolute ideology, would not be compatible with the Christian vision of the human being as responsible for carrying out a temporal project, and with its vision of the State as the administrator of the common good" (DP 549). This ideology

enrolls the individual in unlimited service to the alleged total war against cultural, social, political, and economic strife—and thereby against the threat of communism. In the face of this permanent danger, be it real or merely possible, individual freedoms are restricted as they are in any emergency situation; and the will of the State is confused with the will of the nation. Economic development and the potential to wage war are given priority over the dire needs of the neglected masses [DP 314].

In order to explain and justify the abuses committed in the name of national security, this ideology "elaborates a repressive system, which is in line with its concept of 'permanent war' " (DP 547). It is appropriate, then, to apply here the general judgment of the bishops: "When an ideology appeals to violence, it thereby admits its own weakness and inadequacy" (DP 532). The bishops are not sparing in their description of the consequences of such ideologies, consequences that can be summed up as the anxieties of our people:

There are the anxieties based on systematic or selective repression; it is accompanied by accusations, violations of privacy, improper pressures, tortures, and exiles. There are the anxieties produced in many families by the disappearance of their loved ones, about whom they cannot get any news. There is the total insecurity bound up with arrest and detention without judicial consent. There are the anxieties felt in the face of a system of justice that has been suborned or cowed [DP 42].

The bishops go on to state, "In many instances the ideologies of National Security have helped to intensify the totalitarian or authoritarian character of governments based on the use of force, leading to the abuse of power and the violation of human rights" [DP 49].

The ideology of national security, like other ideologies, suffers from a further ambiguity: its tendency to *absolutization*. It too involves a government by elites who arrogate to themselves the right to make decisions in the name of everyone else and to impose these decisions. According to the bishops, as an ideology national security "is bound up with a specific politico-economic model with elitist and verticalist features, which suppresses the broad-based participation of the people in political decisions" (DP 547). "It puts the people under the tutelage of military and political elites, who exercise authority and power; and it leads to increased inequality in sharing the benefits of development" (DP 549).

The absolutization also has a religious dimension. When absolutized, the value of national security turns into an idol. "The totalitarian use of power is a form of idolatry; and as such, the Church completely rejects it" (DP 500). National security "presents itself as an Absolute holding sway over persons; in its name the insecurity of the individual becomes institutionalized" (DP 314). As an idol, national security demands human sacrifices: "Assassinations, disappearances, arbitrary imprisonment, acts of terrorism, kidnappings, and acts of torture throughout the continent indicate a complete lack of respect for the dignity of the human person. And some try to justify themselves in this, even going so far as to appeal to the demands of national security" (DP 1262).

As far as the instrumentalization of Christianity as a means of disguising a dehumanizing logic is concerned, it is in this ideology that the abuse shows itself most clearly, according to the bishops. "In some instances they [the ideologies of National Security] presume to justify their position with a subjective profession of Christian faith" (DP 49). "In some countries of Latin America this doctrine [of national security] justifies itself as the defender of the Christian civilization of the West" (DP 547). Very often integrist groups hope to reconstruct "a Christian culture of a medieval cast. This would be a new Christendom, in which there was an intimate alliance between civil authority and ecclesiastical authority" (DP 560).

The third tendency of every ideology, although not expressly mentioned in this context at Puebla, is nonetheless verified here again in the *pseudoevidentiality* with which national security is said to demand its sacrifices as a means of preserving Christian values. This conviction is very often found in certain circles which regret the harshness and excesses of repression, but regard these nonetheless as the lesser evil. They do not realize that Christian values can never be defended by means which directly negate these very values.

REFLECTIONS ON IDEOLOGIES

I wish to reflect further on ideologies and to prove the need of distinguishing between ideology as doctrine (I-1) and ideology as a consensus that directly motivates action (I-2).

I shall discuss four points: (1) the permanence or mutability of ideologies; (2) the need of them for political action; (3) the extent to which Christians need ideologies; (4) levels of ideologies.

1. With regard to the permanence or mutability of ideologies we find two seemingly contradictory kinds of statements in the church's social teaching. On the one hand, it is said that ideologies are fixed and immutable and that they do not change once they have been formulated. This trait distinguishes them from historical movements, which evolve (see PT 159; OA 30).

On the other hand, we read: "Many systems of thought have been developed and committed to writing: some of these already have been dissipated as mist before the sun; others have changed radically; still others now elicit less and less response from men" (MM 213).[3] In addition, it must be said that historical movements, as distinct from the doctrines from which they take their rise, need an ideology that will support them at a given point in their history; they therefore need ideologies that are flexible. The distinction between I-1 and I-2 can clarify this seeming contradiction.

2. Ideologies are needed for political action. All political action requires the support of an ideology (see PP 39), and even Puebla says: "Viewed in this positive sense, ideologies seem to be necessary for social activity, insofar as they are mediating factors leading to action" (DP 535).

I must therefore call attention to the fact that a pastoral presentation of the Puebla documents cannot limit itself to pointing out the ambiguities and dangers of ideologies, but must also show the need of them and their positive aspects. Laypersons who accept responsibility for changing structures—an activity that requires political action which is directed and supported by some ideology or other—would be very confused were the teaching church to do nothing but warn them of dangers and not provide them with stimulus and guidance for a proper use of ideologies. They might well take away the impression that since it is so difficult to escape contamination from ideologies, it is better to avoid them completely and therefore to renounce all political activity. Such a pessimistic view of political action advances the interests of those who do not want politics to be purified and who always present it as by nature Machiavellian and dirty.

3. To what extent do Christians have need of ideologies? If political action has need of ideologies and if Christians are urged to accept their responsibility for the political transformation of our society, the conclusion seems evident

that Christians too need ideologies. Nonetheless, John Paul II clearly states that the church does not need ideologies: "The Church therefore does not need to have recourse to ideological systems in order to love, defend, and collaborate in the liberation of the human being" (OAPC III, 2).

How are these opposing statements to be harmonized? One possible explanation must be rejected: that ideologies are in fact not necessary simply because the Christian or the church should not be involved in these tasks of human advancement. Such an explanation clearly contradicts the whole message of Puebla on political activity.

May we say, then, that the church does not need (other) ideologies because it has one of its own? But then we would have to ask: What is this ideology? No body of teachings within the overall compass of church teaching would be closer to an ideology than the social doctrine of the church, but the church denies precisely that this teaching is an ideology (DP 540). What is more, this social teaching is to be a norm for critical judgment on all ideologies (ibid.). It would hardly serve as a norm if like the ideologies it were itself always a reflection of the special interests of a group, according to Puebla's definition of an ideology (see DP 535).

On the other hand, we have seen that precisely at the level of ultimate convictions about humankind and its destiny the social teaching of the church asserts a vision of humankind in the light of faith and, in so doing, sets itself against other doctrines and shows them to be incompatible with faith. Here, then, the church's teaching is an I–1.

But when the social teaching is compared with an I–2, it denies that it is to be put on the same level, for it does not supply guidance for action in function of the interests of a group nor by applying technical formulas or conceptions. At this level the social teaching stands in criticism of the ideologies and of the interests they represent.

If, then, the statement of the pope is to be harmonized with the various other texts that speak to us of ideologies, I think a distinction of levels must be made.

4. In accordance with the definition given by the bishops of Puebla, we may distinguish various levels in an ideology:

a. The level of *motivation*. It is at this level that the church has no need of ideologies. The context of the statement that the church does not need ideologies makes this quite clear. For John Paul II immediately adds:

> At the center of the message of which the Church is the trustee and herald, it finds inspiration for acting in favor of brotherhood, justice, and peace; and against all forms of domination, slavery, discrimination, violence, attacks on religious liberty, and aggression against human beings and whatever attacks life [OAPC III, 2].

Faith-inspired convictions about the dignity of the human person, an attitude of faith before the presence of Christ in the needy—these are the deepest motives a Christian has for promoting justice in the world. If these motives are not enough, we can rightly say that the person's faith is weak and lacks vigor and that the existence of serious injustices in a continent which has received the faith is therefore indeed scandalous. I have already referred to this key problem of evangelization (see MPLA 2; DP 10, 15, 28, 31, 90, 281, 431).

b. The level of *conceptions of the person*. The church has its own conception of the human person and therefore already has a series of answers and explanations at this level, so that it has no need of other ideologies. On the contrary, thanks to what it has of its own, it is able to compare its teaching with other ideologies and doctrines and even point out possible incompatibilities.

c. The level of *practical action*. At this level the purpose of an ideology is to provide more detailed and concrete explanations (penultimate answers, as distinct from ultimate answers that explain the meaning of human life in transcendent terms). At this level, the church itself recognizes the difficulty of moving to action (see MM 229: the passage from theory to action; the difficulty of determining the demands of justice in each concrete case). Here is where the Christian is faced with I-2. When Paul VI offers criteria for discernment of trends already existing in the world, he is aware that Christians do not have direct, technical answers of a temporal kind which they can defend as necessarily following from the doctrine they hold or from revelation; no, the Christian must discern the concrete possibilities.

In conclusion, let me call attention to the prudence that must be exercised in judging ideologies. The church must indeed remain faithful to the truth of its teaching; but this fidelity is exercised primarily in regard to I-1. It is not possible, on the other hand, to pass a static judgment on an ideology that is in movement inasmuch as it supports changing movements. If we confuse these two levels, we may come to illegitimate conclusions: either to avoid politics or to look for a Christian ideology that will lend sacrality to technical options.

11

POLITICS

The social teaching of the church provides guidance and inspiration for the social action of Christians. Pope John Paul II has indeed strongly insisted that the church must not intervene in politics and must respect the autonomy of this area of the temporal order. In saying this he was, however, referring quite specifically to party politics and the exercise of civil power, these being areas in which the pope judged it inappropriate for those representing the church (bishops, priests, religious, pastoral agents) to play an active part.

It is not easy to draw the line between a proper presence of the church in the political order (a presence that is a consequence of its mission to evangelize this order; see DP 528) and unsuitable kinds of presence or intervention; this is especially so because the communications media, imbued as they are with the liberal capitalist ideology, describe as "political meddling" the action of the church in defense of the poor and in preaching and struggling for justice. That the pope's prohibition of partisan activity is not to be interpreted in that fashion is clear from the example of John Paul II himself in his addresses to the Indians of Oaxaca and the workers of Guadalajara and Monterrey.

Faith and politics are mutually related, for if the faith is lived in a coherent way, it will find expression in the political order as elsewhere, while politics is one of the areas in which the fruitfulness of the faith must be proved. For this reason the "evangelization of the political" is a necessary part of the proclamation of God's reign. When that which is at issue in this proclamation (assuming we have properly grasped it) is put in such political terms ("kingdom") it implies the need of moving beyond purely individual relations between God and humankind (all the more since this basic relation entails a personal conversion, which is the first requirement of the kingdom to be proclaimed). The purpose and practice of those who preach the reign of God (John the Baptist, Jesus, his disciples) is to form a community of disciples together with those who accept the invitation to enter the kingdom.

Unless the analogy between the kingdom of God and human kingdoms is unfounded (or even erroneous), it can be said that the political order is a privileged area for manifesting the historical fruitfulness of the teaching of

Jesus. Once again, a faith that does not find expression in justice is a contradiction and a scandal.

A correct judgment on the political order as a place for the epiphany of God's reign (in some of its manifestations) implies a basic theological presupposition: the unity of history. It seems appropriate therefore to start with Pope John Paul II's first explicit and formal act of teaching, the encyclical *Redemptor hominis*, and to develop those implications of his thinking which seem to point precisely in the direction of the unity of history.

The pope reminds us that through the incarnation "God himself entered human history and, as a human being, became one of its 'subjects,' one among countless others and, yet, always one who was unique" (RH 1). The salvation God offers us in the Son is not located on the periphery, or even outside, of the history of the human race; God offers it to us in the Son as one who acts in our history in order to transform it. What Christ came to accomplish is the salvation of the one and only history of the human race.

It would make no sense to link, as the pope does, the crises of our history and the person of Jesus Christ as sole solution of them, if there were in fact two parallel histories: the history of the human race and the history of salvation. If there were this separation, then the person, work, and redemptive action of Jesus would have nothing to contribute in the crises caused by the distortion of a technological progress that lacks any ethical dimension. If there were indeed parallel histories, it could be said with complete truth that human history with its successes and failures is of no interest to the history of salvation and conversion, which would be played out within the consciences of individuals as the only place where Christ is truly Lord. But such an interpretation with its exclusive focus on interiority is expressly rejected by the bishops at Puebla: "We cannot distort, factionalize, or ideologize the person of Jesus Christ . . . by restricting him, the Lord of history, to the merely private realm" (DP 178). The interesting thing about this statement is that it adds to and completes the pope's earlier statement on avoiding a distortion of the person of Jesus. The pope had mentioned only one of the possible forms of reductionism: the limiting of the person of Jesus to the realm of the political, prophetic, and revolutionary and by this reduction distorting or ideologizing him (see OAPC I, 4).

In an effort to understand the sense of Puebla's statements about politics, I want first of all to explain the problem of the political order as conceived in Christian thinking prior to Puebla.

THE PROBLEM OF THE POLITICAL ORDER IN TRADITION

The political order has been regarded as the field of human responsibility in seeking and promoting the common good. Tradition has also emphasized the importance of respecting the autonomy of the political order. These facets of Christian thought are taken over in Puebla, as is the problem of partisan political activity.

As in the case of ideologies, so here in dealing with politics the church distinguishes two levels of action which can be brought into unity by means of two seemingly contradictory undertakings: (1) to show the unqualified value of politics; and (2) to relativize politics.

If politics is the process in which are embodied options leading to justice, then political commitment is a duty the Christian owes to God and not simply to a state or a human community. When Christians make their choice of a political option in accordance with evangelical criteria and give expression therein to their response to the challenges of history, they accept not only fidelity to a political party but also a demand of faith. Their response is (also) a response to God and as such is located on the level of the absolute (see DP 321–29), since, depending on the choice made, the result will be situations of greater or lesser justice and a greater or lesser objective realization of the values of the kingdom of God. Paul is thinking along this line when he says that an obedience "in conscience" is owed to the civil authorities, although in this matter we must make the reservation that the Roman state of that time had functions different from those of modern states (e.g., to exact taxes, put down crime, and administer certain forms of justice: Paul appeals to Caesar [Acts 25:11] and demands justice when he is about to be scourged [Acts 16:37–38]).[1]

On the other hand, politics tends to make absolute claims; systems tend to justify the status quo. Politics will therefore be relativized, first of all, when it is no longer seen as the sole human activity; in other words, when emphasis is put on the fact that there are other levels of human relations at which the requirements of charity, solidarity, justice, and so on must also be lived, for instance, the family, the neighborhood, activities of work and profession. It will be relativized, secondly, when persons become aware that the response given in conscience (having, therefore, an absolute value) is neither the only possible response (pluralism) nor an unqualifiedly definitive one (but is subject to ongoing critical revision, without any effort at ideological self-justification).

If we relate these two principles (absolutization/relativization) to the age-old practice of the church in politics, we will understand, for example, that in the age of "Christendom" the church should have strongly emphasized the first but not the second principle, so that the demand was made for the embodiment of the kingdom of God in political society (absolutization), without the critical reservation that this embodiment was not the only possible one. Therefore, in that situation of "Christendom," the evangelization of the world started with the principle that the rest of the world had to be "educated" (or "civilized")—in other words, forced to accept Western culture—in order that it might then be able to accept and live Christian values. There were no critical tools available at that time for deideologizing this justification for combining the economic, political, and cultural expansion of Europe with the mission of evangelization.

When, under the influence of secularism, modern society emphasizes the autonomy of the political order (in reaction to the subordination of politics in the society of Christendom), it too is in danger of absolutizing politics (by rejecting any ethical judgment on politics) or even of relativizing it but without seeing it as a field for the expression of faith and evangelical values (privatization of faith; absence of Christian motivations and values from politics).

A correct relationship between faith and politics is based on the understanding that, in contrast to what happened in Christendom and what is happening now in secularized society, the legitimate autonomy claimed for the temporal (political) order can only be relative and not absolute. This means that in the perspective of the kingdom of God the church has something to say in the political order, inasmuch as in this order values proper to the kingdom are at stake, but that on the other hand the church may not intervene in what is properly the field of the science or art of politics.

The church provides a relativization (theologically based, this time) that is distinct from any sociological relativization (which we shall see further on). It is based on the fact that no political system can be an adequate and complete intrahistorical expression of the eschatological utopia that is the kingdom of God.

But the church also provides a motive for an absolutization of the political order, inasmuch as it forms the consciences of Christians to see the political order as a field in which the lordship of Christ over history is to be exercised, as a place where the values of the kingdom of God receive concrete historical embodiment, at least at the political level (see DP 513–14).

POLITICS ACCORDING TO PUEBLA

The teachings of Puebla on this subject can be grouped under four headings: (1) view of the political situation in Latin America; (2) mission of evangelization in politics; (3) meaning of politics; and (4) roles and functions of Christians in politics.

View of the Situation

The Latin American bishops observe that "recent years have seen a growing deterioration in the sociopolitical life of our countries" (DP 507). This deterioration is an expression of "economic and political crises, and clear symptoms of corruption and violence" (DP 508).

We must attend to other passages in the Puebla document if we are to gain a more detailed description of this deterioration. We are told that "much harm has been done to the participation of citizens in the conduct of their own affairs and destiny" (DP 46), a situation that brings frustration to one of the deepest aspirations of the Latin American people, namely, "to be truly taken into account as responsible people and subjects of history, who can freely participate in political options, labor-union choices, and the election of rulers" (DP 135).

The bishops regard the political violation of union rights as a particularly serious manifestation of political deterioration.

In many of our countries the lack of respect for human dignity also finds expression in the lack of social participation on various levels. We want to allude, in particular, to labor unionization. In many places labor legislation is either applied arbitrarily or not taken into account at all. This is particularly true in countries where the government is based on the use of force. There they look askance at the organizing efforts of laborers, peasants, and the common people, and they adopt repressive measures to prevent such organizing. But this type of control over, or limitations on, activity is not applied to employer organizations, which can exercise their full power to protect their interests [DP 44].

Another especially serious symptom is the spread of violence that is "generated and fostered by two factors: (1) what can be called institutionalized injustice in various social, political, and economic systems; and (2) ideologies that use violence as a means to win power" (DP 509).

Mission of Evangelization in the Political Order

The church claims a mission in the political order: "The Church must examine the conditions, systems, ideologies, and political life of our continent" (DP 511). There are various grounds for this duty and right: "Christianity is supposed to evangelize the whole of human life, including the political dimension" (DP 515); "The need for the Church's presence in the political arena flows from the very core of the Christian faith . . . from the lordship of Christ over the whole of life" (DP 516); "From the integral message of Christ there flows an original anthropology and theology that takes in 'the concrete personal and social life of the human being' (EN 29)" (DP 517).

In this perspective we can understand the criticism made of certain ways of living the Christian life which refuse to acknowledge the evangelizing mission of the church in the political sphere: "The Church criticizes those who would restrict the scope of faith to personal or family life; who would exclude the professional, economic, social, and political orders as if sin, love, prayer, and pardon had no relevance in them" (DP 515). There are efforts to manipulate the church which "may derive from Christians themselves, and even from priests and religious, when they proclaim a gospel devoid of economic, social, cultural, and political implications. In practice this comes down to a kind of complicity with the established order, however unwitting" (DP 558).

Meaning of the Political Order

The church esteems and accepts politics: "Far from despising political activity, the Christian faith values it and holds it in high esteem" (DP 514). The reason for this esteem is to be found in the very nature of the political order: "The political dimension is a constitutive dimension of human beings and a relevant area of human social life. It has an all-embracing aspect because its aim is the common welfare of society. But that does not mean that it exhausts the gamut of human relationships" (DP 513).

The political order by its nature enjoys a certain autonomy: "The Church acknowledges the proper autonomy of the temporal order (GS 36). This holds true for governments, parties, labor unions, and other groups in the social and political arena" (DP 519).

Puebla distinguishes two concepts of politics.

We must distinguish between two notions of politics and political involvement. First, in the broad sense politics seeks the common good on both the national and international plane. Its task is to spell out the fundamental values of every community—internal concord and external security—reconciling equality with freedom, public authority with the legitimate autonomy and participation of individual persons and groups, and national sovereignty with international coexistence and solidarity. It also defines the ethics and means of social relationships. In this broad sense politics is of interest to the Church, and hence to its pastors, who are ministers of unity. It is a way of paying worship to the one and only God by simultaneously desacralizing and consecrating the world to him (LG 34) [DP 521].

There is another and more limited concept of politics:

Second, the concrete performance of this fundamental political task is normally carried out by groups of citizens. They resolve to pursue and exercise political power in order to solve economic, political, and social problems in accordance with their own criteria or ideology. Here, then, we can talk about "party politics." Now even though the ideologies elaborated by such groups may be inspired by Christian doctrine, they can come to differing conclusions. No matter how deeply inspired in church teaching, no political party can claim the right to represent all the faithful because its concrete program can never have absolute value for all [DP 523].

Later on in the Puebla document it is said that politics includes a wide range of activities: "Among these temporal activities we cannot fail to place special emphasis on political activity. This covers a wide range of activities: from voting, becoming politically active, and exercising party leadership, to holding political offices on various levels" (DP 791).

Roles and Functions of Christians in Politics

Puebla distinguishes various roles for Christians: political militancy is reserved to the laity; and religious, priests, and bishops must avoid this type of commitment, although they should be concerned with politics insofar as the latter aims at the common good (see DP 521, 526–29). The laity should look to their pastors for enlightenment on their party commitment from the teaching of the church (DP 525). Apostolic movements for the laity should help their members to give a Christian meaning to their political commitment (DP 810). Formation for political life includes a range of activities which the church can undertake as an institution: for instance, the education the church offers in its centers of learning (DP 1012–62) or, more concretely, the advancement of marginalized groups. Therefore the following pastoral suggestions are made:

> To combine literacy training of marginal groups with educational activities that will help them to communicate effectively; to take cognizance of their rights and duties; to understand the situation in which they are living and its causes; to organize effectively in the fields of civil life, labor, politics, and government power; and hence to participate fully in the decision-making processes that affect them [DP 1045].

Evidently, these suggestions are directly concerned with formation for the exercise of political rights and duties, although there is no question of partisan indoctrination.

In order to encourage those who have made a commitment to political life, the bishops say explicitly of them:

> We affirm the nobility and dignity of involvement in an activity aimed at consolidating internal concord and external security. We encourage the sensible, intelligent activity of politicians to give the State better government, to achieve the common good, and to effectively reconcile freedom, justice, and equality in a truly participatory society [DP 1238].

REFLECTIONS ON POLITICS

The framework of faith-justice, an interpretative key supplied by Puebla, has already proved its fruitfulness by showing in what sense justice is an essential or integral part of evangelization and by giving a hermeneutical perspective for reading the social teaching of the church.

In our present Latin American context it again provides a key enabling us to perceive a certain novelty in Puebla's treatment of politics. I shall focus here on the problem of the discernment of ideologies and the real conditions for such discernment, as well as on the new concentration in the church's political practice in Latin America, namely, on the defense and advancement of human rights.

Ideologies, politics, and the church's mission of evangelization are interrelated inasmuch as the church offers criteria for the discernment of ideologies. But this task can turn into a form of retreat for the church itself, a temptation to avoid real confrontations with the actual exercise of politics. It is easier to move on the level of principles and doctrine, without adopting concrete positions that may turn out to be sources of profound conflict. I believe, however, that the Latin American church has not yielded to this temptation, at least in certain areas of political life: "Its firm defense of human rights and its committed effort to real societal improvement have brought the Church closer to the people; but it is still misunderstood in some instances, and some social groups have moved away from it" (DP 83).

But the discernment of ideologies, which is an important part of the church's service to human beings, must pay heed to the real situation in which the discernment is to be exercised in Latin America. The need in Latin America is not to guide the *manner of exercise* of the right to engage in politics through one or other ideological option; there is a prior and much more radical problem: how to secure the *possibility of the exercise* of that right. The issue is the practice of politics as such, at least as a real possibility for a genuine popular participation. It is useless to give criteria for an ideological option if there is no political room in which these ideologies may find expression in the form of concrete movements. In addition, the possibility that political experience may help to change historical movements and bring about their development (PT 159) is itself dependent on the identification of ideology and movement not being perpetuated, as it is when a movement has not been forced to revise its presuppositions as a result of challenges from the real world. Yet precisely here the point must be made that after the bishops at Puebla acknowledge (in DP 507-9) a notable deterioration in the political life of Latin America, along with clear symptoms of corruption and violence, their ensuing teaching seems to suppose a completely normal situation in which ideologies present themselves for examination and are not imposed by institutionalized violence, the claims of national security, or subversion.

But, I must add, a positive step forward is also taken at Puebla. For in addition to the teaching set forth (especially on the roles of the laity, the clergy, etc., in politics), a teaching that reflects the traditional views of the church, Puebla finds itself obliged to face up to a new task: the defense and advancement of human rights. We may say, therefore, that in Latin America the relation of the church to politics is not simply a matter of the discernment of ideologies but calls for unambiguous actions of confrontation with those in power.

Nor is this simply a matter of defending the right to the free exercise of religion on the grounds that this right creates room for evangelization. The church is claiming something more than freedom to proclaim the kingdom of God; when it explains in what the reign of God consists it is asserting that human rights are evangelical values (see OAPC III, 2 and 3) and therefore demanding respect for all the rights of the person and of all human beings. If it is a sin to violate human dignity, then the reign of God, which is a reign of grace, justice, and love, also means respect for the dignity of the human being who is a child of God. The defense of human rights represents an explication of evangelical values and of Christian teaching, but an explication that is not an abstract commentary on the nature of the person but a concrete denunciation of existing conditions, situations, and violations of human rights.

The defense of human rights is bringing with it various consequences which Latin American theological thought will have to clarify in the time ahead:

1. The (abstract) assertion of doctrine is making way for a (concrete) denunciation of injustice.

2. The (atemporal) affirmation of values is turning into a (historical) confrontation with political power as presently exercised.

3. The (traditional) position which reserves militant and partisan concrete action to the laity is being brought into question by concrete steps taken by the institutional church (actions of the hierarchy or hierarchical organizations, such as the Vicaría de Solidaridad in Chile or the Commissions for Justice and Peace which exist at least at the archdiocesan level in San Salvador, São Paulo, and elsewhere).

4. The absence of the church from the concrete political arena at the party level is being changed into a real presence there. For the church is denouncing concrete governments and accusing them not simply of an ineffective use of power (the accusation a party might make as it offered alternative formulas) but of inhumanity in the exercise of power (this is a much more radical criticism of political authority).

The preaching of human rights is a legitimate way for the church, even the church as institution, to be present in the political arena. This practice is not contradicted by the nonpartisan principles which the church offers for guidance in the political sphere. The church continues to maintain its universality and independence, but we must not think that universality is a synonym for abstract ideas. The church follows its call to serve all human beings not only when it enunciates human values in the abstract (see DP 521), but also when it denounces in concrete terms the existence of inhuman practices, without seeking to have this form of presence be realized through a particular group (see DP 523).

The existence of a political party is not the only way of achieving the concrete presence which the church needs in addition to the abstract guidance it offers regarding social values. A kind of "concrete universal" (not partisan, nor benefiting this or that power group) comes into being when the church, through its teachers, descends to particulars in order to pass judgment on facts or events that are embodiments of inhumanity, and to show that these are incompatible with what is human and Christian. The pope provides an example of this "descent" when he denounces the existence of vast estates at a time when so many families lack food. This criticism might have been made by one or other party as a way of winning the votes of the peasants for a land reform. It was neither partisan intention nor ambition for power that led the pope to point out concrete facts and situations, but rather the presence in these facts of what is inhuman and anti-Christian.

The denunciation of violations of human rights enables the church to move beyond the moralism for which it has been so severely criticized. Moralism consists in proclaiming a just society without paying heed to the necessary concrete mediations. But when the church denounces such forces as institutionalized violence (see DP 509), it helps to clarify the conditions for the possibility of social change.

The church's social teaching, properly understood, read carefully, and welcomed with personal interest, is a norm for the liberating activity of Christians in Latin America. May the place where these Christians are to be found in the process of liberation be also the place where the teaching of the church is continually read and meditated on.

ABBREVIATIONS

AIOC	Address to the Indians of Oaxaca and Chiapas. Jan. 29, 1979, Oaxaca. John Paul II
APR	Address to Priests and Religious in Mexico. Jan. 27, 1979, Basilica of Guadalupe, Mexico City. John Paul II
ARW	Address to Religious Women in Mexico City. Jan. 27, 1979, College of San Miguel. John Paul II
AWG	Address to the Workers in Guadalajara. Jan. 30, 1979. John Paul II
AWM	Address to the Workers in Monterrey. Jan. 31, 1979. John Paul II
DH	*Dignitatis humanae.* Vatican II
DP	Final Document of Puebla Conference
DS	Densinger-Schönmetzer, *Enchiridion symbolorum definitionum et declarationum*
EN	*Evangelii nuntiandi.* Paul VI
ES	*Ecclesiam suam.* Paul VI
GS	*Gaudium et spes.* Vatican II
HBG	Homily at the Basilica of Guadalupe. Jan. 27, 1979. John Paul II
HCMC	Homily at the Cathedral in Mexico City. Jan. 26, 1979. John Paul II
I–1	Ideology 1. See p. 147 for definition.
I–2	Ideology 2. See p. 147 for definition.
IP	*Il Programma.* Pius XII
LE	*Laborem exercens.* John Paul II
LG	*Lumen gentium.* Vatican II
LS	*La Solennità.* Pius XII
Med-P	Medellín Document on Peace
MH	Message to Humanity. Vatican II
MM	*Mater et magistra.* John XXIII
MPLA	Message to the Peoples of Latin America. Puebla Conference
MV	*Mirari vos.* Gregory XVI
NRPP	Natural Right of Private Property
OA	*Octogesima adveniens.* Paul VI
OAPC	Opening Address at the Puebla Conference. John Paul II
PB	*Puebla and Beyond*
PG	*Patrologia graeca* (Migne's)

PL	*Patrologiae latinae* (Migne's)
POCG	Private ownership of consumer goods
POMP	Private ownership of the means of production
PP	*Populorum progressio.* Paul VI
PT	*Pacem in terris.* John XXIII
QA	*Quadragesimo anno.* Pius XI
QC	*Quanta cura.* Pius IX
RH	*Redemptor hominis.* John Paul II
RN	*Rerum novarum.* Leo XIII
ST	*Summa theologiae.* Thomas Aquinas
TPS	*The Pope Speaks*

NOTES

CHAPTER 2

1. See J.M. Robinson, "Hermeneutic since Barth," in *The New Hermeneutic,* ed. J.M. Robinson and J.B. Cobb (New York: Harper and Row, 1964), 1–77. Cf. G. Ebeling, "Hermeneutik," in *Religion in Geschichte und Gegenwart,* ed. Kurt Calling, 3rd ed. (Tübingen: Mohr, 1959).

2. See Robinson, "Hermeneutic," 2.

3. Karl Lehmann, "Hermeneutics," *Sacramentum mundi* (New York: Herder and Herder, 1969), 3:23.

4. *Diccionario de la Biblia* (Barcelona: Herder, 1963), s.v. "hermenéutica."

5. Ibid.

6. Carlos Bravo, "Hermenéutica y método histórico-crítico," *Theologica Xaveriana* 26 (1976):28.

7. Anton Vögtle, "Qué significa la interpretación de la Escritura," in *La interpretación de la Biblia* (Barcelona: Herder, 1970), 28. (Span. trans. of *Was heisst Auslegung der Hl. Schrift* [Regensberg: Fredrich Pustet, 1966].)

8. Norbert Lohfink, *Exegésis bíblica y teología* (Salamanca: Sígueme, 1969). (Span. trans. of *Bibelauslegung im Wandel: Ein Exeget ortet seine Wissenschaft* [Frankfurt: Knecht, 1967].)

9. Carl E. Braaten, *History and Hermeneutics,* New Directions in Theology Today, No. 2 (Philadelphia: Westminster, 1974), 150.

10. Rudolf Bultmann, *Jesus and the Word*, trans. L.P. Smith and E.H. Lantero (New York: Scribner's, 1962), 152.

11. Bultmann, *Jesus*, 3.

12. Bernardus Delfgaauw, *La historia como progreso* (Buenos Aires: Lohle, 1968), 1:20. (Span. trans. of *Geschiedenis en vooruitgang,* 3 vols. [Baarn, 1961–64]).

13. Ibid., 1:144–45.

14. Bultmann, "New Testament and Theology," in *Kerygma and Myth: A Theological Debate,* ed. H.W. Bartsch, trans. R.H. Fuller (New York: Harper, 1961), 10, n. 2.

15. Dietmar Eickelschulte, "Hermenéutica y teología en Rudolf Bultmann," *Selecciones de teología* 20 (1966): 287–97.

16. René Marlé, *Introduction to Hermeneutics,* trans. E. Froment and R. Albrecht (New York: Herder and Herder, 1967), 53.

17. Edward Schillebeeckx, *God the Future of Man,* trans. N.D. Smith (New York: Sheed and Ward, 1968), 7.

18. Cited in E. Coreth, *Grundfragen der Hermeneutik: Ein philosophischer Beitrag* (Freiburg: Herder, 1969), 27.

19. Braaten, *History,* 132.

20. Wilhelm Dilthey wrote: "We explain [*erklären*] nature, we understand [*verstehen*] the life of the soul"; cited in Coreth, *Grundfragen,* 28–29, and in Robinson and Cobb, *New Hermeneutic,* 19.

21. Braaten, *History,* 133.

22. Martin Heidegger, *Being and Time*, trans. J. Macquarrie and E. Robinson (New York: Harper and Row, 1962).

23. Coreth, *Grundfragen,* 32.

24. Heidegger, *Unterwegs zur Sprache* (Pfullingen: Neske, 1960).

25. Hans-Georg Gadamer, *Truth and Method,* trans. G. Barden and J. Cumming (New York: Seabury, 1975).

26. Cf. Lehmann, "Hermeneutics," 3:25.

CHAPTER 3

1. *Amadísimos hijos* (March 11, 1951), in F. Rodriguez, ed., *Documentos sociales,* vol. 3 of *Doctrina pontificia,* Biblioteca de autores cristianos, no. 178 (Madrid: Editorial Católica 1969), 1098.

2. Modern Technology and Peace (Christmas Message, 1953), 2:181, in V. Yzermans, ed., *The Major Addresses of Pope Pius XII,* 2 vols. (St. Paul: North Central Publishing Co., 1961), 2:181.

3. *Avec une égale sollicitude* (May 7, 1949), in Rodriguez, *Documentos,* 1071.

4. *Mit dem Gefühl* (September 4, 1949), Yzermans, *Major Addresses,* 129.

5. *Conforto, letizia* (September 7, 1947), in ibid., 111.

6. *Mit dem Gefühl,* in ibid., 129.

7. Jean-Yves Calvez and Jacques Perrin, *The Church and Social Justice: The Social Teaching of the Popes from Leo XIII to Pius XII,* trans. J. R. Kirwan (Chicago: Regnery, 1961), 1–3.

8. QA 41; MM 1–5, 262; GS 42; EN 16, 60, 66; DP 4, 51, 85, 271, 272, 338, 349, 351.

9. QA 41; cf. QA 96; RN 12, 20; MM 15, 220; GS 42; DP 515, 178, 516.

10. RN 12; QA 11, 41, 138; LS 27, 28; MM 6–9, 16, 28, 42, 239.

11. RN 12; QA 41–43; MM 42; QA 96.

12. LE 5; MM 195; RN 12; QA 32.

13. QA 132, 135, 139.

14. MM 176; RH 18.

15. QA 88, 105; MM 11.

16. Puebla adopts this perspective: DP 28, 69, 70, 73, 90, 138, 186, 253, 281, 323, 349, 358, 452, 517, 793, 864, 1154, 1257, 1258.

17. QA 130, 135; MM 11.

18. RN 31; QA 101, 124–25; PP 9, 21–22, 30; RH 16; cf. DP 40–44, 47, 50, 87, 134, 1261.

19. QA 135, 144; MM 176, 208; PP 19; OAPC III, 4; PB 67; RH 15, 16; DP 55, 56, 95, 312, 314, 543.

20. Pius X, *Singulari quadam* 2; Pius XII, *Conforto, letizia,* 113; MM 222; QA 42; AWM; OAPC III, 2–7.

21. Pierre Bigo, *Doctrina social de la Iglesia* (Barcelona: ICES, 1967), 109–10.

22. Ibid., 104.

23. Gregory Baum, "The Magisterium in a Changing Church," in *Man as Man and Believer,* Concilium, no. 21 (1967), 67.

24. According to the context, "magisterium" means either teaching authority or those who possess and exercise this authority—Tr.

25. Karl Rahner, "Magisterium," *Sacramentum Mundi* (New York: Herder and Herder, 1969), 3:351, 358.

26. Franz Böckle, "Zur Krise der Autorität (Kommentar zum Buch von A. Müller)," *Wort und Weisheit* 2 (1965): 809.

27. Rahner, "Magisterium," 356.

28. This pastoral letter is cited by Rahner, ibid., 356-57.

29. J. Salaverri, in *Theologia Fundamentalis,* vol. 1 of *Sacrae theologiae summa,* Biblioteca de autores cristianos, no. 61 (Madrid: Editorial Católica, 1958), 685.

30. L. Billot, *De ecclesia Christi,* 5th ed. (Rome: Gregorian University Press, 1927), 446, cited in Salaverri.

31. Rahner, "Magisterium," 3:357-58.

32. Oswald von Nell-Breuning, *Soziallehre der Kirche: Erläuterungen der lehramtlichen Dokumente* (Vienna: Europa, 1977).

CHAPTER 5

1. Josef Blank, "Does the New Testament Provide Principles for Modern Moral Theology?" in *Understanding the Signs of the Times,* Concilium, no. 25 (1967), 10 (citing *Summa theologiae* I-II, q. 19, a. 9c).

2. Ibid.

3. Ibid., 10-11.

4. Ibid., 21.

5. Ibid., 21-22.

6. Ibid., 22.

7. Ibid., 20.

8. Ibid.

9. Franz Furger, "Prudence and Moral Change," in *The Social Message of the Gospels,* Concilium, no. 35 (1968), 119-31.

10. Theo Beemer, "The Interpretation of Moral Theology," in *Dilemmas of Tomorrow's World,* Concilium, no. 45 (1969), 148.

11. A. G. M. Van Melsen, "Natur und Moral," in *Das Naturrecht im Disput,* ed. Franz Böckle (Düsseldorf: Patmos, 1966).

12. F. X. Kaufmann, "Die Ehe in sozialanthropologischer Sicht," in Böckle, *Das Naturrecht.*

13. Wihelmus A. M. Luijpen, *Phenomenology of Natural Law,* trans. H. J. Koren (Pittsburgh: Duquesne University Press, 1967).

14. Böckle, *Das Naturrecht.*

15. The first reference is in the Council of Arles (DS 336, 341); see also DS 1375, 2148, 2149, 2302. See Gregory XVI: *Mirari vos;* Pius IX: *Qui pluribus; Syllabus* 56, 57; *Quanta cura* 2; Leo XIII: *Diuturnum* 16; *Immortale Dei* 13; *Aeterni Patris; Libertas; Rerum novarum.* For a more complete list see E. Nova, *¿Que queda del derecho natural?* (Buenos Aires and Santiago de Chile: Depalma, 1967).

16. Rom. 13:8-10; Col. 3:14; 1 Cor. 12:31f.; John 13:24; 1 John 4:7-11; James 2:9; 1 Peter 1:22.

17. Eduardo Hamel, "El cristiano de hoy frente al magisterio," *Criterio* 44 (1971): 425.

CHAPTER 6

1. Edward Schillebeeckx, *God the Future of Man,* trans. N. D. Smith (New York: Sheed and Ward, 1968), 153.

2. Ibid., 154.

3. Leonardo Boff, "Qué es hacer teología desde América Latina," in *Liberación y cautiverio: Encuentro latinoamericano de teología* (Mexico City: Organizing Committee, 1975), 129–54.

4. Justice 1; Peace 1, 5; Catechesis 7; Laity 2; Formation of the Clergy 1; Poverty of the Church 3, 7.

5. Peace 2; Family 2b; Education 3; Justice 1; Joint Pastoral Planning 1.

6. Laity 2; Justice 1, 11, 13, 16, 20; Peace 2, 5, 8, 14a, 22.

7. Justice 2; Poverty of the Church 2, 16, 19.

8. Paul VI, Address to the Participants in the 13th National Congress of the Italian Women's Center (February 12, 1966), in TPS 11 (1966), 7.

9. John XXIII, *Humanae salutis* (December 25, 1961), in TPS 7 (1961): 354.

10. Clodovis Boff, *Sinais dos tempos* (São Paulo: Loyola, 1979).

11. C. Boff, *Teologia e pratica* (Petrópolis: Vozes, 1979).

12. See, n. 7 and DP 70, 73, 186, 517, 1258.

13. Schillebeeckx, *God,* 162.

14. Ibid.

CHAPTER 8

1. LS, p. 32.

2. LS, p. 33.

3. Oswald von Nell-Breuning, *Soziallehre der Kirche* (Vienna: Europa, 1977), 43.

4. LS, p. 34.

5. LS, p. 31.

6. See Charles Avila, *Ownership: Early Christian Thinking* (Maryknoll, N.Y.: Orbis Books, 1983), 50.

7. Pierre Bigo, *Doctrina social de la Iglesia* (Barcelona: ICES, 1967).

8. José M. Díez Alegría, *Actitudes cristianas ante los problemas sociales* (Barcelona: Estela, 1973), 26–28.

9. LS, p. 33.

10. O. von Nell-Breuning, in *Stimmen der Zeit* 139 (1946–47): 426.

11. Celso Furtado, "La hegemonía de los Estados Unidos y el futuro de América Latina," in *La dominación de América Latina* (Lima: Moncloa, 1968), 61–62.

12. J. M. Díez Alegría, "La lettura del magisterio pontificio in materia sociale alla luce del suo sviluppo storico," in *Magisterio e morale* (Bologna, 1970).

13. Guillermo Múgica, *Los pobres en los Padres de la Iglesia,* 2nd ed. (Lima: CEP, 1978).

14. Clement of Rome, *First Clement* 16, in *The Apostolic Fathers,* The Fathers of the Church (New York: CIMA, 1947).

15. John Chrysostom, PG 35:864, 49:535, 55:504.

16. Polycarp, *Letter to the Philippians* 6; Hermas, 38:10; Ambrose, PL 16:148; Ignatius of Antioch, *Letter to the Smyrnaeans* 6; *Letter to Polycarp* 4.

17. Chrysostom, PG 57, 58; Theodoret, PG 83:646; Basil, PG 31:294; Ambrose, PL

17:780; 14:770; Polycarp, *Letter to the Philippians* 4; Chrysostom, PG 52:561.

18. Ambrose, PL 17:780; 14:779; Chrysostom, PG 58:761.

19. Basil, PG 29:152; Chrysostom, PG 61:94; Ambrose, PL 14:784; Chrysostom, PG 62:561; Basil, PG 29:277–78, 273, 267; Ambrose, PL 14:788, 770; Zeno, PL 11:286.

20. Clement of Alexandria, PG 8:437, 592; Basil, PG 31:323; Gregory of Nyssa, PG 44:708; Chrysostom, PG 62:563; 77:87; 62:563; Cyril of Alexandria, PG 72:816.

21. Lactantius, PL 6:598; Ambrose, PL 14:770; 16:66–67; 16:158; Augustine, PL 31:1718.

22. Basil, PG 29:261; 31:915, 928–29; Lactantius, PL 6:667; Augustine, PL 40:373.

23. Gregory of Nazianzus, PG 35:891; Chrysostom, PG 62:563; Ambrose, PL 14:767, 783; 16:63; Gregory of Nyssa, PG 44:664; Lactantius, PL 6:598.

24. *Didache* 2; Tertullian, PL 1:1372; Lactantius, PL 6:565; Basil, PG 31:276, 928–29; Gregory of Nyssa, PG 44:708; Chrysostom, PG 62:563.

25. Basil, PG 29:261; 31:267–68, 321; Gregory of Nyssa, PG 44:1251; Chrysostom, PG 48:591; 58:7–8; 77:87; Augustine, *De Trinitate,* XIII, 9 (PL 42:1045).

26. Bigo, *Doctrina,* 43.

27. Thomas Aquinas, *Summa theologiae* (hereafter ST), trans. M. Lefébre (New York: McGraw-Hill, 1975), II–II, q. 66, a. 1.

28. ST II–II, q. 66, a. 2.

29. Bigo, *Doctrina,* 57.

30. ST II–II, q. 66, a. 7.

31. Ibid.

32. F. Kluber, *Katholische Eigentumslehre* (Osnabruck: Fromm, 1968).

CHAPTER 9

1. ST II–II, q. 57, a. 3 ad 2.

2. *A voi, lavoratori* (May 22, 1966), in TPS 11 (1966), 328.

3. Ibid., 329.

CHAPTER 10

1. André Manaranche, *Existe uma ética social crista?* (São Paulo: Loyola, 1973), 122.

2. DP 83, 342, 393, 418, 433, 434, 435–36, 456, 622, 851, 1014, 1052, 1300.

3. The translation has been slightly altered here in order to accurately reflect the meaning of the original Latin.

CHAPTER 11

1. R. Mehl, *Pour une éthique sociale chrétienne,* cited in Manaranche, *Existe,* 110.

REFERENCE LIST
OF TRANSLATIONS
OF CHURCH DOCUMENTS

John Paul II. Address to the Indians of Oaxaca and Chiapas; Homily at the Basilica of Guadalupe; and Opening Address at the Puebla Conference. In *Puebla and Beyond: Documentation and Commentary*, ed. John Eagleson and Philip Scharper. Maryknoll, N.Y.: Orbis Books, 1979.

———. Address to the Workers in Monterrey; Homily at the Cathedral in Mexico City; and *Redemptor hominis*. In *The Pope Speaks* 24 (1979).

———. *Laborem exercens*. In *The Pope Speaks* 26 (1981).

John XXIII. *Mater et magistra*; and *Pacem in terris*. In *The Gospel of Peace and Justice: Catholic Social Teaching since Pope John*, ed. Joseph Gremillion. Maryknoll, N.Y.: Orbis Books, 1976.

Leo XIII. *Rerum novarum*. In *The Great Encyclicals of Leo XIII*. New York: Benziger, 1903.

Medellín documents. In *The Church in the Present-Day Transformation of Latin America in the Light of the Council*, ed. Louis M. Colonnese. Washington, D.C.: Latin American Bureau, USCC, 1969.

Paul VI. *Ecclesiam suam*. In vol. 5 of *The Papal Encyclicals*, ed. C. Carlen. 5 vols. Wilmington, N.C.: McGrath, 1981.

———. *Octogesima adveniens*; and *Populorum progressio*. In *The Gospel of Peace and Justice*. See John XXIII.

Pius XI. *Quadragesimo anno*. Washington, D.C.: National Catholic Welfare Conference, 1942.

Pius IX. *Quanta cura*. In vol. 1 of *The Papal Encyclicals*. See Paul VI.

Pius X. *Singulari quadam*. In vol. 3 of *The Papal Encyclicals*. See Paul VI.

Pius XII. *Conforto, letizia* (Now Is the Time for Action); *Mit dem Gefühl* (The Social Problem); Modern Technology and Peace; *La Solennità* (The Anniversary of *Rerum novarum*). In *The Major Addresses of Pope Pius XII*, ed. V. Yzermans. 2 vols. St. Paul: North Central Publishing Co., 1961.

———. *Il Programma*. In *The Pope Speaks* 2 (1955).

Puebla documents. The Final Document; and Message to the Peoples of Latin America. In *Puebla and Beyond*. See John Paul II.

Vatican II documents. *Dignitatis humanae; Lumen gentium;* and Message to Humanity. In *Vatican II: The Conciliar and Postconciliar Documents*, ed. A. Flannery. Collegeville, Minn.: Liturgical Press, 1975.

THE GOSPEL OF PEACE AND JUSTICE
Catholic Social Teaching Since Pope John
edited by Joseph Gremillion

"This source book and survey of social problems contains 22 documents—encyclicals, conciliar decrees, and papal and episcopal addresses—which have appeared during the reigns of Pope John XXIII and Paul VI. Gremillion introduces them with a 140 page outline of the world situation today, the role the Catholic Church has played and should play in promoting justice and peace, and the development of papal thought on these questions."   *Theology Digest*

"Gremillion's study is not just four star work, it is four star plus. It should be preached, studied, meditated, and read. It is without equal. It is a must for anyone seeking to live the social Gospel."   *Religious Media Today*

no. 166-7   **637pp. pbk.**   **$14.95**

OPTION FOR THE POOR
A Hundred Years of Vatican Social Teaching
by Donal Dorr

This is a careful examination of the social teaching of the Catholic Church over the past century to find out what Church leaders have to say about poverty and social injustice. Dorr makes a thorough and balanced study of the teaching of popes, councils and synods—and shows that the notion of an "option for the poor" has a solid traditional basis.

"Highly recommended."   *Commonweal*

no. 365-1   **336pp. pbk.**   **$11.95**

PUEBLA AND BEYOND
edited by John Eagleson and Philip Scharper

An excellent history of the struggle leading to Puebla by Penny Lernoux and an introduction to the event by Archbishop Marcos McGrath precede full texts of Pope John Paul II's addresses in Mexico and the final document of the conference. The volume concludes with analyses of the significance of Puebla by Jon Sobrino, Robert McAfee Brown, and Joseph Gremillion.

no. 399-6   **383pp. pbk.**   **$9.95**

SOCIAL ANALYSIS
Linking Faith and Justice
by Joe Holland and Peter Henriot

This study describes the task of social analysis and its relevance to social justice action. According to Joe Holland and Peter Henriot, the way people see a problem determines how they will respond to it. Social analysis is a result of "seeing a wider picture" of the problem—exploring structural issues, examining causal linkages, identifying key factors, and tracing long term trends. This approach, they assert, will initiate action capable of affecting profound social change. The book provides illustrations of analytical approaches to various problems and explores the suggestions and questions they raise for pastoral response.

". . . a provocative essay that is particularly valuable in highlighting the role of the social sciences in effective applications of faith values."   *Sociological Analysis*

no. 462-3   **118pp. pbk.**   **$7.95**

THE TRUE CHURCH AND THE POOR
by Jon Sobrino

This unusual scholarly venture into ecclesiology focuses on the poor as the channel through which God's spirit is manifesting itself today. For Jon Sobrino, the shift in Latin American churches to a mission centered on the poor has led to vicious persecution but also to hope, and hence, to "a recovery by the Church of the memory of Jesus."

". . . a challenging and controversial book."   *Sojourners*

no. 513-1   **384pp. pbk.**   **$13.95**

SPIRITUALITY AND JUSTICE
by Donal Dorr

The author of *Option for the Poor* (Orbis, 1983) examines the link between spirituality and justice in response to the dilemmas of two groups: social activists alienated by a traditional, individualistic spirituality and people deeply concerned with spirituality but intimidated by the demands of an effective commitment to justice. Donal Dorr attempts to help each group in their search for a synthesis.

no. 449-6   **264pp. pbk.**   **$10.95**